T.E. Lawrence
in
Lincolnshire

John Pateman

The Pateran Press
11 Windsor Close
Sleaford
Lincolnshire
NG34 7NL

2012

ISBN 978-1-4717-6243-7

Acknowledgements

College Hall Library, RAF College Cranwell

The T.E. Lawrence Society

Lincolnshire Library Service & Archives

Cranwell Aviation Heritage Centre

RAF Digby

Friends of Metheringham Airfield

Dedication

This book is dedicated to the memory of T.E. Shaw and his fellow 'irks' in B Flight at RAF Cranwell, August 1925 – November 1926

Contents

Introduction

This book looks at the time which T.E. Lawrence (Lawrence of Arabia) spent in Lincolnshire between August 1925 – November 1926. Lawrence was an enigmatic character who rose to fame during the Arab Revolt in the Great War and then chose to reduce himself to the ranks in the Army and the RAF where he assumed the name T.E. Shaw. We are fortunate to have Lawrence's own perspective on his time in Lincolnshire as recorded in *The Mint* and in the letters which he wrote to friends and family while serving as an Aircraftman at Cranwell. We also have the accounts of people who knew Lawrence at Cranwell such as Leslie Webb, Sergeant Pugh and Rupert de la Bere.

T.E. Lawrence

Lieutenant Colonel Thomas Edward Lawrence, CB, DSO (16 August 1888 – 19 May 1935), known professionally as T. E. Lawrence, was a British Army officer renowned especially for his liaison role during the Arab Revolt against Ottoman Turkish rule of 1916–18. The extraordinary breadth and variety of his activities and associations, and his ability to describe them vividly in writing, earned him international fame as Lawrence of Arabia, a title popularised by the 1962 film based on his life.

Lawrence was born at Gorphwysfa in Tremadog, Caernarfonshire (now Gwynedd), Wales. His Anglo-Irish father, Thomas Robert Tighe Chapman, who in 1914 inherited the title of seventh Baronet of Westmeath in Ireland, had abandoned his wife Edith for his daughters' governess Sarah Junner (born out of wedlock to a father named Lawrence, and who had styled herself 'Miss Lawrence' in the Chapman household). The couple did not marry but were known as Mr and Mrs Lawrence.

Thomas Chapman and Sarah Junner had five sons born out of wedlock, of whom Thomas Edward was the second eldest. From Wales the family moved to Kirkudbright in Scotland, then Dinard in Brittany, then to Jersey. From 1894–96 the family lived at Langley Lodge (now demolished), set in private woods between the eastern borders of the New Forest and Southampton Water in Hampshire. Mr Lawrence sailed and took the boys to watch yacht racing in the Solent off Lepe beach. By the time they left, the eight-year-old Ned (as Thomas became known) had developed a taste for the countryside and outdoor activities.

In the summer of 1896 the Lawrences moved to 2 Polstead Road (now marked with a blue plaque) in Oxford, where, until 1921, they lived under the names of Mr and Mrs Lawrence. Ned attended the City of Oxford High School for Boys, where one of the four houses was later named *"Lawrence"* in his honour; the school closed in 1966. As a schoolboy, one of his favourite pastimes was to cycle to country churches and make brass rubbings. Lawrence and one of his brothers became commissioned officers in the Church Lads' Brigade at St Aldate's Church.

Lawrence claimed that in about 1905, he ran away from home and served for a few weeks as a boy soldier with the Royal Garrison Artillery at St Mawes Castle in Cornwall, from which he was bought out. No evidence of this can be found in army records.

From 1907 Lawrence was educated at Jesus College, Oxford. During the summers of 1907 and 1908, he toured France by bicycle, collecting photographs, drawings and measurements of castles dating from the mediaeval period. In the summer of 1909, he set out alone on a three-month walking tour of crusader castles in Ottoman Syria, during which he travelled 1,000 mi (1,600 km) on foot. Lawrence graduated with First Class Honours after submitting a thesis entitled *The influence of the Crusades on European Military Architecture – to the end of the 12th century* based on his own field research in France, notably in Châlus, and the Middle East.

On completing his degree in 1910, Lawrence commenced postgraduate research in mediaeval pottery with a Senior Demy at Magdalen College, Oxford, which he abandoned after he was offered the opportunity to become a practising archaeologist in the Middle East. Lawrence was a polyglot who could speak English, French, German, Latin, Greek, Arabic, Turkish and Syriac. In December 1910 he sailed for Beirut, and on arrival went to Jbail (Byblos), where he studied Arabic. He then went to work on the excavations at Carchemish, near Jerablus in northern Syria, where he worked under D. G. Hogarth and R. Campbell-Thompson of the British Museum. He would later state that everything that he had accomplished, he owed to Hogarth. As the site lay near an important crossing on the Baghdad Railway, knowledge gathered there was of considerable importance for military intelligence. While excavating ancient Mesopotamian sites, Lawrence met Gertrude Bell, who was to influence him during his time in the Middle East.

In late 1911, Lawrence returned to England for a brief sojourn. By November he was en route to Beirut for a second season at Carchemish, where he was to work with Leonard Woolley. Prior to resuming work there, however, he briefly worked with Flinders Petrie at Kafr Ammar in Egypt.

Lawrence continued making trips to the Middle East as a field archaeologist until the outbreak of World War I. In January 1914, Woolley and Lawrence were co-opted by the British military as an archaeological smokescreen for a British military survey of the Negev Desert. They were funded by the Palestine Exploration Fund to search for an area referred to in the Bible as the "Wilderness of Zin"; along the way, they undertook an archaeological survey of the Negev Desert. The Negev was of strategic importance, as it would have to be crossed by any Ottoman army attacking Egypt in the event of war. Woolley and Lawrence subsequently published a report of the expedition's archaeological findings, but a more important result was an updated mapping of the area, with special attention to features of military relevance such as water sources. Lawrence also visited Aqaba and Petra.

From March to May 1914, Lawrence worked again at Carchemish. Following the outbreak of hostilities in August 1914, on the advice of S.F. Newcombe, Lawrence did not immediately enlist in the British Army; he held back until October, when he was commissioned on the General List.

Arab revolt

At the outbreak of World War I Lawrence was a university post-graduate researcher who had for years travelled extensively within the Ottoman Empire provinces of the Levant (Transjordan and Palestine) and Mesopotamia (Syria and Iraq) under his own name. As such he became known to the Turkish Interior Ministry authorities and their German technical advisors. Lawrence came into contact with the Ottoman–German technical advisers, travelling over the German-designed, -built, and -financed railways during the course of his researches.

Even if Lawrence had not volunteered, the British would probably have recruited him for his first-hand knowledge of Syria, the Levant, and Mesopotamia. He was eventually posted to Cairo on the Intelligence Staff of the GOC Middle East.

Contrary to later myth, it was neither Lawrence nor the Army that conceived a campaign of internal insurgency against the Ottoman Empire in the Middle East, but rather the Arab Bureau of Britain's Foreign Office. The Arab Bureau had long felt it likely that a campaign instigated and financed by outside powers, supporting the breakaway-minded tribes and regional challengers to the Turkish government's centralised rule of their empire, would pay great dividends in the diversion of effort that would be needed to meet such a challenge. The Arab Bureau had recognised the strategic value of what is today called the "asymmetry" of such conflict. The Ottoman authorities would have to devote from a hundred to a thousand times the resources to contain the threat of such an internal rebellion compared to the Allies' cost of sponsoring it.

At that point in the Foreign Office's thinking they were not considering the region as candidate territories for incorporation in the British Empire, but only as an extension of the range of British Imperial influence, and the weakening and destruction of a German ally, the Ottoman Empire.

During the war, Lawrence fought with Arab irregular troops under the command of Emir Faisal, a son of Sherif Hussein of Mecca, in extended guerrilla operations against the armed forces of the Ottoman Empire. He persuaded the Arabs not to make a frontal assault on the Ottoman stronghold in Medina but allowed the Turkish army to tie up troops in the city garrison. The Arabs were then free to direct most of their attention to the Turks' weak point, the Hejaz railway that supplied the garrison. This vastly expanded the battlefield and tied up even more Ottoman troops, who were then forced to protect the railway and repair the constant damage.

The capture of Aqaba

In 1917, Lawrence arranged a joint action with the Arab irregulars and forces under Auda Abu Tayi (until then in the employ of the Ottomans) against the strategically located but lightly defended town of Aqaba. On 6 July, after a surprise overland attack, Aqaba fell to

Lawrence and the Arab forces. After Aqaba, Lawrence was promoted to major. Fortunately for Lawrence, the new commander-in-chief of the Egyptian Expeditionary Force, General Sir Edmund Allenby, agreed to his strategy for the revolt, stating after the war:

"I gave him a free hand. His cooperation was marked by the utmost loyalty, and I never had anything but praise for his work, which, indeed, was invaluable throughout the campaign."

Lawrence now held a powerful position, as an adviser to Faisal and a person who had Allenby's confidence.

The fall of Damascus

The following year, Lawrence was involved in the capture of Damascus in the final weeks of the war and was promoted to lieutenant-colonel in 1918. In newly liberated Damascus—which he had envisioned as the capital of an Arab state—Lawrence was instrumental in establishing a provisional Arab government under Faisal. Faisal's rule as king, however, came to an abrupt end in 1920, after the battle of Maysaloun, when the French Forces of General Gouraud under the command of General Mariano Goybet, entered Damascus, breaking Lawrence's dream of an independent Arabia.

As was his habit when travelling before the war, Lawrence adopted many local customs and traditions (many photographs show him in the desert wearing white Arab dishdasha and riding camels).

During the closing years of the war he sought, with mixed success, to convince his superiors in the British government that Arab independence was in their interests. The secret Sykes-Picot Agreement between France and Britain contradicted the promises of independence he had made to the Arabs and frustrated his work.

In 1918 he co-operated with war correspondent Lowell Thomas for a short period. During this time Thomas and his cameraman Harry Chase shot a great deal of film and many photographs, which Thomas used in a highly lucrative film that toured the world after the war.

Post-war years

Immediately after the war, Lawrence worked for the Foreign Office, attending the Paris Peace Conference between January and May as a member of Faisal's delegation. He served for much of 1921 as an advisor to Winston Churchill at the Colonial Office.

In August 1922, Lawrence enlisted in the Royal Air Force as an aircraftman under the name John Hume Ross. He was soon exposed and, in February 1923, was forced out of the RAF. He changed his name to T. E. Shaw and joined the Royal Tank Corps in 1923. He was unhappy there and repeatedly petitioned to rejoin the RAF, which finally readmitted him in August 1925. A fresh burst of publicity after the publication of *Revolt in the Desert* (see below) resulted in his assignment to a remote base in British India in late 1926, where he remained until the end of 1928. At that time he was forced to return to Britain after rumours began to circulate that he was involved in espionage activities.

He purchased several small plots of land in Chingford, built a hut and swimming pool there, and visited frequently. This was removed in 1930 when the Chingford Urban District Council acquired the land and passed it to the City of London Corporation, but re-erected the hut in the grounds of The Warren, Loughton, where it remains, neglected, today. Lawrence's tenure of the Chingford land has now been commemorated by a plaque fixed on the sighting obelisk on Pole Hill.

He continued serving in the RAF based at Bridlington, East Riding of Yorkshire, specialising in high-speed boats and professing happiness, and it was with considerable regret that he left the service at the end of his enlistment in March 1935.

Lawrence was a keen motorcyclist, and, at different times, had owned seven Brough Superior motorcycles. His seventh motorcycle is on display at the Imperial War Museum. Among the books Lawrence is known to have carried with him on his military campaigns is Thomas Malory's *Morte D'Arthur*. Accounts of the 1934 discovery of the Winchester Manuscript of the *Morte* include a report that Lawrence followed Eugene Vinaver—a Malory scholar—by motorcycle from Manchester to Winchester upon reading of the discovery in *The Times*.

Death

At the age of 46, two months after leaving the service, Lawrence was fatally injured in an accident on his Brough Superior SS100 motorcycle in Dorset, close to his cottage, Clouds Hill, near Wareham. A dip in the road obstructed his view of two boys on their bicycles; he swerved to avoid them, lost control and was thrown over the handlebars. He died six days later on 19 May 1935. The spot is marked by a small memorial at the side of the road.

The circumstances of Lawrence's death had far-reaching consequences. One of the doctors attending him was the neurosurgeon Hugh Cairns. He was profoundly affected by the incident, and consequently began a long study of what he saw as the unnecessary loss of life by motorcycle dispatch riders through head injuries. His research led to the use of crash helmets by both military and civilian motorcyclists.

Moreton Estate, which borders Bovington Camp, was owned by family cousins, the Frampton family. Lawrence had rented and later bought Clouds Hill from the Framptons. He had been a frequent visitor to their home, Okers Wood House, and had for years corresponded with Louisa Frampton. On Lawrence's death, his mother arranged with the Framptons for him to be buried in their family plot at Moreton Church. His coffin was transported on the Frampton estate's bier. Mourners included Winston and Clementine Churchill and Lawrence's youngest brother, Arnold.

A bust of Lawrence was placed in the crypt at St Paul's Cathedral and a stone effigy by Eric Kennington remains in the Anglo-Saxon church of St Martin, Wareham.

Writings

Throughout his life, Lawrence was a prolific writer. A large portion of his output was epistolary; he often sent several letters a day. Several collections of his letters have been published. He corresponded with many notable figures, including George Bernard Shaw, Edward Elgar, Winston Churchill, Robert Graves, Noël Coward, E. M. Forster, Siegfried Sassoon, John Buchan, Augustus John and Henry Williamson. He met Joseph Conrad and commented perceptively on his works. The many letters that he sent to Shaw's wife, Charlotte, offer a revealing side of his character.

In his lifetime, Lawrence published four major texts. Two were translations: Homer's *Odyssey*, and *The Forest Giant* — the latter an otherwise forgotten work of French fiction. He received a flat fee for the second translation, and negotiated a generous fee plus royalties for the first.

Seven Pillars of Wisdom

Lawrence's major work is *Seven Pillars of Wisdom*, an account of his war experiences. In 1919 he had been elected to a seven-year research fellowship at All Souls College, Oxford, providing him with support while he worked on the book. In addition to being a memoir of his experiences during the war, certain parts also serve as essays on military strategy, Arabian culture and geography, and other topics. Lawrence re-wrote *Seven Pillars of Wisdom* three times; once "blind" after he lost the manuscript while changing trains at Reading railway station.

The list of his alleged "embellishments" in *Seven Pillars* is long, though many such allegations have been disproved with time, most definitively in Jeremy Wilson's authorised biography. However Lawrence's own notebooks refute his claim to have crossed the Sinai Peninsula from Aqaba to the Suez Canal in just 49 hours without any sleep. In reality this famous camel ride lasted for more than 70 hours and was interrupted by two long breaks for sleeping which Lawrence omitted when he wrote his book.

Lawrence acknowledged having been helped in the editing of the book by George Bernard Shaw. In the preface to *Seven Pillars*, Lawrence offered his "thanks to Mr. and Mrs. Bernard Shaw for countless suggestions of great value and diversity: and for all the present semicolons."

The first public edition was published in 1926 as a high-priced private subscription edition, printed in London by Roy Manning Pike and Herbert John Hodgson, with illustrations by Eric Kennington, Augustus John, Paul Nash, Blair Hughes-Stanton and his wife Gertrude Hermes. Lawrence was afraid that the public would think that he would make a substantial income from the book, and he stated that it was written as a result of his war service. He vowed not to take any money from it, and indeed he did not, as the sale price was one third of the production costs. This left Lawrence in substantial debt.

There is a proof copy of *The Seven Pillars Of Wisdom* at Cranwell College which Lawrence had bound and placed at the disposal of the then Commandant, Air Commodore Borton. Here is a description of the book that accompanied the Lawrence exhibition at the National Portrait Gallery in 1988:

'Proof copy of *Seven Pillars of Wisdom*, 1926. The working reference copy of the subscribers' edition assembled by Lawrence as the sections were printed. It was widely read by officers and fellow aircraftmen at Cranwell, where he served from August 1925 until November 1926. The proof was originally bound up roughly by Lawrence himself, and titled mischievously "The complete aircrafthand". Before leaving Cranwell he presented it to the College Library, which commissioned the present binding.

It was inscribed by Lawrence: 'Copy placed at disposal of Air Commodore Borton. This is a spoiled set of proofs of the complete text of my book Seven Pillars of Wisdom. It includes two pages in their original form – pages which have been modified for the edition as distributed. This copy lacks title page, fly-leaves, table of contents, table of illustrations, nine "arguments" prefaced to sections, many woodcuts and line blocks, all the plates, and two appendices; these, being trimmings of the text, are supplied only to subscribers / 18.X.26 TES.'

Revolt in the Desert

Revolt in the Desert was an abridged version of *Seven Pillars*, which he began in 1926 and was published in March 1927 in both limited and trade editions. He undertook a needed but reluctant publicity exercise, which resulted in a best-seller. Again he vowed not to take any fees from the publication, partly to appease the subscribers to *Seven Pillars* who had paid dearly for their editions. By the fourth reprint in 1927, the debt from *Seven Pillars* was paid off. As Lawrence left for military service in India at the end of 1926, he set up the "Seven Pillars Trust" with his friend D. G. Hogarth as a trustee, in which he made over the copyright and any surplus income of *Revolt in the Desert*. He later told Hogarth that he had "made the Trust final, to save myself the temptation of reviewing it, if *Revolt* turned out a best seller."

The resultant trust paid off the debt, and Lawrence then invoked a clause in his publishing contract to halt publication of the abridgment in the UK. However, he allowed both American editions and translations, which resulted in a substantial flow of income. The trust paid income either into an educational fund for children of RAF officers who lost their lives or were invalided as a result of service, or more substantially into the RAF Benevolent Fund.

The Mint

Lawrence left unpublished *The Mint*, a memoir of his experiences as an enlisted man in the Royal Air Force. For this, he worked from a notebook that he kept while enlisted, writing of the daily lives of enlisted men and his desire to be a part of something larger than himself: the Royal Air Force. The book is stylistically very different from *Seven Pillars of Wisdom*, using sparse prose as opposed to the complicated syntax found in *Seven Pillars*. It was published posthumously, edited by his brother, Professor A. W. Lawrence.

After Lawrence's death, A. W. Lawrence inherited all Lawrence's estate and his copyrights as the sole beneficiary. To pay the inheritance tax, he sold the U.S. copyright of *Seven Pillars of Wisdom* (subscribers' text) outright to Doubleday Doran in 1935. Doubleday still controls publication rights of this version of the text of *Seven Pillars of Wisdom* in the USA. In 1936 Prof. Lawrence split the remaining assets of the estate, giving Clouds Hill and many copies of less substantial or historical letters to the nation via the National Trust, and then set up two trusts to control interests in T. E. Lawrence's residual copyrights. To the original Seven Pillars Trust, Prof. Lawrence assigned the copyright in *Seven Pillars of Wisdom*, as a result of which it was given its first general publication. To the Letters and Symposium Trust, he assigned the copyright in *The Mint* and all Lawrence's letters, which were subsequently edited and published in the book *T. E. Lawrence by his Friends* (edited by A. W. Lawrence, London, Jonathan Cape, 1937).

A substantial amount of income went directly to the RAF Benevolent Fund or for archaeological, environmental, or academic projects. The two trusts were amalgamated in 1986 and, on the death of Prof. A. W. Lawrence, the unified trust also acquired all the remaining rights to Lawrence's works that it had not owned, plus rights to all of Prof. Lawrence's works.

Letters

T.E. Lawrence was also a prolific letter writer. Clifford Irwin has estimated that, altogether, there are a little over 5,000 letters in existence. They have been described as the autobiography Lawrence never wrote. Many of these letters were published in:

- *The Letters of T.E. Lawrence* edited by David Garnett (1938)
- *The Home Letters of T.E. Lawrence and his brothers* (1954)
- *T. E. Lawrence to his Biographers Robert Graves and Liddell Hart* (1963)
- *Solitary in the Ranks* by H. Montgomery Hyde (1977)
- *The Letters of T.E. Lawrence* selected and edited by Malcolm Brown (1988 & 2005)
- *T.E. Lawrence Letters Volume One: Correspondence with Bernard and Charlotte Shaw, 1922-26,* edited by Jeremy and Nicole Wilson (2000)
- *T.E. Lawrence Letters Volume Two: Correspondence with Bernard and Charlotte Shaw, 1927,* edited by Jeremy and Nicole Wilson (2003)

Some letters are still covered by copyright and these have been summarised, including those which he wrote to Charlotte Shaw in 1925-26. These letters were in many ways life- lines and letter writing in general was his salvation. Without these letters his years in the ranks from 1922 would have been a total drop out.

Malcolm Brown: 'Lawrence was a genius who denied himself full expression, and I believe that letters allowed him to unleash his intelligence and intellect, both of which were constrained by the narrowness of his chosen position...It is perhaps precisely because he was not attempting to make literature that his letters, written uninhibitedly, with scarcely any corrections, often at length and to a remarkably wide range of people, shed so much light on so many aspects of his life, and make him seem so much more of a human being than the figure that emerges from the mass of analysis and psychological dissection to which he has been subjected over the years.'

Cranwell

T.E. Lawrence was posted to RAF Cranwell in Lincolnshire in August 1925 and the next 16 months were among the happiest in his life. He spent time working on *Revolt in the Desert*, an abridgement of *Seven Pillars of Wisdom*, and he enjoyed riding around the local countryside on his Brough Superior. He made regular visits to Lincoln (where there is a plaque on the house he lodged in on Steep Hill), Nottingham (where George Brough had his motorcycle works) and Sleaford (the local market town where he bought provisions). On one of his journeys from Cranwell to Lincoln he raced a bi-plane from RAF Digby. He also made longer journeys to Cambridge and London where he visited friends and acquaintances from the worlds of literature and politics. There are a number of contemporary accounts from Leslie Webb, Rupert de la Bere and Sergeant Pugh who served with Lawrence at Cranwell.

Leslie Webb

On his 18th birthday in February 1923, Leslie Webb enlisted in the RAF. He was posted to RAF Depot, Uxbridge where the Camp Commandant was a Group Captain, a much feared one legged casualty from the Great War. Leslie was then posted to the RAF Cadet College, Cranwell West camp:

'In August 1925 a new arrival presented himself at the QM stores to draw bedding, plates and mugs etc. and was allocated to B Flight. It was 352089 AC2 T.E. Shaw (Lawrence of Arabia)...Through the 18 months I served with T.E. Shaw at Cranwell he was just one of the "irks" and never sought or expected to be more than one of us.

The only social difference between us was he owned a Brough Superior motor bike on which he belted down the straight Leadenham road at around 70-80 mph, sometimes with the diminutive Smudge Smith riding pillion, while we tinkered with our AJS's and Douglas's. Shaw was less than complimentary about his short spell of service with the Tank Corps and always evasive if questioned about his wartime exploits, the subject, strange as it may sound, was avoided.

The last I saw of T.E. Shaw was a picture in the Daily Mirror of him climbing a rope ladder to board a troopship sailing for India, the media had caught up with him again. Many are the stories I have been told and read about him, some of which were sheer fantasy. I am now [written on 14 November 1997] within reach of my 93rd birthday and I wonder how many of the "irks" are still alive to remember those happy days at Cranwell West Camp.'

Rupert de la Bere

In his *Letters of T.E. Lawrence* (1938), David Garnett includes only one letter from Lawrence to Rupert de la Bere, described in a footnote as, 'Professor at Royal Air Force College, Cranwell'. Yet it is clear from Lawrence's correspondence that he was on very good terms with de la Bere during his time at Cranwell. They remained in touch and, in 1935, when Lawrence was cycling south from Bridlington to Clouds Hill, he made a detour to Cranwell to see 'the Prof.' again. Following de la Bere's death in March 1946, his life was briefly summarised in a letter which appeared in *The Times*. Air Vice-Marshal Frederick Halahan writes:

'Rupert de la Bere, who died at his home on Ventnor recently, will always be remembered by his RAF colleagues who served at the RAF College, Cranwell, in its earliest days...On the formation of the RAF College at Cranwell in 1921 he was appointed to the staff as Professor of English subjects, and there it was that he devoted his whole time to the Flight Cadets. Many of those who passed through his hands are now Air officers of high rank, though many have paid the supreme sacrifice during and before the late war – but one and all would testify to the encouragement, both by precept and example, and the personal interest and friendship which 'the Prof.', as he was affectionately called, had for everyone. Work or sport came alike to him, and he did as much to teach us the King's English as he did in encouraging and fostering all types of sports and games. His own living quarters were always available to all, as he was a wonderful host, and had the gift of understanding human weaknesses and helping those in trouble. His 17 years at Cranwell were ended in 1938, when he was appointed to the Staff of Headquarters, Fighter Command...'

Halahan had also written a warm tribute to de la Bere in 1938, when 'the Prof.' retired from his work at Cranwell. This was printed in the Autumn 1938 issue of the *Journal of The Royal Air Force College* – a publication which de la Bere had edited to a very high standard:

'The bald announcement that Captain Rupert de la Bere was being transferred from the College came as a shock to his countless friends and admirers. Somehow 'the Prof.' has been, and is, very much a part of the College. Often has one heard ex-cadets and ex-officers discussing a visit to it, saying "I don't expect I shall know a soul; but anyhow the Prof. will be there."

One can truly say that 'the Prof.' never made an enemy among all those who had served in the College with him during the past 18 years. We shall miss him for his profound interest in all which appertains to the *genus* Cadet – past or present – whether to referee a Rugger game; or raise a Soccer side to give practice to the XI; or act as judge, at Athletics, Cross-Country, Running, Boxing, Hockey, Cricket; he was always there to help and encourage.

What of us ourselves – this College Magazine? The work as Editor-in-Chief is difficult and continuous. We have grown under his supervision from very small beginnings until now we are – modesty forbids us to continue. We shall miss our Editor. Nor must we forget, in this connection, his activities to promote the welfare of Old Cranwellians. The Coat of Arms and the Old Cranwellian Book at the College owe their inception to him alone.

We shall miss those cheery teas in his quarters, where one met many friends, and had such interesting and instructive talks and arguments. Many a cadet – aye, and officer too, will hold him in high esteem for sage advice and kindly criticism, which so often enabled them to 'find their bearings' and keep their thumbs in the tram lines.

A man of very high academic attainments – with a shrewd and sometimes apparently simple manner – we shall always look on 'the Prof.' as a friend – and a sahib – using the latter word in its highest sense. He never thrust his personality upon anyone: yet all felt that here was one person in the College to whom all could go in time of trouble – always to receive his help and advice – and a square deal.

He taught us to speak the King's English (we hope most fervently that there are no split infinitives or other enormities in this screed) – to write a decent letter and to speak correctly and logically. The Debating Society will miss him – with his kindly smile at our errors, and his simple and friendly correction of the same. And the Hunting Filed will miss him – even though at times of great stress and risk he may have used quite a different language from that which we were accustomed to associate with him in the Lecture Rooms! And so on – his activities embraced, in varying degree, the whole life of the College.

Above all we learnt from him unselfish devotion to the job in hand – a fine tolerance for human frailty (although he could never "suffer fools gladly") – and loyalty to our companions and leaders. We wish him all the best in his new endeavours and environment.'

These appreciations by Halahan give some idea of the man Lawrence liked. He also liked Sergt. Pugh and wrote him a number of letters after leaving Cranwell in November 1926.

Sergeant Pugh

Sergeant Pugh was in B Flight with Lawrence at Cranwell. His memories of Lawrence were recorded by Robert Graves in *Lawrence and the Arabs* (1927). These vignettes of life at Cranwell were: Arrival at Cranwell; First Fatigue; Credit from the Tank Corps; Church; S. Joins Up in RAF Second Time; B Flight, Cranwell; A Gramophone Was Bought; He Starts;

Broughs; 'Office Boy'; Fires; Nights Out; Promotion; Night Riding; Offer of Air Officer Commanding; Flying and Scrubbing; Scrounging; Coal; Civil Police; Air Display; Jobs; A Visit.

Graves sent these to Lawrence who commented on them and made some corrections in *T.E. Lawrence to His Biographer Robert Graves* (1938). Overall Lawrence enjoyed Sergt. Pugh's account and described it as 'great fun'. Graves also published some additional notes from Sergeant Pugh which he had not included in the biography: Tate Art Gallery and Tax Collectors.

Lawrence wrote a number of letters to Sergt. Pugh after leaving Cranwell for India in November 1926. Lawrence went east without enthusiasm. 'I squat on deck with Smith, C.J.' he wrote on 16 December 1926 from the troopship S.S. *Derbyshire* to Sergeant Pugh, 'lamenting Cranwell and England, and all good things.'

When the long unpleasant voyage was over he found himself in an RAF Camp at Drigh Road just outside Karachi, where he wrote to Sergt. Pugh on 30 June 1927: 'Do you remember how that tray on the table used to get blocked solid: and how then I'd stuff the new-coming letters into those pigeon holes on my left, till they were too tight: and then we'd light the stove, & I'd chuck the time-expired ones by armfuls into the fire, and groan over answering the rest?'

Also from Drigh Road on 13 April 1928 he wrote to Sergt. Pugh; 'A publisher wrote & asked if I had any little poems I'd let him publish (a hen might as well lay cabbages as me write poetry) because if so he'd send me the latest Brough Superiors for the years 1928-29-30-31-32. I told him a) that I had no poems b) that Karachi had no roads.'

Letters were Lawrence's only method of contact in India. He received so many letters that he could only answer a small proportion of them, but to those to whom he wished to write he gave generous measure: his letters to Sergeant Pugh are sometimes many pages long. On 9 June 1928, for example, he wrote a long letter to Sergt. Pugh from RAF Detachment, Miranshah:

'This is more like B Flight, only as it happens their number is A...The Flight Lieutenant commanding this flight is the CO of the Station, during his first spell of duty:- so I get a change of CO every few weeks. That is part profit, and part loss. At Cranwell, it would have been a dead loss. At Karachi it would have been a gain...If Mrs Shaw and the others send me out, to here, as many books as they used to send to Cranwell, why then the local library will not hold them all...we are 3000 feet up, and as cool as cool can be. Nearly midsummer, and the temperature probably not over 100. We do not know for certain as we have no thermometer. Happy Miranshah. But in winter we may be as cold as Cranwell. Heaven forbid...They say however that there is no snow, ever, on the ground: but rain in buckets, and the hills about all snow-tipped, and cold winds and other horrors.'

Postscript

Memories of Lawrence's time at Cranwell have been published in a number of local history books and journals and articles have appeared in the local newspapers. Here are a selction:

Lincoln links with Lawrence of Arabia (1972)

'Major Frank Darroch, of Ingham, whose death at the age of 74 was announced last week, played a small part in the story of Lawrence of Arabia. He had left the RAF several months previously when, in May 1935, he had an accident while motorcycling in Dorset. An ambulance was summoned from Bovington military camp nearby and aboard that ambulance that went to bring in the unconscious, fatally injured Lawrence was Sgt. Major Darroch of the RAMC. And later, Frank Darroch was one of the bearers who carried the great man's coffin to the hearse for the journey to Moreton church where the funeral service was held.

A brother in Majorca was the only relative who could be traced and he came over to England. But he shunned publicity and turned down an offer of a Westminster Abbey funeral for Lawrence. He insisted, according to Major Darroch, on the funeral taking place in the village cemetery and on one other thing – no photographs. The brother, however, unbent so far as to allow a local photographer to take one picture of the coffin being carried from the hospital mortuary to the hearse. Major Darroch adds: "Two prints only were made by the photographer before, under instructions from Lawrence's brother, he smashed the negative. One print was given to the brother; I have the other".

In addition to Major Durroch, two other local people knew Lawrence of Arabia – Mr W. Dodd, the manager of the Regal Cinema, and Mrs E. Cousans of Hykeham Road, Lincoln. Mr Dodd was at Cranwell for a time while Lawrence was there and remembered him as a very "matey" sort of bloke. Mrs Cousans husband was Lawrence's driver in Egypt. She once had tea with Lawrence whom she recalled as "a perfect gentleman". (*Sleaford Standard*, 22 December 1972).

Hero's halcyon days at Cranwell (1988)

'A county of extremes and suddenness – Lawrence of Arabia's impressions of Lincolnshire from his Cranwell letters.

In August 1925 Lawrence wrote from RAF College, Cranwell, that a Bovington friend at Cranwell recognised him as "Colonel Lawrence". Aldington in his book, *Lawrence of Arabia 1955*, says that this was one of many stories Lawrence concocted. It was very unlikely a man from the Royal Tank Corps should also be in the RAF.

Lawrence wrote: "People who come to Cranwell often stay there for five years. I will go over to Nottingham on Saturday week, and try to see Brough, who has a 1926 BS 110 waiting for me. After that I'll get a room in some near village, and begin work."

Lawrence wrote to Mrs Thomas Hardy on 26 August, "Cranwell is not really near anywhere (nor is it anything in itself); and the disorder of falling into a new station is yet upon me. The RAF is home to me. My known past always rouses curiosity in a new station."

On 27 August Lawrence wrote to Buchan, 'This is a very comfortable, peaceful, cleanly camp, and will be glorious when I have settled into it."

He wrote to a friend, "There are no bugles in the camp and no reveille". He found the meals "good enough. Alternate weekend passes, church parade every Sunday in camp. I miss very much the quietude of the office for working in; music; colour, Lincolnshire is only green".

He enjoyed travelling long distances on his motorbike, having been given "the keys to a flat in London" and visiting "a bearded bookseller of Lincoln".

Lawrence wrote graphically of the winter, in December. "Lincolnshire is like a picture of dead earth in green and grey. You feel the curve of the great ball in the wideness of all the local views. It freezes, it snows, it blows, I'm as cold as cold".

Lawrence had offers for his Canadian sweater. "It must have been made for work in the Flights at Cranwell. They offer me huge prices here for it; packets and packets of woodbines, spare pairs of boots, a civvy suit. I refuse them all".

At Christmas "drunkenness goes unpunished". Scholarly Lawrence was reading TS Eliot's collected poems. "Lincolnshire is very wintry weather. Cranwell is the coldest place on earth and the windiest".

Lawrence thrilled with the love of speed. "Crashed off the Brough last Monday: knee, ankle, elbow being repaired. Tunic and breeches being replaced. Front mud guard, name plate, handle bars, foot rest, renewed. Skid on ice at 55 mph. Dark, wet, most miserable. Hobble like a cripple now."

Another time he stopped to help start a car. The car's starting handle suddenly flew back and broke his arm. Lawrence limped back to Cranwell on his Brough.

Lawrence sometimes waxes lyrical. In summer 1926 he wrote to Mrs Hardy, "We are very busy just now...the inclination is to lie in the grass and watch its greenness turning slowly into yellow. Lincolnshire has a severe winter and a severe summer: a county of extremes and suddenness. The RAF are sending me to India this Autumn, in November probably".

Lawrence's last Cranwell letter on 27 September 1927 enclosed his testimonial to George Brough "for five successive Brough superiors...the jolliest things on wheels".

Cranwell, where Lawrence found "the camp, fellows and the life, very good", [featured in *The Mint*]. "The Cadet College parts are as sincere as the rest. There is decent treatment, and a very real measure of happiness, to those who do not look forward or back". (Michael Dawney, *Sleaford Standard*, 18 August 1988)

Well, now we know (1992)

'Just where did Lawrence of Arabia stay when he visited Lincoln? City councillor Trevor Rook wanted to know the location in the hope that a plaque could be placed on the wall. Herbert Smith remembers seeing a sign in a Steep Hill boarding house which said "Lawrence of Arabia stayed here". By checking back in his 1922 copy of a Ruddock's street directory, he found the boarding house was at 33 Steep Hill, and in those days it was kept by Mrs E.E. Dugdale.' (*Lincolnshire Echo*, 11 May 1992).

Plaque marks historic spot (1993)

'A new plaque has been sited at Brown's Pie Shop in Steep Hill to mark the place where T.E. Lawrence, known as Lawrence of Arabia, stayed while serving at RAF Cranwell. T.E. Lawrence's plaque reads: Lawrence of Arabia 1888 – 1935. Around the time Lawrence stayed in Steep Hill, he wrote *Seven Pillars of Wisdom*, the legendary account of Arab insurgence against the Turks in Syria during the First World War.' (*Lincolnshire Echo*, 19 July 1993).

Week in Ancaster (1994)

'Bob Hardwick, Ancaster's former blacksmith, knew Lawrence of Arabia. Bob said "It was when he came to Cranwell in 1925. I was 21 and lived in North Rauceby." In those days the cadets had a half day on Wednesday. On one such afternoon Bob saw a big motorbike parked in the village. He saw an airman. "I could see he was a bit superior, someone with some money" he said.

Another Wednesday he saw the same cadet. Bob admired the motorbike, said "Is this yours? It's a smasher." Bob noticed that the cadet was about five feet six inches tall and probably 12 years older than he was. Later he was told by an RAF Sergeant who lived nearby, "That's Lawrence of Arabia". Another Wednesday Bob spoke to Lawrence who told him he had ordered a new motor bike, another Brough as always. Although the Broughs were made in Nottingham he had to go to a distributor in London for the new ones. This one would be his sixth. Bob said, "I saw it when he came with it, it was an immaculate machine".

One day he came and told Bob, "I'm going to have a race with an aeroplane". He said it would be from Sleaford to Lincoln. Later when Bob asked him about it he said, "It was level all the way". He told Bob he got onto the Sleaford – Lincoln Road, the aeroplane came up to him and the race started. The race finished at Bracebridge and afterwards the pilot told Lawrence that they would call it a draw. Bob said "He went after that and I didn't see him any more".

In Lawrence's own book written about his RAF life called *The Mint*, he makes reference to this time. Referring to the motorbike he said the "first glad roar at being alive again nightly jarred the huts of Cadet College". He described the race with the aeroplane. "A Bristol Fighter from nearby Whitewash Villas, our neighbour aerodrome was banking sharply round. I checked my speed an instant to wave...the pilot pointed down the road towards Lincoln". He described the high speed race where the plane was "zooming along the trees and telegraph poles with my scurrying pot only 80 yards ahead. I gained though, perhaps five miles per hour faster...I closed down and coasted to the cross roads by the Hospital. He caught, banked, climbed and turned home. 14 miles from camp and 15 minutes since I left the hut door."

He finished by going into Lincoln, "along tram lines, through the dirty streets and uphill to the aloof cathedral where it stood in frigid perfection above the cowering close". He bought bacon and then to Newark and Nottingham for sausages. "Home via Sleaford, our squalid, purse proud local village. Its butcher had six penn'orth of dripping ready for me". He concluded by saying "For months I have been making my round of marketing, riding a hundred miles for the joy of it and picking up the best food cheapest, over half the countryside". (Shelagh McIntyre, *Sleaford Standard*, 3 June 1994).

Lawrence of Cranwell (1996)

'The Cranwell posting was an idyllic time for Lawrence and when he was sent to India in 1926 he left behind fond memories. In a letter to a friend he wrote "The RAF is still my spiritual home and I'm awfully sorry to leave Cranwell where I've had the best year I ever remember to have had". (Pat Nurse, *Lincolnshire Echo*, 9 November 1996).

Monday is Market Day (1997)

'During the late 1920s my late husband (Tom) and his elder brother (Lal, as he was known) invested in a garage on East Road...During his posting at RAF Cranwell in 1925, T.E. Lawrence – "Lawrence of Arabia" – was a regular customer at the garage with his Brough Superior motorcycle known affectionately as *Boanerges*.' (C. Boon, *Memories of Sleaford*, 1997)

Back on map as plaque restores Lawrence link (1998)

'A new plaque celebrating the city's connection with one of the First World War's most famous heroes has been unveiled after the original one was stolen. The plate marking the place where Lawrence of Arabia stayed was stolen from above Brown's Pie Shop, in Steep Hill, Lincoln, in April. It was never recovered, but a new one has now been put up in its place.' (*Lincolnshire Echo*, 27 October 1998)

Former postman mourned (1999)

'One of Ancaster's oldest residents has died at the age of 94. Robert McLean Hardwick, former village postman, born 14 June 1904, died 31 December 1998. At one time he operated a blacksmith's in North Rauceby, Wilsford and Ancaster. His memory of meeting T.E. Shaw (Lawrence of Arabia) fascinated those who heard it. Mr Hardwick saw many RAF cadets as they bought petrol at the blacksmiths. It came in two gallon tins and it was sold at ten old pennies a gallon.' (*Lincolnshire Echo*, 17 February 1999).

Thomas Edward Lawrence (2002)

'Twice a week he would ride on *Boanerges,* his particular Brough at the time, to Lincoln, Sleaford and Nottingham on a "supply run" buying bacon, sausages, dripping and fresh eggs on behalf of his flight to supplement the mess and canteen food.' (J.R. Ketteringham, *Lincolnshire Natives and Others*, 2002).

Mystery woman in life of Lawrence of Arabia (2002)

'Confidential files made public for the first time today show that for more than a year he paid out two thirds of his salary to a woman living in Newark while he served in the RAF in Lincolnshire. He arranged for two shillings a day from his daily pay of three shillings to be paid to a Miss Ruby Bryant of 31 Portland Street, Newark. The payments began in September 1925 and continued for just over year until November 1926, while Lawrence was serving at RAF Cranwell. Miss Bryant has never been mentioned in any of Lawrence's biographies and his relationship with her and the reason for the payments can only be a matter of speculation.

Whatever the truth of their relationship, Miss Bryant was aware of Lawrence's real identity (he was serving at the time as Aircraftman TE Shaw). A letter she wrote to the Air Ministry complaining she had not been paid makes this clear. "Kindly note the allotment made out to me on behalf of Colonel Lawrence (going under the name of Aircraftman Shaw) has not yet come to hand. This should have been due last Thursday", she wrote.

To add to the intrigue, the day he cancelled the payments to Miss Bryant, Lawrence ordered a new set of payments of sixpence a day to another mystery character, W.J. Ross of 76 Marsham Street in London. They continued for another year. The files also show a further set of payments of nine pennies a day, again lasting over a year, to John Bruce, a Scots lad he had befriended in London in the early 1920's.' (*Lincolnshire Echo*, 29 May 2002).

How Lincolnshire legend still inspires film makers (2006)

'A new movie about one of Lincolnshire's famous residents, Lawrence of Arabia, has been announced. The new movie will focus on his years in England, including his time at RAF College Cranwell in the 1920's. He served at Cranwell for a year and during that time lodged in a house in Lincoln's Steep Hill. He was also apparently a regular drinker in the City Vaults pub in the High Street.' (Emma Pearson, *Lincolnshire Echo*, 23 May 2006)

Lawrence Sale

'Original negatives of one of Lincoln's most famous residents, Lawrence of Arabia, have been sold at auction for £6,572. They had been discovered by a collector who bought them for £32. The pictures show the First World War hero posing in India in the 1920s. A spokesman for Duke's Auction House in Dorchester, Dorset, said the negatives were sold to a UK based private collector over the telephone. The anonymous seller found them among items he had bought at auction 7 years ago in Bournemouth.

In 1925 Lawrence joined the RAF as an ordinary aircraftman and was based at RAF College Cranwell serving there for a year. During that time he lodged in a house in Lincoln's Steep Hill. He was also apparently a regular drinker in the City Vaults pub in the High Street. Official documents released in 2002 show that while he was at Cranwell he paid out two thirds of his salary to a woman in Newark.' (*Lincolnshire Echo*, 12 April 2008)

Lawrence's lost letter for sale (2010)

'A lost letter from Lawrence of Arabia describing his experiences at RAF Cranwell is to be sold at auction. The letter from TE Lawrence to Francis Rennell was found inside a rare copy of his book *The Seven Pillars of Wisdom*. One of 170 written by the author in 1926, the letter dated 3 November 1925, talks of his recent move to cadet college at RAF Cranwell. He describes the county as "a picture of dead earth in green and grey", although he was upbeat about his time there. He wrote: "The camp is good. Also the fellows, also the life. Mark me down for a further spell of quite happy existence". The author also attempts to persuade his friend not to buy *The Seven Pillars of Wisdom* book, telling him it was too expensive. The letter reads, "You don't really want one, you know. Thirty guineas is an absurd price. Wash out the idea".

The letter and the book are valued at £28,000 [they sold for £33,000] and will be auctioned at Lyon & Turnbull in Edinburgh. The auctioneer's book specialist Simon Vickers said, "The book, a signed copy of Lawrence's *Seven Pillars of Wisdom*, was brought in by the vendor, which is exciting enough as they are very rare, but it was when I was leafing through the book I noticed the letter. It is a wonderful everyday letter from Lawrence discussing his move to RAF cadet college Cranwell, as well as trying to dissuade Lord Rennell from buying the very copy of *Seven Pillars* we are selling". (Lisa Porter, '', *Sleaford Target*, 26 May 2010)

Cranwell

When Lawrence rejoined the RAF in 1925 he was sent first to RAF West Drayton to be processed as a recruit, then after a brief spell in Uxbridge, where he had begun his RAF career just three years earlier, he was posted to the Cadet College at Cranwell, Lincolnshire, arriving there on 24 August1925. He was now and would remain for the rest of his service years 338171 Aircraftman Shaw.

Lawrence's time at RAF Cranwell is described by all of his major biographers including John Mack, *A Prince of our Disorder: the life of T.E. Lawrence* (1976); H. Montgomery Hyde, *Solitary in the Ranks* (1977); and Jeremy Wilson, *Lawrence of Arabia: the authorised biography of T.E. Lawrence* (1989).

The life of Aircraftman Shaw in B Flight at Cranwell is also referenced in a wide range of other biographies and books about T.E. Lawrence including: S. Weintrab, *Private Shaw and Public Shaw* (1963); P. Marriott & Y. Argent, *Last Days of T.E. Lawrence* (1996); and P. Tunbridge, *With Lawrence in the Royal Air Force* (2000).

Aircraftman T.E. Shaw at RAF Cranwell, 24 August 1925 – November 1926

Lawrence rejoined the RAF at Uxbridge on **18 August 1925**, just after his 37th birthday. On 21 August, after only a few days at Uxbridge, orders came for Lawrence's immediate posting to the RAF Cadet College at Cranwell in Lincolnshire. He was delighted with the news. When he arrived there three days later, he celebrated by ordering a Brough motorcycle of the latest type. It would be his fourth Brough Superior.

A/c2 Shaw arrived at Cranwell on **24 August 1925** to enjoy a bath and a heavenly sleep. Baths were very important to Lawrence - as Sergeant Pugh put it 'Baths are his God'. Lawrence would even bribe the 'stoker' at Cranwell to tend to the fires for his bath before those of the others.

'Well, you're in luck here: this place is cushy. Any bed you like,' was the pleasant greeting Lawrence received at Cranwell. He was assigned to B Flight which, consisted of 15 men, a sergeant, and a corporal. Their duties were to look after six of the aircraft used for training cadets, and consequently their workload was much lighter during the college vacation than in term time. Ten of the flight were technicians, and five were unspecialised aircraftmen. Lawrence acted as runner and clerk. They were accommodated in Hut 103, into which Shaw shifted his kit after he had seen the Adjutant.

He wrote to Mrs Hardy on **26 August 1925**: 'Cranwell is not really anywhere (nor is it anything in itself): and the disorder of falling into a new station is yet upon me.'

Lawrence seemed at the Cadet College to be, at least outwardly, cheerful and happy. Sensing the suspiciousness with which the men there regarded his unusual past, Lawrence broke the ice socially by playing the most awful-sounding records he could find on his gramophone, and listening without any facial expression while the men suffered. When they realised it was a leg pull the tension was relaxed and he was accepted into the Flight. 'Everywhere a relationship: no loneliness anymore,' he wrote contentedly.

He wrote to John Buchan on **27 August 1925**: 'I feel like a person home at last...This is a very comfortable, peaceful, cleanly camp, and will be glorious when I have settled into it'.

The Commandant at Cranwell Cadet College was Air Commodore A.E. 'Biffy' Borton who had flown with the Royal Flying Corps in the desert and had Lawrence there. But Borton had no idea that Lawrence was being posted to Cranwell until he happened to catch sight of him a few days after his arrival: 'I walked in one day and saw Lawrence in an airman's uniform. I was furious with Trenchard for not letting me know. Fortunately I kept my head and didn't say anything, but being taken by surprise like that I could have easily let the cat out of the bag. I went to my quarters and sent for him.'

Although he was happy to return to the RAF he missed the beauty of the countryside around Bovington and the friends he had made there. On **7 September 1925** he wrote to E. Palmer: '. Odd that a man should be so ungrateful, for the R.T.C. was very good to me, and I've jilted her without a regret.' One link with Bovington remained. His younger brother Arnold had recently married, and the couple had moved into Clouds Hill during July. Lawrence had great affection for the college, and his brother, now an archaeologist working mainly overseas, wanted a base for his possessions in England. They soon decided to buy Clouds Hill, and Arnold began negotiations with the Moreton estate.

The mission of the station – to maintain the aircraft which the cadets were learning to fly – was meaningful to Lawrence. He made a point of flying with the officers in the Flight whenever he had the opportunity, so that each knew him well and were proud of the fact judging by their smiles when he climbed in with them.

Although he was assigned to an office, he would 'leave the office at times, shove overalls on,' and scrub and wash machines in the hangar despite the fact that 'there was never any need to do so.'

Sergeant Pugh of B Flight at Cranwell reported that in his clerk's job Lawrence mastered and took care of 'every conceivable kind of job. His sheer force of personality got him undreamed of odds and ends necessary for us in our work, which seemed unobtainable to any Segeant to say the most, and never an aircrafthand. Lawrence would not, however, hear of promotion and there is no suggestion on the part of Sergeant Pugh, who slept in Hut 103 with the airmen in the Flight, that any of them considered his manner at all superior or that his behaviour was in any way that of a 'posh' person.

As at other bases, despite his often exaggeratedly literal obedience to authority, Lawrence was the champion of the men against unreasonable authority or regulations. Although he liked, for example, the church at Cranwell, he had no use for the sermons and amused the enlisted men with his employment of the device of 'apparent stupidity' in his resistance to mandatory church going. He also astounded the other men by his successful protest to the superintendent of police at Cranwell over being unjustly held up on his motorcycle by the 'copper' in Sleaford. Such arguments with civilian authority were unheard of for enlisted men in uniform at that time and provided them with an exhilarating example with which to identify.

Sometimes, according to Sergeant Pugh, Lawrence would head off into the night on his Brough, summer or winter. He would return 'loaded up with good things for his roommates,' but then make his own supper of 'Smith's crisps' at the camp canteen. At other times he would 'smoke' down to London on the Brough to look after the printing of his book and would sleep at the Union Jack Club. On at least one occasion, when the club was full, he was packed among other enlisted men in varying states of drunkenness.

Sergeant Pugh offered this summary of Lawrence at Cranwell: 'It seemed his sole purpose was to be an airman of the lowest grade and rank and to be left alone with his Brough at B Flight, Cranwell. He was hero worshipped by all the flight for his never failing cheery disposition, ability to get all he could for their benefit, never complaining, and his generosity to all concerned till at times it appeared that he was doing too much for everyone and all were out to do the best for him. Quarrels ceased and the flight had to pull together for the sheer joy of remaining in his company and being with him for his companionship, help, habits, fun and teaching one and all to play straight. He fathered us and left us a sorrowful crowd awaiting letters or his return.'

Lawrence was now working on the last pages of *Seven Pillars*. As he told E. Candler on **22 September 1925**: 'I cut it off at the end like a knife: since that was how I cut myself off the Arabian adventure.'

Now that Lawrence was back in the RAF and the subscribers' *Seven Pillars* was nearing completion, he had time to take stock. There was no longer an easy escape route from service life: he had so frequently rejected the idea of accepting any benefit from the Arab Revolt that he could not take any profit from Cape's abridgement, however successful. Moreover, he would now be morally compelled to stay in the RAF, having fought so hard to return to its ranks. In effect, he had been trapped by his own actions and would have to make the best of his five remaining years of enlistment. He professed to be happy with this prospect, yet within five weeks of reaching Cranwell he sent Charlotte Shaw one of his most despairing letters on **28 September 1925**:

'Do you know what it is when you see, suddenly, that your life is all a ruin? Tonight it is cold, and the hut is dark and empty, with all the fellows out somewhere. Every day I haunt their company, because the noise stops me thinking. Thinking drives me mad, because of the invisible ties about me which limit my moving, my wishing, my imagining. All these bonds I have tied myself, deliberately, wishing to tie myself down beyond the hope or power of movement. And the deliberation, this intention, rests. It is stronger than anything else in me, than everything else put together. So long as there is breath in my body my strength will be exerted to keep my soul in prison, since nowhere else can it exist in safety. The terror of being run away with, in the liberty of power, lies at the back of these many renunciations of my later life. I am afraid, of myself. Is this madness?'

Lawrence went on to tell how he had gone to London, seen Feisal, who was visiting there, and Winterton, and spent a solitary night in a rooming house, but realised only how much that life was behind him, although Winterton had attempted to recall old times. 'From henceforward my way will lie with these fellows here, degrading myself (for in their eyes and your eyes and Winterton's eyes I see that it is degradation) in the hope that someday I will feel really degraded, be degraded, to their level. I long for people to look down upon me and despise me, and I'm too shy to take the filthy steps which would publicly shame me, and out me in their contempt. I want to dirty myself outwardly, so that my person may properly reflect the dirtiness which it conceals...and I shrink from dirtying the outside, while I've eaten, avidly eaten, every filthy morsel which chance threw in my way. I'm too shy to go looking for dirt. I'd be afraid of seeming a novice in it, when I found it. That's why I can't go off stewing into the Lincoln or Navenby brothels with the fellows.'

Despite this deep unhappiness about his present course, the majority of Lawrence's letters show that he soon found contentment at Cranwell. He made no secret of his identity, and the men's curiosity soon wore off. The Cadet College was an attractive station in other ways. Lawrence made friends among members of the teaching staff and helped one of them, Rupert de la Bere, to edit the college journal.

On **17 October 1925** Lawrence advised Charlotte Shaw on her proof reading of *Seven Pillars*: 'Don't spend much time on VIII and IX: they are only incidentals. X is important, in its way'.

On **21 October 1925** Lawrence corresponded with Robert Graves about the position of Professor of English Literature at the newly founded Egyptian University at Cairo. Lawrence had put Grave's name forward to the Foreign Office for this post: 'So altogether I hope that you will take it. The harm to you is little, for the family will benefit by a stay in the warm (Cairo isn't warm in winter) and the job won't drive you into frantic excesses of rage.'

The *Seven Pillars* printing went on steadily, Lawrence had less free time for proof reading than at Bovington, and allowed himself more distractions. On **3 November 1925** he wrote to Edward Garnett: 'I'm in the RAF. Absurdly happy. Such content feels *brittle*, in the light of my past histories. Perhaps it will last. *The Seven Pillars* are at Book VIII. The joy of living is hindering its road. People only work when profoundly miserable. Profoundly but not hopelessly. In March perhaps it will be ready for issue. The poor subscribers...Have read again: *War and Peace, The House of the Dead, The Brothers Karamazov*.'

He had placed a brief epilogue after the end of the narrative in *Seven Pillars*, and on **17 November 1925** he sent a revised draft of this to Charlotte Shaw: 'Isn't it wonderful? The job is nearly over.'

Two incidents described by Lawrence in *The Mint* are worthy of mention. The first was the late arrival in Hut 103 of a fellow airman who had been to a dance and met a girl who he paid for with 'that dollar I borrowed off you Monday'.

The other incident was the parade service on **27 November 1925** day that Queen Alexandra was buried beside her late husband in St George's Chapel at Windsor.

As the typesetting of *Seven Pillars* progressed there were more opportunities to use tailpieces, many of which were drawn by William Roberts. Lawrence sent him a batch of proofs on **10 December 1925**: 'I don't suggest your reading all this, but the pages [indicated] would do with tail-pieces and if your imagination prompts you to anything fitting – why fire away! Designs needn't be *illustrations*. Abstract designs will do. Ditto remote things, like vegetables or trees, hills, sunsets, clouds: dead fishes, apples on a plate. *Not* Pierrots a la Beardsley. *Not* Ballet dancers a la Laura Knight. *Not* cafe scenes a la Sickert.'

Early in December 1925 Lawrence had a crash while riding his motorcycle, which, in retrospect, seems to anticipate the accident that led to his death 10 years later. Letter to E. Palmer, **10 December 1925**: 'Crashed off the Brough last Monday: knee: ankle; elbow: being repaired. Tunic and breeches being replaced. Front mudguard, name-plate, handlebars, footrest, renewed. Skid on ice at 55 m.p.h. Dark: wet: most miserable. Hobble like a cripple now.

Borton often invited Lawrence to his private quarters at Cranwell and they spent many enjoyable evenings together. When the Bortons went away for Christmas 1925 they invited Lawrence to live at their house, but he gratefully declined. Lawrence spent Christmas alone, since the rest of B Flight were on leave. He was still wrestling with the Deraa passages during the final corrections of the subscribers' edition of *Seven Pillars*. 'That's the "bad" book [Book VI] he wrote Charlotte Shaw on **26 December 1925**, 'with the Deraa Chapter. Working on it always makes me sick. The two impulses fight so upon it. Self-respect would close it: self-expression seeks to open it. It's a case in which you can't let yourself write as well as you could.'

His mother looked to him at this time for more expressions of closeness, but Lawrence could not, would not, give them and held her away firmly and abruptly in a letter on **28 December 1925**: 'You talk of "sharing my life" in letters: but that I won't allow. It is only my own business. Nor can anybody turn on or off the tap of "love" so called. I haven't any in me, for anything. Once I used to like *things* (not people) and *ideas*. Now I don't care for anything at all.'

He passed the time correcting proofs and reading *TS Eliot's Poems 1909-1925*: 'It's odd, you know, to be reading these poems,' he wrote to Sydney Cockerell on **29 December 1925**, 'so full of the future, so far ahead of our time; and then to turn back to my book, whose prose stinks of coffins and ancestors and armorial hatchments. Yet people have the nerve to tell me it's a good book! It would have been, if written a hundred years ago: but to bring it out after *Ulysses* is an insult to modern letters - an insult I never meant of course, but ignorance is no defence in the army!'

And to his agent Raymond Savage he wrote on **30 December 1925**: 'The book. It crawls. The distractions are too many, and I hate the beastly thing.' At the end of 1925 Wing Commander Sydney Smith arrived at Cranwell with his wife Clare to take up the post of Chief Staff Officer. They had previously met Lawrence at the Cairo Conference in 1921 when they had all three become friends and Lawrence was very pleased to see them again at Cranwell.

By the close of the year it seemed that the new text would be completed, at long last, within a month. But there was still work to be done on the illustrations. Lawrence suggested that the cost of extra tailpieces should be covered by accepting more subscribers. In any case, as he explained to R.V. Buxton on **4 January 1926**, he didn't 'want to make the number exactly a hundred, for one of my many dislikes is the bibliophile, and that sort of man makes a fetish of numbers. To defeat him I am not numbering my copies, nor disclosing to anyone quite how many have been printed, nor making any two just alike.'

Under the terms of his contract with Jonathan Cape, Lawrence had to deliver the new abridgement of *Seven Pillars* by the end of March 1926. He began work on it in January, deleting passages in pencil on a proof of the subscriber's *Seven Pillars*. Success with the abridgement would be extremely important because he was relying on the shortened version to clear his debts.

Cranwell brought Lawrence a period of calm he had not experienced for many years, especially during the 'interim misfortunes' of the Tank Corps period. On **15 January 1926** he wrote to Charlotte Shaw like an exultant schoolboy bringing home a good report card: 'My RAF character has been assessed (for last year) as "exceptional". This is the highest grade. It shows you how I can behave for four months. Down with the Sam Hoares!'

Cranwell lacked only privacy. Francis Rodd lent him the keys of his London flat during his absence abroad, but Lawrence only used the place once for four nights. 'Four, you will say, is too few to justify my holding those keys all the weeks,' he wrote thanking Rodd for his hospitality on **28 January 1926**, 'but consider the quality of those nights. The place so quiet, so absolutely mine, and the door locked downstairs, so that it was really mine. Why there isn't a lock in my power at Cranwell, not even on the shit-house door! The happiness and security of those nights were very keen.'

A letter written to H.J. Cape on **28 January 1926** shows that Lawrence had already given a good deal of time to the abridgement of *Seven Pillars*: 'I'm not pleased with the abridgement...as now in my hands; I've done the first 500 pages, and it reads queer. The details are too large for the body. How would you view my dictating a more colloquial contracted narrative to some shorthand scribe? I'd take the subscriber version, page by page, and miss out or boil down rapidly in my mind each sentence as it came to the eye. The result would be unceremonious, swift moving, rough perhaps.'

'Cranwell is not a good winter station,' Lawrence told Charlotte Shaw on **8 February 1926** after he had been there for six months. 'Yet technically it is so good and peaceful that I hope they will leave me here a long time.'

As work on *Seven Pillars* drew to a close, Lawrence began to consider further literary projects. The scheme to edit Hardy's early autobiography was especially attractive. He told Mrs Hardy on **13 February 1926**: 'I had been reading it deliberately, tasting it all over: and I swear that it's a very good thing. There is a strange *individual* taste about the story of those old days. . It's very beautiful. Rarely so...I was seeing, every page I read, little things which might be done to polish the jewel more excellently. I do hope you will send it me back. I'll tackle it most humbly and honestly.'

Cape too thought that Lawrence should start some new project. CM Doughty had died in January (Lawrence had taken a day's leave in order to attend the funeral in Golders Green). Shortly afterwards Cape suggested a biography to Lawrence, who replied on **22 February 1926**: 'I've thought of that "life" idea, up and down: and I'm sorry that I can't touch it. I would not have delayed so in considering the life of anyone else: but for CMD I have a very real regard.'

Lawrence was able at Cranwell to permit himself once more the sensuous yet objective appreciation of the qualities of the world around him as he had not for years. One Sunday he cycled over to Nottingham on Boanerges (his Brough motorbike) and saw large crowds going into a Wesleyan Mission Hall. 'I went instead to a Lyons tea shop and ordered tea,' he told Charlotte Shaw on **22 February 1926**, 'the other people were amusing. They hadn't come from my planet, I think. The only friendly person was a black cat, who sat beside me, and was exceedingly insistent upon the point of food. I bought an éclair, and split it open down its length, like two little dugout canoes. The cat flung himself upon them, and hollowed out all the pith with its grating tongue. When it got down to the brown shell it sat back on its hind legs and licked its face lovingly. A man on the opposite seat, also had cream on his cheek and tried horribly hard to lick it. Only his tongue was too short. Not really short, you know: only for that...the cat was a very excellent animal. The human beings were gross, noisy, vulgar: they did the same things as the cat, but in a clumsy blatant way...Heaven knows that I've bothered to write you this nonsense. The moral spoils it.'

To a new friend and reader of *Seven Pillars*, the Cambridge poet F. L. Lucas, Lawrence wrote on **14 March 1926**: 'I always had the ambition to write something good, and when the Revolt gave me a subject I tried to make up for what I felt to be my lack of instinct by taking immense pains: by studying how other people got their effects, and using their experience. So I built an enormous mass of second hand ornaments into my skeleton...and completely hid the skeleton under them...It sounds very conceited, that I should go on believing the book rotten, when you have written in the contrary sense. S.S. [Siegried Sassoon] also called it epical (though an epic hasn't yet been built on the feelings, as aside from the actions of men.'

Lawrence finished correcting the last proofs of the *Seven Pillars* text, but the illustrations were still well behind. Whittingham & Griggs told him they could not complete their part of the work before July, and he replied on **15 March 1926** that this was too late: 'Will you let me know which are the laggard plates? And I'll cancel them, if possible...I want all the illustrations completed by the first week in June.'

It was well that he had finished the text corrections, for 10 days later he broke his right arm while trying to help out in a car accident. He was turning the starting handle of a car when the engine backfired, breaking his radius and dislocating his wrist. Fortunately, by this time he had also completed the Cape abridgement as far as the final Book of *Seven Pillars*. He was never to recover full movement of his right hand, and for the next month could only write with difficulty, often asking one of the other aircraftman to act as secretary. On **18 March 1926** he wrote to Charlotte Shaw in what he described as 'a drunken script'.

When he finished making the Cape abridgement in late March he decided to keep the pencil working draft. With help from two friends, another proof of *Seven Pillars* was marked up with all the cuts and linking passages for the abridgement. This operation, which consisted mainly of blacking out the deleted passages with Indian ink, provided the basis for a deliberately misleading statement Lawrence later gave to Cape's house journal *Now and Then*: 'The abridgement...was made by him in seven hours at Cranwell in Lincolnshire on **March 26** and **March 27 1926**, with the assistance of two airman friends, A/A Knowles and A/c Miller'. The text they produced was submitted to Cape on **30 March 1926**.

In making his abridgement Lawrence ignored Edward Garnett's earlier abridgement and reduced the text to less than half by obliterating 'whole slabs of the text.' Omitted were the emotionally laden, introspective or personal parts, or any sections which might reveal himself or otherwise provoke, shock, or disturb his readers. 'I cut out all the high emotion,' Lawrence wrote Edward Garnett, 'and whittled it into non-entity.' Since most of his self-criticism derived precisely from these personal elements of the narrative, and from the disturbing occurrences they described, it is not surprising that Lawrence declared the abridgement on occasion to be better than the complete text. 'Half a calamity is better than a whole one.' He wrote Edward Garnett on **6 April 1926.** 'By exercising heights and depths I have made a balanced thing: yet I share your difficulty of seeing the shorter version's real shape across the gaps.' Yet remarkably, according to Howard, 'his cuts required scarcely any interpolations to form linkages and very few words were written in.'

When Lawrence first agreed to the cape abridgement, he had planned that it would appear several months after *Seven Pillars* had been issued; but work on the illustrations was still holding up the subscribers' edition. In April 1926 Whittingham & Griggs postponed their completion date until August, and Lawrence heard that the Ordnance Survey was too busy to tackle his maps, so he had to look for an alternative printer. In the meantime he had commissioned more tailpieces, including a group from Blair Hughes-Stanton.

He told his mother about his broken wrist on **20 April 1926**, two months after it happened, 'The tip of the radius was cracked off and the wrist dislocated. Now they have put it nearly straight again: but it still cramps me badly after a few minutes in one position holding anything small like a pen or a knife. They say that in another month it will be quite fit; though I have lost the power of twisting my hand round very far. It goes about half way now.'

The Medical Officer was an old Wing Commander who looked after Lawrence well. 'He is 70 odd: ex-surgeon to the King as a civil practitioner. Courtly: a wonderful bedside manner – so sympathetic. Rather nice too. He has been very good to me', Lawrence told Charlotte Shaw on **20 April 1926**.

On **29 April 1926** Lawrence sent Charlotte Shaw a postcard of Queen Eleanor of Castile, Edward I's wife, whose statue is above the chantry in Lincoln Cathedral: 'She is exceedingly lovely: just the sort of woman you meet at tea, constantly. Interested faintly, in church work, and has a pet dog'.

At the beginning of May 1926 progress with the remaining work on *Seven Pillars* was briefly held up by the General Strike, but Lawrence felt that the end was in sight. He expected to issue *Seven Pillars* in September. Friends in the rare book trade told him that its value would go up to £50 within a month.

'So far we have not been done anything with,' he wrote to Charlotte Shaw on **10 May 1926**, the seventh day of the strike, 'All leave is cancelled and we just wait in camp till the Government want to use us'.

During the General Strike coal issues were stopped and B Flight only had a lot of coal dust and slack. Lawrence found the name of the officer who had stopped the issue (but not stopped his own coal ration) and exchanged the dust and slack for some wonderful pieces of coal from the officer's supply.

In late May he learned that he was to be posted to India that autumn. This seemed to be for the best, because it meant that he would be out of reach of the publicity surrounding Cape's issue of the abridgement. But the posting did not please him personally; he wrote to H.H. Banbury, a Tank Corps friend then serving at Quetta, on **25 May 1926**: 'I will be low in

India. Living on my pay, and trying to be an airman. The *Seven Pillars* will have been built by then, and my hybrid existence ended. In some way it will be a relief. So long as I am in England I cannot avoid sometimes bridging the classes. The writers and artists are intoxicating to meet and talk to. For a while with them I imagine myself to be an artist: they feel somehow (presumptuous it sounds) to be of my own sort. With these fellows in the service I'm very happy; but the play times are rather a strain. I don't play – not at anything: so that the more hours work they give us the better life goes.'

The subscribers to *Seven Pillars* included King George V, whose cheque was sent to Lawrence's friend J.G. Wilson. 'The Windsor copy will be duly sent,' Lawrence wrote to Wilson on **25 May 1926**, 'but I'm an old fashioned person, to whom it seems improper that Kings should buy and sell among their subjects'. The cheque was discreetly returned.

On **17 June 1926** he wrote to Charlotte Shaw: 'I can only keep happy in the RAF by holding myself a little below par: if it's much below I mizzle: grow sorry for myself. This happens if I get ill or hurt, or am chased over much by some NCO with a grievance to hand on.'

Within two months of receiving the abridgement draft, Cape produced a set of galley proofs for correction; as a result Lawrence had this additional preoccupation in June. Work on *Seven Pillars* was not going so smoothly. The continuing industrial unrest was affecting power supplies, and Whittingham & Griggs were held up still further. He resigned himself to the possibility that they might not finish the plates until September. On **21 June 1926** he wrote to Florence Hardy: 'Everything else is printed and ready, and I'll send the copies out before I go abroad, whether all the possible pictures are finished or not.'

On **3 July 1926** Lawrence took B Flight and their wives to Hendon by charabanc to see the annual air display.

On **6 July 1926** he told his mother of the plans for India, explaining that 'the Air Force authorities drag too slowly and that he wished to be definite before letting her know the news. 'It is always difficult to get away and I've been long drawing in my horns inch by inch, like a snail. India will let me finish the business.'

On **15 August 1926** Lawrence gave a copy of *Seven Pillars* to 'Biffy' Borton at RAF Cranwell. Rupert de la Bere, the editor of the college magazine, asked Lawrence for permission to make a substantial quotation from *The Seven Pillars* which he proposed to preface with a short biographical appreciation of the author.

In mid August he went to Edinburgh to see Bartholomews, the map publishers, who had agreed to adapt and print the War Office maps he wanted to use for *Seven Pillars*. By then the colour printers were working on their last three plates. He wrote to Charlotte Shaw on **22 August 1926**: 'One has twenty-three colours upon it. Lord save us! Kelman, a Constable partner, was admiring some of the prints at Chiswick and said to the printer "Now why shouldn't you give *us* some work of that quality?" "We will," said Newbery [of Whittingham

& Griggs], "if you'll pay ten shillings a print"! Exit K.' Most of the plates were to be placed at the end of Seven Pillars, and Lawrence, who had the idea of making each copy different, thought of changing their order. Later, however, he abandoned the idea since it would have made a nonsense of the list of illustrations.

On **24 August 1926** he sent Charlotte Shaw a description of his journey back from Edinburgh which conveys both the pleasure he took in motor-cycling, and his happiness that work on *Seven Pillars* was so nearly over. On Boanerges he travelled from Durham to 'Cranwell (160 miles) in 2 hrs 58 minutes...The Great North Road: (what a dream, what a drunkenness of delight of a name!) is, as you know, very wide and smooth, and straight. So that you can biff along it safely, without any tactics in meeting or overtaking traffic.'

On **28 August 1926**, in preparation for leaving the country, Lawrence had his solicitors draw up a Last Will and Testament (of me Thomas Edward Shaw otherwise called Thomas Edward Lawrence or John Hume Ross of Clouds Hill, Moreton'). He appointed his younger brother and his solicitor as executors and willed each of them £100 and a copy of Shelly's poems in the Kelmcott Edition by William Morris. He left the land and buildings at Pole Hill, Chingford, in Essex to Vyvyan Ricahrds and the residue of his property to his younger brother Arnold and Arnold's children.

Lawrence thought that copies of *Seven Pillars* would be ready for dispatch to the binders on **15 September 1926**. However, there were yet further delays and the text was still not ready on **25 September 1926** when he learned that he had inadvertently libelled Ronald Storrs. The offending passage had to be rewritten, and then, since the type had been distributed, four pages had to be reset, proofed and reprinted. To add to his problems Kennington found fault with some of the plates. As a result, the binding date had to be postponed until the end of October. There was good news, however, when Raymond Savage obtained offers worth £2000 from the *Daily Telegraph* and *Asia Magazine* for serial rights in the Cape abridgement. This would help greatly with the *Seven Pillars* overdraft and Lawrence accepted.

On **27 September 1926** he sent a letter and testimonial to George Brough, the motorcycle manufacturer in Nottingham, writing that 'Yesterday I completed 100,000 miles, since 1922, on five successive Brough Superiors, and I'm going abroad very soon, so that I think I must make an end, and thank you for the road-pleasure I have got out of them. In 1922 I found George I (your old Mark I) the best thing I'd ridden, but George V (the 1922 SS 100) is incomparably better. In 1925 and 1926 (George IV & V) I have not had an involuntary stop, and so have not been able to test your spares service, on which I drew so heavily in 1922 and 1923. Your present machines are as fast and reliable as express trains, and the greatest fun in the world to drive:- and I say this after twenty years experience of cycles and cars.'

On **14 October 1926** he wrote to Mrs Friedlow that Cranwell had become his 'home for lost dogs'. He was already planning how he would spend the time between leaving Cranwell and going to India. This would be a combination of finishing the production of *Seven Pillars* and saying goodbye to people. He wrote to D. Knowles on **18 October 1926**: 'Then I'll be free for ten days to say goodbye to everyone: then a week distributing the bound volumes.' He also wrote to M. Pike on **18 October 1926**: 'Keep at it. We are really last lapping. Get the Table of Contents done: make a title page which pleases you, and don't send it me: and then print and print and print.'

On **26 October 1926** Lawrence told T.B. Marston, 'the RAF is still my spiritual home, and I'm awfully sorry to leave Cranwell, where I've had the best year I ever remember to have had'. Marston had a son John who was a cadet at Cranwell, but Lawrence had not seen much of him as he was in another squadron. 'I hope he will like the RAF', Lawrence said. 'From my point of view it is the perfect existence: but then I've been battered so much elsewhere.'

On **4 November 1926** Lawrence began the month's leave to which he was entitled before going to India He had planned a last visit to many friends before this five year absence overseas. But work on *Seven Pillars* took priority, and he meant to spend the first few days helping Pike get the sheets off to the bookbinders. A few copies of the English *Seven Pillars* were completed by the binders during November. Lawrence sent the very first of these to the Royal Library at Windsor.

When Hugh Trenchard (who had got Lawrence back into the RAF in 1925) heard that Shaw was being posted to India, he told him that it was not necessary for him to go if he did not wish to. Lawrence wrote back on **20 November 1926** explaining 'I volunteered to go, deliberately, for the reason that I am publishing a book (about myself in Arabia) on March 3 1927. I'm sorry you should have been unnecessarily troubled. It had been my ambition that you shouldn't hear of or from me, after my readmission to the RAF. I'm perfectly happy in it, on the ordinary terms: and if the other fellows knew that I used to know you, my character would be ruined.'

He also told Trenchard: 'I've got everything I want: and nearly every morning when I wake up a little rush of delight comes over me, at finding myself still in the RAF. The only regrettable thing is that I have this feeling of delight at 6.30am in winter. It would be more moving if they let us lie in till 8.' But, as he explained in The Mint, there was a great consolation in the summer when 'we race over in the first dawn to the College's translucent swimming pool, and dive into the elastic water which fits our bodies as closely as a skin:- and we belong to that too. Everywhere a relationship: no loneliness any more'.

Trenchard's specially bound copy of *Seven Pillars* in air force blue was sent direct to its recipient with a covering letter on **22 November 1926**, in which Lawrence wrote, 'It is not the right blue of course: but then what is the right blue? No two airmen are alike: indeed it is a miracle if the top and bottom halves of one airman are the same colour. So perhaps you are not particular'.

Trenchard's copy of *Seven Pillars* was inscribed by the author: 'Sir Hugh Trenchard, from a contented, admiring and, whenever possible, obedient servant.' This gratified and amused the Chief of the Air Staff who replied to Lawrence on **22 November 1926** saying that it was 'a delightful touch from the most disobedient mortal I have ever met...I would very much like to have seen you before you actually sailed, but I suppose that is not possible, and perhaps it would be inadvisable from your point of view: but if you want to be put up for a night, my wife and children would be delighted to see you before you went out at Dancers Hill. Let me know'.

'Many thanks,' Lawrence replied on **29 November 1926**, 'but I will not trouble Lady Trenchard. It wouldn't do in uniform: and I've no other clothes fit to wear. This has been a hard-working, rushed month for me: and yesterday I had a crash on my bicycle. Broke the poor thing, and scratched my knee! First crash for 11 months. Hard luck'.

The month's leave passed very quickly. Lawrence had to spend most of it helping Pike collate the remaining copies of Seven Pillars, making up the individual sets of pages and plates. He managed a brief visit to Clouds Hill in Dorset and arranged to let the cottage (to two service friends for 12 shillings a week) and collect some books for reading in India. During this visit he went over to Max Gate to say good-bye to the Hardys. Kennington had asked him to pose for a bronze portrait bust, and somehow Lawrence made time for five sittings.

During the last days in London, Lawrence sold his motorbike and made over the copyright of the Cape abridgement, to be called *Revolt in the Desert*, to a charitable trust, appointing Robin Buxton, DG Hogarth and Edward Eliot (a London solicitor recommended by Buxton) as Trustees.

On **1 December 1926** he wrote to his mother, who was with Robert Lawrence in China on medical missionary work: 'This is my last free night in England, & I'm writing to you, very late, in the top of Barton Street, where [Sir Herbert] Baker has let me stay during this month. It should have been leave, preparatory to going overseas: but for me it has been a very hard month of work on that book of mine...Thank you for suggesting my leaving the RAF and living quietly somewhere: but I cannot be quiet, and so the bustle and enforced duty of the RAF is good for me.'

He then lectured them both – the first of a series of dressings down he gave them – about the evils of missionary work and medicine in general and interfering with the destiny of other peoples, all of which his medical missionary brother not unexpectedly cut from the printed edition of these letters.

He sent his mother's copy of *Seven Pillars* to Arnold Lawrence (his brother) to await for her return from China. 'Getting it over has been a big relief,' he told her. 'I have spent £13,000 on it altogether, and the responsibility of that has been heavy, since my own resources would not meet the liability'. He added that he was relying on the abridgement to bring him in enough to cover the deficit.

In London he saw the Shaws and a few other friends. As a leaving present Charlotte gave him a notebook she had filled with philosophical meditations. He wrote to thank her on **2 December 1926:** 'We managed that good bye occasion very well, I think. They are so difficult. Your little book will be very valued, for your sake, and I hope for its own. I tremble rather, upon this second head, for my tastes are not very catholic and not speculative. However I'll write and tell you just how it takes me, after I've studied it.'

On **3 December 1926** he wrote to Francis Rodd: 'I had an awful month, real hard labour upon my old man of the sea: final printings, plates, collection, collation, issue to binders, correction of subscribers' lists, allotment of copies. Yet though I sweated it at every possible hour of the day and night, seeing no one and doing nothing else, even now it is not finished. About 20 copies have gone out, and most of the rest will go out about Christmas time ['my Christmas pudding' he called it in another letter] but the very special copies will hang on till the New Year. I think my experience is almost a conclusive demonstration that publishing is not a suitable hobby for an airman.'

'It is a strange empty feeling to have finished with it, after all these years,' he wrote to Dick Knowles, his Clouds Hill neighbour on **3 December 1926.** Lawrence gave many of his books to Vyvyan Richards and a gift copy of *Seven Pillars* in heavy morocco binding to Robert Graves.

Stanley Baldwin's incomplete copy of the *Seven Pillars* was sent through John Buchan on **14 December 1926.** 'This copy is one of those which I am giving to the fellows who did the Arab revolt with me,' he wrote in the covering letter to Buchan. 'If he likes books, as I am told, he may prefer a broken copy to none at all. The thing is, anyhow, a rarity'.

On board ship he wrote to Sergeant Pugh (of his Flight at Cranwell) on **16 December 1926** of Trenchard's last minute offer of a choice about whether or not to go to India, but 'I had to choose to go, of course, damn it. I'm always hurting myself or my interests.'

The trip to India aboard the crowded troopship *Derbyshire* was a foul and fetid one, with 'wave upon wave of the smell of stabled humanity' from which Lawrence sought to isolate himself by writing further auto-biographical notes. What seemed to represent for him the quintessence of its horrors was the problem of unplugging a latrine in close quarters stopped up by a sanitary napkin ('the horror of almost final squalidity'). The only relief was a brief affectionate meeting in Port Said with the Newcombes, who took him away for several hours into the harbour where he could escape the smell of the ship.

Clare Sydney Smith: *The Golden Reign: the story of my friendship with Lawrence of Arabia* (1940)

'At the end of 1925 Sydney was moved to Cranwell from the Staff College, Cambereley, where he had been during 1924-25. He was now appointed Chief Staff Officer at the Royal Air Force Cadet College.

All this time I had heard little of Lawrence, who was serving as an aircraftman at Cranwell, but as soon as we arrived there and had settled into the wooden hut which was our official 'house', he came to tea and we renewed our acquaintance. The blue suit and white topee had changed into a Service uniform. 'Lawrence of Arabia' was now Thomas Edward Shaw.

At tea we talked over Egypt and our first meeting. Although physically he looked the same, he was far more restless than when I had met him at Cairo. Sitting on his chair he would rub its sides with his hands, up and down, up and down, and he would sometimes pass two fingers over his mouth and chin, or rumple up the crest of fair hair which was still unruly and refused to lie down.

The Commandant at Cranwell was Air Vice Marshal A. E. Borton, who was in command of the Air Force in Palestine when the war ended. Lawrence had a great affection for 'Biffy', as he is known to his friends, and refers to him in *Seven Pillars* and in some of his letters to me. His immediate officer in command was Flight Lieutenant Green who told Sydney that he was delighted to have Shaw with him and that his presence was invaluable, both to him and to the men.

At Cranwell he spent much of his spare time working on the second manuscript of *Seven Pillars*. Nearly all of the first draft had been lost or stolen in 1919 while he was having a cup of coffee in a refreshment room at Reading station. He was travelling to Oxford to spend the first Christmas at home after his father's death and had put it down at his feet unthinkingly. He offered £100 at once for its return – there were letters addressed to him in the bag as well as the manuscript – but to this day it has never turned up. Now, at Cranwell, he was near the end of the heart breaking labour of rewriting it, and his health and nerves were suffering accordingly. Every moment he could snatch from his duties as an airman he devoted to the final details of his laborious task, over which he had spent something like seven years.

One day he turned up at our house carrying the finished manuscript. In size and bulk it was tremendous – a great thick quarto mass written in his own small, neat hand writing and with many corrections. 'Would you leave it for us to read?' I asked him. 'Well, it's terribly long and dull; you'll never get through it!' 'I can try, at any rate. But does it matter how long I keep it?' 'Oh, no; you can keep it as long as you like.'

The deprecating attitude towards himself and his achievements was typical of him. He was genuinely humble about anything he did. As soon as the manuscript was off his hands I noticed a great change in him. He seemed altogether freer and lighter in spirit. In it he had finally worked his Arabian experiences – some of which were so terrible – off his mind, and it was as if he had got rid of a heavy burden that had been weighing him down. Added to that,

36

the actual writing of the book had worried and obsessed him. Now the child was born and he was free.

The bulky manuscript that Sydney and I read with so much interest was printed in a room behind Whiteley's by Lawrence with the help of a man called Pyke. There was no profits from it; in fact, he was £15000 in debt to his bank over it. Subscribers paid £30 a copy, but each one had cost him £90. To pay off this debt was the reason why he allowed the abridged edition *Revolt in the Desert* to be published.

Afraid of the publicity it would entail for him, he applied to be sent overseas to escape it. Lord Trenchard, fully appreciating the situation, agreed to his request and had him posted to the RAF depot at Karachi.'

A.W.H.M : 'Aircraftman Shaw – A Memory' (1949)

[*Journal of the Royal Air Force College*, November 1949].

'Sight of the Lawrence relics in the College library reminds me of my own fleeting glimpses of that most remarkable man. I first saw him in the old M Squadron dining hall at Uxbridge. In those days the big annual overseas drafts assembled there. Large numbers of men bound for India, Iraq and Egypt were caught in the turmoil of "kitting out" and otherwise preparing for five years overseas. Lawrence remained through it all, serene, reserved, having little intercourse with any but his immediate neighbours. That would be in 1926.

The usual descriptions of Lawrence are generally correct. His physique was slight, almost shadowy, and he moved and spoke quietly. He could easily have been lost in a crowd. But somehow he never was. Not that the force of his personality was immediately obvious. He was no high-pressure salesman. He had, in a large measure, the faculty of withdrawal. He could make a praiseworthy attempt to take the colours of his surroundings. He did desire, if we are to believe his own words, complete obscurity. But great as might be his power of withdrawal, and anonymous as was his physique, he could not hide his features, at least, in European clothes. The clear blue eyes could be veiled, but that cliff-like brow was still obvious beneath a 'cap, S.D.'

I think Lawrence realised that he had made a mistake. Complete anonymity is not to be found in the Royal Air Force. He had shed responsibility perhaps, but he had overlooked the fact that the RAF was, and, one hopes, still is, a close-knit band with common aims and abundant mutual interest. Every member of the team is a matter of great interest to a greater number of people. He could have hidden himself so much more easily in Islington or Charing Cross Road. In the RAF he was a walking query. He knew it and hated it. He could do nothing about it. He bore it cheerfully. Perhaps is ministered to that masochism which was in him and which largely shaped his course.

The draft sailed in the old *Derbyshire*, long since defunct. The vessel swarmed with humanity; by day the deck was a market place – it was hard to find squatting room. But

Lawrence could usually find a perch for his small frame and quietly read Pepys. Like deck space, topics of conversation were limited. The troops quickly exhausted the officers (whom they did not know) and the officers' ladies and the nursing sisters who regarded them from the distant heights of the upper deck. Lawrence was in the midst of the troops. What was he doing in the RAF? Was it true that he was a spy? Why was he going to India? Was he snooping for Air Ministry? The queries arose and buzzed on the troop decks. One afternoon they were put to me by a group tight-packed against the rail. I replied that I didn't know and didn't care. There was nothing we could do anyway. Lawrence's business was his own. He obviously wanted to be left alone: the best and kindest thing would be to leave him so. I noted the expressions of my companions. Turning, I saw Lawrence. Clearly, he had heard. He grinned rather boyishly and walked away.

Thereafter he and I met several times on deck in the cool of the morning before the swarm arose. We chatted, but I do not recall that we said anything significant. He disliked "Helmets Wolseley, N.P." and thought them ridiculously unnecessary. "I travelled thousands of miles up and down the coast," he once said, indicating the red burnt desolation of Arabia, "and I never wore one. I let my hair grow long down the back of my neck." But mostly I think we preferred to be silent.

The last time I saw him was in the Union Jack Club a year before he died. He sat behind a newspaper in the reading room. He lowered the paper and I saw his features fully. He had matured. He had developed eyebrows at the base of that great brow. His nose and chin were more set. The likeness to George Bernard Shaw was startling. We half grinned and I passed on.

No doubt had I been a little less reserved with him, my memories of Lawrence might have been more valuable. But on the whole I am glad that I did not hammer on his shell.'

S. Weintraub: *Private Shaw and Public Shaw* (1963)

'By the end of August, Private Shaw had become Aircraftman Shaw...He was beside himself with joy and triumph: "How can any man describe his happiness?" he wrote in the preface to the RAF journal he renewed making...But Cranwell was far from both Clouds Hill and Max Gate...There would now be little chance to visit his cottage on the heath, and little time left to visit with the ageing Thomas Hardy...

[In] his B Flight...there were a sergeant, a corporal and 14 aircraftmen to service a hangar and 6 training planes used by 15 cadets. As junior man he was runner and bookkeeper for his flight....In his new peace he wrote little , except in his RAF journal, in which life at Cranwell appeared much more bleak than in his joyous letters.

In September King Feisal of Iraq visited England, and Aircraftman Shaw, who had known Feisal well when both were in highly different circumstances, received a pass to see him...By November the revision [of Seven Pillars] was nearly completed...Early in December he wrote to the Shaws that he wanted to see them...Lawrence never got to Ayot in December, and work on Seven Pillars slowed down...At Christmas leave time he had the hut to himself...

Writing again on New Year's Day, 1926, he wondered when the Shaws would return from Falmouth...January weather was bad, with temperatures dropping at night to zero, and many roads still snowbound; but Lawrence had promised to spend a week end at Ayot. Before the end of the month he had done so...

Other distractions occupied Lawrence in February of 1926. Early in the month Doughty died, and TE had gone, in the cold rain, to the funeral...Lawrence became a victim of an epidemic of measles at the camp...In mid March he fractured his writing (right) arm, an event which drastically curtailed his correspondence...While his arm was still mending, he chanced the long journey from Lincolnshire to Max gate. A few months later Virginia Woolf heard about the visit when she was there, and noted in her diary how:

Colonel Lawrence, bicycling with a broken arm "held like that" from Lincoln to Hardy, listened at the door to hear if there was anyone there. "I hope he won't commit suicide," said Mrs Hardy pensively, still leaning over the tea cups, gazing despondently. "He often says things like it, though he has never said quite that perhaps. But he has blue lines around his eyes. He calls himself Shaw in the army. No one is to know where he is. But it got into the papers." "He promised me not to go into the air," said hardy. "My husband doesn't like anything to do with the air," said Mrs Hardy. [25 July 1926].

GBS was still not well, and ailed through April...[Lawrence] had to help the RAF cheer the King on his official birthday (Saturday 5 June). After the ceremony TE raced southward to Ayot. The Shaws had passed up the opportunity to visit HG Wells on the chance that Lawrence might turn up...Toward the end of June, with everything going well, he sent them a facetious foreword he had written, supposedly for the Cape abridgement [*Revolt in the Desert*]...In July the news belatedly broke that Lawrence was back in the Air Force, but the information was romantically garbled, and created no stir at Cranwell...'

Phillip Knightley & Colin Simpson: *The Secret Lives of Lawrence of Arabia* (1969)

Lawrence had become friendly with Arthur Lippet, who worked in the station's X-ray department and had treated Lawrence for a fractured wrist. According to Lippet, 'One afternoon after tea time Lawrence was waiting for me outside our mess. He told me he needed my help. About six o'clock a parcel would be dropped from a motor cycle on to the road passing through the camp or on to the road passing outside. Lawrence said, "You go to the outside road and keep watch. If anything is dropped bring it back to me. Don't stay after dusk." I did as he asked, but the drop was made on the road Lawrence was watching. It was a parcel containing hundreds of subversive pamphlets. Lawrence took them away.' Lippet said that it was common knowledge that there were a number of Irish Republican Army sympathisers in the camp and minor explosions had occurred. It seems clear that Lawrence, either on his own initiative, but more probably with the knowledge of the authorities, had made it his business to keep an eye on the IRA elements and, when possible, upset their schemes.

E.B. Haslam: *The History of Royal Air Force Cranwell* (1982)

'AC2 Shaw...reported to Cranwell on 24 August 1925 and was posted to B Flight (South airfield) and lived in Hut 105 in West Camp....There are several testimonies to his behaviour at Cranwell. The Commandant, "Biffy" Borton...often invited Lawrence to the Lodge in the evening for talks. "He did a lot for the library at Cranwell", said Borton...

A fellow airman at Cranwell in 1925-26 was Mr Cyril Hobbs who had lately passed out from Halton as a Carpenter Rigger AC1. He remembered Shaw reading or writing in his hut while the others disported themselves in Lincoln or Newark. "He was a good airman and comrade".

Wing Commander Sydney Smith, who had known Lawrence at the Cairo Conference in 1921 and his wife, Clare, arrived at Cranwell in late 1925 and renewed their friendship with him. But for the most part Shaw kept away from officers while he was at Cranwell. It was not surprising therefore that the General Committee Meeting of the Old Cranwellian Association on 19 March 1935 decided that "Although A/c Shaw had written the book [Revolt in the Desert] when he was stationed at the College, he had an insufficiently close connection with the College to warrant his being invited to become an honorary member of the Association." The chances are that Shaw would have declined the offer had it been made.'

Michael Yardley: *T.E. Lawrence: a biography* (1986)

'A/c Shaw's duties were chiefly clerical, but whenever the chance arose, he would work on the aeroplanes maintained by other members of his Flight. Similarly, several of the instructing officers, eager to have Lawrence of Arabia as their passenger, would allow him to fly with them when machines needed checking out or when they were not busy with cadets. Lawrence loved aeroplanesw. He would even sneak into the hangars to wash them down, not because they needed cleaning or because he had been ordered to, but because he enjoyed it.'

P.J. Marriott & Y. Argent: *Last days of T.E. Lawrence* (1996)

'The Long Ride Home, 26 February – 5 March 1935' [Lawrence left the RAF at Bridlington, Yorkshire, on 26 February 1935 to start his journey by bicycle to his cottage, Clouds Hill, in Dorset].

Lawrence left Bridlington at 10.00 hours on Tuesday 26 February, on a sunny day with a moderate westerly breeze. He cycled south, probably along the coastal road to Beverley and Hull, covering 32 miles and arrived at Hull in the early afternoon. He caught the Humber ferry, which took an hour to cross the Humber. Travelling south for the rest of the daylight,

Lawrence passed through Caistor and Market Rasen. Just south of here was then sited the Youth Hostel at Lynwode, a possible night stop.

Rain, heavy at times, with a south-easterly gale, continued all through Wednesday the 27th making cycling very arduous. Lawrence would have covered only a small distance, say 15 or so miles. It seems highly probable that drenched through he travelled to his old favourite haunt, Lincoln, where he might have lodged overnight (27-28 February). It is quite possible that he stayed at a guest house on Steep Hill - one used often in his Cranwell days.

Conditions were ideal on Thursday morning (the 28th). The rain had passed over and only a mist and overcast sky greeted Lawrence as he pushed south the 17 or so miles to RAF Cranwell. He went to visit Rupert de la Bere, an old friend he had known for about 15 years...He arrived at the mid-morning break (10.00 – 11.00 hours). They walked around the College for "about an hour and a half...he was just going off on his push bike from Cranwell to Cambridge."
It is highly probable that...de la Bere mentioned that the author Frederic Manning had died on 22 February. As all newspapers were available in the College, de la Bere would have read Manning's only obituary, which was first published in the early editions of *The Times* newspaper on the morning of 28 February...

On leaving RAF Cranwell around lunchtime Lawrence avoided Bourne and cycled through Sleaford and Swineshead the 30 miles to Holbeach to stay at the *Talbot Hotel*. This was a public house situated in the High Street; in 1935 it was run by Andrew Keight. At that time it possessed a large rear yard connecting through to Cross Street. It had been an inn-cum-hotel since the early 19th century but was eventually boarded up in the early 1970s, and finally demolished in about 1975 to make way for three modern shops.

Lawrence wrote to the publisher Peter Davies on Thursday 28 February, saying "On Tuesday [26 February] I took my discharge from the RAF and started southward by road, meaning to call at Bourne and see Manning: but today [28th] I turned eastward, instead, hearing that he was dead". The letter was written on headed notepaper from the Talbot Hotel, where he obviously stayed the night...arriving there in the late afternoon – darkness then fell around 17.30 hours.

After staying the night of Thursday / Friday (28 February / 1 March) Lawrence cycled through the morning fog southward to Wisbech, then routing to Cambridge via Chatteris or Ely. Both roads were of similar distance making the journey Holbeach to Cambridge a round 54 miles. This would have taken about 6 hours arriving at Cambridge around 15.00 hours, when he visited the Fitzwilliam Museum...Later he arrived at his brother's house (A.W. Lawrence's home) at 31 Madingley Road, Cambridge...

After Cambridge, Lawrence cycled to Oxford. He left his brother's house early on Saturday morning, 2 March. It was cloudy with a fine rain and mist. He probably took the slightly shorter route (76 miles) through Bedford and Buckingham. Later in the day the rain became heavier, so he must have reached Oxford after dusk. He visited E.T Leeds, Curator of the Ashmolean Museum, at his home at 88 Woodstock Road, Oxford, where he most probably stayed the night (Saturday/Sunday, 2 – 3 March)....[He arrived at Clouds Hill on 5 March].

P. Tunbridge: *With Lawrence in the Royal Air Force* (2000)

'Lawrence rejoined the Royal Air Force on 18 August 1925, a memorable date for him. On his arrival at West Drayton, the RAF Records Centre, he walked over to the recruits hut with the notes of his favourite song 'The Lass of Richmond Hill' drifting from a nearby barrack-room. That evening he began his letter to Mrs Bernard Shaw "a happy day". A corporal – with strict instructions to obtain a receipt for his charge – accompanied Lawrence to the RAF Depot Uxbridge where a store man issued him with the familiar blue uniform and equipment. He spent the evening there in the company of other recruits scrubbing his webbing equipment and burnishing his bayonet.

In the morning with a kitbag over his shoulder he reported to the Guardroom where the NCO insisted on hanging a full water bottle beneath his full pack. When he protested the sergeant reminded him it was still Uxbridge and to shut up or be "put inside". At the railway station, sweating in tight puttees and smelling of mothballs, Lawrence happily collapsed in the London train. Oblivious to the upturned water-bottle gurgling its contents onto the seat, he relaxed for the first time in years. As he boarded the bus to Victoria Station, the friendly conductor remarked how he too had served in uniform, "but a bit before your time, sonny". Lawrence politely acknowledged this with a "Yes, dad."

On arrival at RAF Cranwell, Lawrence found himself attached to B Flight of the Cadet Training College, under Flight Lt FCB Green. As an aircrafthand – the lowest trade group in the RAF – Lawrence's duties included pushing aircraft in and out of hangars, recording flying times in the Cadets' logbooks, and hand swinging propellers of the training aircraft. The flying instructors respected Lawrence's desire to be treated as an ordinary aircraftman. An Air Marshal, then Flying Officer Pendred, recalls being warned against any "hob-nobbing" with Lawrence who apart from popping in and out of the instructors' office to stoke the fire or tidy up the table, spent part of his time in the Flight Sergeant's office. Pendred remembered Lawrence from the Cairo Conference when he had flown him over the Suez Canal area in a Bristol Fighter. He was not surprised when Lawrence shyly approached him on the tarmac and asked to accompany him on his next flight. Although on the way back to the flight office, Pendred asked Lawrence whether he recalled their previous flight, Lawrence refused to be drawn and changed the subject.

In addition to four instructors, B Flight comprised two NCO's and fifteen airmen to maintain the Avro 504K's, Bristol Fighters, DH9A's and Sopwith Camels in which the cadets received their training. Lawrence, who shared the hut with four other aircrafthands, five engine fitters and five riggers, began his day at 6.30 am followed by a leisurely breakfast and colour hoisting parade at 8 am before marching to the hangars. On Lawrence's first morning, after having "squared off" the folded blankets and sheets on his Macdonald bed, the hut corporal asked whether he was "bobbing" for promotion. Lawrence stood to attention but relaxed when the corporal told him this was not necessary. "Righto, Corporal" Lawrence said, but received another shock on being told to drop the "Corporal" and to cut out the bullshit. With the Tank Corps bugle calls and shouting sergeants rapidly fading in his memory, Lawrence enjoyed the morning boot and button polishing routine. His only other chore was the weekly inspection when the table and forms had to be scrubbed and the hut entrance brightened up. A flick with a duster and a quick sweep round his bed space sufficed to satisfy the orderly officer's morning rounds.

After collecting his red "monster" SS110 motorcycle from the Brough works at Nottingham, Lawrence, Lawrence began making nightly runs to the Lincolnshire countryside to purchase sausages, eggs and bacon for the evening fry up in the hut. He sometimes parked his Brough – which the flight cadets admired but could not even begin to afford – against a 'P' model Triumph belonging to Sgt C. Mayhew of C Flight who occasionally marched Lawrence's flight to the hangars. After being posted to RAF Henlow, Mayhew again bumped into Lawrence in the refreshment room on Grantham station. "Hello Sergeant" said Lawrence with a grin "you've come to see us again?" When he learned that Mayhew was on route for Lincoln, Lawrence offered him the pillion seat of his Brough. "I guarantee you a good freezing" he laughed, but Mayhew declined the offer.

As an unskilled aircrafthand, Lawrence sometimes assisted the riggers in setting up the machines for inspection, when wings were removed for checking prior to reassembly and rigging. The fitter corporal entrusted him with scraping the carbon encrusted piston heads from dismantled engines. But Lawrence preferred his self appointed task of straightening out the clerical work of B Flight office and making up the cadets' log books. Lawrence had the greatest respect for the flying instructors, King Tim (flight commander), John, Crasher and Ginger, but occasionally an over-zealous NCO interrupted their working hours with drill periods. At such times Lawrence persuaded the flight to practice the ultimate in submission until their chiefs understood that "the soldier and the mechanic were mutually destructive ideals." Such "working to rule" tactics did not exactly correspond with his professed desire for discipline! Nevertheless, his sense of humour and personal example achieved results from the other airmen which was freely acknowledged by the officers and NCO's.

In December 1925 Lawrence acted for a time as runner to the Accounts Section. His duties included the passing of files and messages between the occupants of a row of dingy offices and handing out cups of tea to airmen clerks and their supervisors who enjoyed this "high level" service. On his return to B Flight he assisted in running the office. One morning a Bristol Fighter landed and the air gunner passenger, LAC Allen remembered being greeted on the tarmac by a small airman whose first question was whether he would like "tea and wads". They walked over to the flight office where Lawrence was drawing up a leave roster for the Xmas holidays. He was surprised when the corporal told him it was Lawrence of Arabia. "King Tim", the flight commander, sometimes administered "bull sessions" on the tarmac when he found a dirty aircraft or skimped work. The airmen endured this with stoic indifference for every man knew that Tim was getting his own back. Such "punishment" Lawrence knew was essential for airmen, as well as soldiers, who occasionally needed encouragement.

Lawrence posted his last souvenir of Tank Corps days, his black beret, to his friend Private "Posh" Palmer at Bovington. He wore the soles of his service issue boots down to the uppers before having them resoled with rubber since aircraft, unlike tanks, did not take kindly to heavy boots. The morning parades at Cranwell were sometimes attended by the AOC "Biffy" Borton who had flown with Lawrence in the desert. Ranks of airmen and aircraft apprentices formed a hollow square reserved for the flight cadets who marched into position before being inspected. Lawrence knew that Biffy's off handed casual manner cloaked a tough and brilliant mind. As Lawrence put it, such aloof shyness from a man who had "governed cities, planned battles, and conferred death on many hundreds of men" saved us from over-much formality. The AOC's nonchalant 'Cawwy on, Sergeant Major" before strolling off the parade ground delighted the ranks of airmen.

Serving at Cranwell at this time was Sir Frank Whittle then a young aircraft apprentice before being selected to a cadetship at the RAF College. Whittle, who had been a keen member of the Model Aircraft Society, was informed that "that bloody man Lawrence is back". It was only years afterwards, while having his portrait painted for the RAF College by Eric Kennington, that Whittle read *The Mint*. Kennington told Whittle that although it was generally assumed that Lawrence had joined the RAF with the sole intention of getting some peace and quiet, in fact he had been "damn well starving".

Whittle asked Lawrence, who often watched the model aeroplanes flying on the aerodrome, what he thought about Lowell Thomas' recently published book *With Lawrence in Arabia*. He was surprised to hear "All lies, all lies". When Whittle had to be flown to the Apprectice School at RAF Halton for a model aircraft competition Lawrence, who met him at the flight office, asked "What can I do for you, child?" Whittle recalled that Lawrence addressed all the apprentices as though they were children but always most amiably. Asked by Whittle to sign an autograph book for his 12 year old girl friend, the conversation went as follows:

"Would you mind signing this autograph book?"
"Certainly, which one would you like?"
"The real one please."
"I am afraid you cannot have that."
"Won't you write T.E. Lawrence?"
"Certainly" Lawrence replied before proceeding to write the three names Lawrence, Ross and Shaw.

He mystified Whittle by pointing out that none of these was his real name – on which fact he would not enlarge. Whenever a new aircraftman arrived on the station he would solemnly be conducted to Lawrence's hut to be formally presented. Gradually Lawrence's presence at Cranwell was accepted but when on guard duty he preferred to patrol his beat than to share the smoke laden atmosphere of the guardroom with the Service police. They remained quite indifferent to Lawrence's reputation and when he booked out of the Camp the "snoop" on duty would look for unauthorised departures from official regulations. With Lawrence standing at "attention", they checked him for dirty boots or buttons, hair correctly cut, walking out cane correctly carried and any unofficial modifications to his service dress cap. As Lawrence put it they ensured that his general attitude was correct.

Lawrence preferred aerodrome duties which included accompanying planes with the cadets taxied in from training flights. Sometimes he assisted with engine starting by hand swinging the propeller. With note pad in hand, Lawrence took down complaints made by pilots on their aircraft. At such times the diminutive Lawrence would politely greet the pilot "Aircraft all right, Sir?" At least one cadet, who retired as an Air Commodore, always felt tempted to reply "Yes thank you, Sir". Lawrence's Brough Superior fascinated the cadets who as motor cycle enthusiasts themselves (encouraged by the authorities) envied his noisy departures from the Camp when he opened up the throttle. One evening a dozen cadets formed up in a "western style" posse and followed Lawrence into the Lincolnshire lanes eventually forcing him to the side of the road. There he patiently submitted to their good natured cross examination on his motor cycling habits. Ex-cadet Philpott remembered Lawrence's poker face expression when, after politely replying to their preliminary enquiries, he maintained a stony silence when the questions turned to his wartime exploits. The cadets were astonished to learn that Lawrence had been invited by the AOC "Biffy" Borton to his house to dine. Ex-cadet Norwood's comment some 50 years later is explicative: "He went!" Another former cadet recalled that Lawrence saw Borton from time to time and certainly did not hide his light under a bushel when things failed to please him.

To meet the cost of the expensive subscriber's edition of the *Seven Pillars*, in April 1926 Lawrence completed an abridged version. This shorter work issued as *Revolt in the Desert* stemmed from a two evening cut and paste stint on a barrack hut table helped by Aircraft Apprentice Dick Knowles (son of his neighbour at Clouds Hill cottage) and Aircraftman Miller. The work was so well done that no subsequent corrections proved necessary. To dodge the publicity which Lawrence foresaw on publication of this abridgement in March 1927 he applied for posting overseas.

Ex-Flight Cadet Cooper only saw Lawrence on their brief meetings in B Flight offices. He did, however, recall one memorable occasion involving Lawrence when on 5 July 1926 the whole station paraded to honour the visit of General Niessel, Inspector General of the French Air Force. The visit, made at the personal invitation of Sir Hugh Trenchard had been arranged at the suggestion of the British Embassy in Paris with a view to strengthening the somewhat strained relations between the French and British forces. The General seemed unimpressed as he watched the Cadets and airmen marching on to the parade ground. Someone must have pointed out Lawrence who as usual stood in the rear rank of B Flight. Suddenly to the astonishment of the whole parade, including Air Cdre Borton, the General darted forward and to Lawrence's obvious embarrassment insisted on embracing him on both cheeks in approved and uninhibited Gaelic fashion.

At the beginning of November 1926, Lawrence proceeded on 28 days embarkation leave. After last visits to his cottage and farewells to his friends at Bovington, Lawrence called on his friend Eric Kennington who had made the portraits for his Seven Pillars. Kennington drove him to the RAF Depot at Uxbridge, which in addition to being a recruit training unit served as a centre for drafts proceeding overseas. On arrival at the Depot, they drove into the camp, past the guardroom. Two lines of airmen stood on the parade ground at the stand easy position. Without a word to Kennington, Lawrence got out of the car and fell in with the troops. "For a few minutes", wrote Kennington, "I watched him shifting, chin thrust forward, turning blindly left and right." The airmen marched to the ding hall before forming up again inside. When Lawrence's name was called he stepped forward to assist the warrant officer who was experiencing difficulties sorting the various nominal rolls. Lawrence's initiative, which went unchecked, surprised the assembled airmen since even in an enlightened service such as the RAF it was not usual for an airman to break ranks.'

Andrew Simpson: *Another Life: Lawrence after Arabia* (2008)

'On a warm day of blue cloudless skies, Thursday 16 July 1925, the Chief of the Air Staff signed the order for Lawrence to return to the Air Force. After recruit processing at RAF West Drayton and Uxbridge, within weeks he was cleaning aircraft at the Cranell Cadet College and living in a hut of 14 men, a corporal and a sergeant. It was tough, but nothing as barbaric as life in the Tanks.

He still had some fondness of his time at Bovington: seven days after rejoining the RAF on 25 August 1925 he wrote to 'Posh' Palmer from the RAF Cadets College: 'When I entered the R.A.F. station at West Drayton (a derelict misery-stricken unfinished factory-place) from its upper windows came 'The Lass of Richmond Hill', violently sung. At once I remembered Clouds Hill, and you, and H.H.B. and I hung my kit-bag on a willow-tree and wept.'

Life was less harsh that at the Uxbridge Depot of 1922. He was exulted by the sound in the early morning of the running up of a 260 hp Rolls Royce engine at 1900 revs. Two Air Force men who encountered Lawrence during this period, an officer and an aircrafthand left accounts. He helped Rupert de la Bere edit the Cadet College Journal and whilst at Cranwell Lawrence attended a lecture course de la Bere was giving on Imperial geography. In the midst of this he gave his own talk on the Middle East that would never be forgotten by those who heard it.

At Cranwell he served in B Flight, billeted in Hut 106. According to R. Hales, also at Cranwell, his duties would be cleaning and tidying the Flight hangar and living quarters. Hales was a Carpenter / Rigger who had a lot of friends in the same hut as Lawrence. De la Bere remembered he was responsible for tidying the Flight office and lighting the fire. They were tasks he did uncomplainingly and Hales concluded that the esprit de corps was so high at the Cadet College that the kindness of his fellow airmen, officers and NCO's completed his rehabilitation.

Other personalities at the College at that time were the Duke of York (later king George VI) and Wing Commander 'Razzo' Rees VC, who radiated coolness and courage in the air and on the ground. B Flight maintained Bristol Fighters, whilst C Flight was more experimental, having training aircraft such as the Avro 504K and Sopwith Snipes and one of the early Gloster Schneider Trophy aircraft.

Both de la Bere and Hales agree that Lawrence wrote part of *Seven Pillars of Wisdom* in his rooms near Lindum Hall, Lincoln, whilst at Cranwell. He also gave a first edition of the book to a fitter in B Flight, Sergeant Pugh. Lawrence contributed a number of articles to the College Journal at de la Bere's request. His capacity for compassion and generosity was well known by his colleagues. One example at the Cadet College of such empathy only came to light in 2002, when his records were released to the public. Lawrence was friendly with an airman at Cranwell named Greyham Bryant. Bryant, like Lawrence, loved racing motorcycles around Lincolnshire. In September 1926 TE attended an RAF dance at the Cadet College and here he met Bryant's 24 year old sister Ruby. The girl was not impressed when they met, later describing him as 'quite a pathetic figure with a weak handshake.'

Lawrence learned somehow of her tragic background. Her father had been a private in the Essex Regiment and was shot in the back on the Western Front by a sniper in 1915. His death overwhelmed his widow and she died a short time later. The girl was cruelly treated and took a job as a maid. But her circumstances worsened. By the time Lawrence met her Miss Bryant was noticeably underweight and he took pity on her. According at an 'Allotment of Pay' order in his RAF pay book, he shortly afterwards set aside two thirds of his pay, two shillings a day, to her. This continued for 14 months, from September 1925 to November 1926 and it transformed her life, enabling her to leave work and attend secretarial college. It was well known amongst her relations that Miss Bryant knew Lawrence, but they did not know of the help he had given her. Ruby Bryant died in 1980, aged 76.'

[The story of Ruby Bryant was widely reported in the national press:]

Gavin Cordon, 'Payments to a mystery Miss Bryan confuse the legend of Lawrence', *Independent*, 29 May 2002

'The mystery surrounding the legend of Lawrence of Arabia, the great romantic hero of the First World war, had deepened with the release of confidential files to the Public Record Office. Further debate among historians and biographers over Lawrence's private life is guaranteed by the revelation that he paid two thirds of his three shillings a day salary to Ruby Bryant of 31 Portland Street, Newark. He made the payments between September 1925 and November 1926 while serving at RAF Cranwell as Aircraftman TE Shaw – an attempt to escape the fame generated by his exploits.'

Neil Tweedie, 'Mystery of woman paid wages by Lawrence of Arabia', *The Daily Telegraph*, 29 May 2002

The life of Lawrence of Arabia, one of the most intriguing of the 20th century, has thrown up a new mystery in the guise of a previously unknown woman to whom he gave two-thirds of his pay while serving under an assumed name in the Royal Air Force. Documents released at the Public Record Office yesterday show that Lawrence made regular payments to a woman called Ruby Bryant, who lived in Newark, Notts, while he was serving in the RAF as T E Shaw in the 1920s. No mention of Miss Bryant is made in biographies of Lawrence, and the Air Ministry files give no clue as to their relationship. But what is clear is that she knew of Lawrence's true identity at a time when he was anxious to conceal it.

Lawrence's records show that deductions from his RAF pay were also made to two men: W J Ross, who lived in Marsham Street, London, and John Bruce, a Scotsman who served with Lawrence in the Royal Tank Corps. Bruce came to prominence in 1968 when he alleged that he had satisfied Lawrence's masochistic urges by administering a number of beatings. The nature of Ross's relationship with Lawrence is another mystery, however. Both men are described on the forms allowing the payments simply as "friend".

Lawrence's payments to Miss Bryant lasted for almost a year, between September 1925 and November 1926, before ceasing suddenly. Lawrence was serving as a lowly aircraftsman at RAF Cranwell at the time, not far from Newark. Almost as soon as the payments to Miss Bryant stopped, payments to Ross began. They continued for a year after Ross requested they cease. Bruce kept on demanding money, even from Lawrence's executors following his death as the result of a motorcycle accident in 1935.

The payments raise further questions about the private life of Thomas Edward Lawrence, an enduring source of controversy. Claims that he was a repressed homosexual have been challenged by those who suggest that the beatings administered by Bruce and others were Lawrence's way of dealing with the trauma of his experiences in Arabia. In particular, Lawrence was seeking a form of penance for the "guilt" of suffering homosexual rape at the hands of Turkish troops following his arrest in Deraa in November 1917. Certainly, Lawrence had few dealings with women during his life, making the case of Miss Bryant all the more interesting.

Why Lawrence opted out of public life, seeking anonymity in the Services, will probably remain a mystery. He had a desperate desire to escape the press, which had imbued him with a mythic status for his exploits while leading the Arab rebellion against the Turkish Empire during the First World War, recounted by Lawrence in *The Seven Pillars of Wisdom*. Following a brief period with the Colonial Office, Lawrence resigned, apparently fearing for his sanity. In 1922 he enlisted with the RAF under the name John Hume Ross, but his cover was blown and he was forced to leave the following year.

The files show how Lawrence pleaded with his friend, Sir Hugh Trenchard, Chief of the Air Staff, to be allowed to return to the ranks. But Trenchard was against it, arguing that the presence of Lawrence, who had retired from the Army as a colonel, would prove embarrassing for officers forced to deal with him as a mere aircraftsman. Instead, Lawrence enlisted in the Royal Tank Corps as Thomas Edward Shaw, but quickly rejoined the RAF as Shaw in 1925. At that time he was earning three shillings a day from the RAF, and was giving Miss Bryant two shillings a day. That she knew his identity is clear from a letter sent by her from 12 Friary Road, Newark, Notts to the Air Ministry on 12 January 1926. She wrote: "Dear Sir, Kindly note, the allotment made out to me on behalf of Colonel Lawrence - going under the name of LAC [Leading Aircraftsman] Shaw - has not yet come to hand.. This should have been due last Thursday. Also kindly note address again. You have already been informed of this, but each time it is sent to the above address. Thanking you in anticipation. Yours faithfully, R. Bryant (Miss). New address: 31 Portland Street, Newark, Notts.'

Lawrence was obsessive about concealing his identity. Deluged with fan mail, he refused to write back. When a German officer tried to engage him in correspondence about the war in Arabia, he wrote to the Air Ministry saying: "I had hoped that the writer would have realised [by my failure to reply] that this proposal did not appeal to me. I do not discuss my part in the war with anyone, nor do I read about it: the whole subject is repulsive."

Worse was to come. In 1934 Lawrence learned that the producer Alexander Korda was proposing to make a film about his exploits. Lawrence was incensed. In a letter to Sir Philip Sassoon, under secretary at the Air Ministry, he wrote: "There is just one consideration that might interest me here - a film merchant called Korda, who announces that he proposes to make a film called 'Lawrence of Arabia'. Presumably he means me, and I have strong views as to the undesirability of any such film. So I have sent him word that perhaps he ought to discuss his intentions with me before he opens his silly mouth again." Korda backed off, leaving David Lean to make the film with Peter O'Toole in the starring role a quarter of a century later.

Despite his genius in harnessing irregular Arab forces to the British cause, Lawrence was an unpromising recruit. The files contain an account of Lawrence's early days at the RAF depot in Uxbridge by a fellow serviceman [A.G. Turner], who wrote: "Ross was a very quiet sort, did not smoke, swear or express an opinion about things going on in the camp. Being very thin, he did not seem to have much strength and used to fumble with his rifle. The drill sergeant would take it from him telling him he was like an old woman who'd never had it, and showed him how to handle the rifle. This used to embarrass Ross very much. It was rumoured later that he was Lawrence of Arabia but we did not believe that. A small, thin man like that leading the Arabs! We thought what a load of bull!"

Lawrence himself was aware of his delicate psychological and physical state, writing to a friend that the experience of writing *The Seven Pillars of Wisdom* had all but exhausted him. In another letter contained in the files Lawrence summed up his feelings about fame and the intrusion that it produced. "That's the worst of having once been 'somebody'. At times I fear that my news value may not end until the day after I am dead," he said. How wrong he was.

John Crosland and Michael Horsnell, 'Did Lawrence of Arabia secretly wed this woman?', *The Times*, 29 May 2002

TE Lawrence gave two thirds of his service pay between 1924 and 1926 to a woman called Ruby Bryant under the marriage allowance and allotment arrangements of the King's regulations. The suggestion that Lawrence had a liaison, let alone a marriage, found little favour with his biographer Jeremy Wilson who said, 'He had no liaisons with women in the modern sense and he never cohabited with anybody of either sex. He regularly gave sums of money away to people whose needs he regarded as greater than his. Much of his royalties as a writer were given away. The chances are that this was a lady in acute need of money. With time we may get closer to the truth of this.'

To add to the intrigue, the day Lawrence cancelled the payments to Ms Bryant he ordered a new set of payments to WJ Ross of 76 Marsham Street, London. Writing on 22 November 1927, Ross says: 'As it is most inconvenient to call at the Chief Office at the Ministry I shall be obliged if the enclosed draft may be made payable at the Post Office at 24 Marsham Street instead of King Edward Street.' They continued for another year until Ross himself told the Air Ministry they were no longer required.

James Bone and Michael Horsnell, 'Landlord link to home of mystery lover', *The Times*, 29 May 2002

The terraced house in Nottinghamshire where Ruby Bryant, TE Lawrence's reputed bride, is thought to have lived in the 20s still stands. The present occupier, Janet Howitt, who has lived at 12 Friary Road, Newark, for 45 years, said 'When I first moved in I paid £1 a week rent to the landlord, who I remember was called Bryant and was very elderly. He owned a lot of properties on this street but he sold them all, including mine, about 30 years ago.'

It is possible that Ruby was a relative of his, but inquiries elsewhere by *The Times* found little proof that Bryant was married to Lawrence. The Public Record Office said that Ruby Ficklin Bryant may have been an American nurse who went on to become chief of the US Army School of Nursing, and that she may have been based in Newark at the right time. But her family was sure that she had not lived in Britain in the 20s.

Bryant died childless on 3 January this year aged 95 in Warsaw, Virginia. Robert McBath, her nephew, said that she would have mentioned any connection to Lawrence. 'I went through all her papers with a fine tooth comb and I would have noticed something like that. Aunt Ruby and I were close and if she had known Lawrence she would have picked up those papers and said, 'Bob, let me show you this.'

Ficklin Bryant, another nephew, said that she graduated from the Army School of Nursing in Washington in 1932. 'If she didn't become a nurse till the 1930s, I don't think she was ever there [in Britain] in the 1920s,' he said.

A search at the Family Records Centre in London failed to locate a marriage certificate between Lawrence or any alias of his and a Bryant. No one by the name of Bryant was on the electoral roll at the two addresses in Newark where Lawrence's pay was sent.'

Maurice Chittenden and Gareth Walsh, 'Secret Lawrence "wife" was just a taxing affair', *The Sunday Times*, 2 June 2002

The mystery of payments by Lawrence of Arabia to a man and woman while he was serving in the RAF have been solved. The main being paid, William Ross, was an Inland Revenue assessor collecting unpaid taxes from Lawrence's other earnings, such as his £200 annual stipend as a research fellow at All Souls College, Oxford.

The payments to the woman, Ruby Bryant, were almost certainly rent for a room in a private house while he was stationed under a pseudonym at RAF Cranwell, Lincolnshire, according to Lawrence experts. In the evening and at weekends he would leave the barracks where he was known as Leading Aircraftman TE Shaw and take off on his Brough Superior motorcycle for the room where he could work on the final drafts of *Seven Pillars of Wisdom*, his classic account of how he led an Arab revolt against the Ottoman Turks a decade earlier.

Bryant appears to have lived as a lodger in two Victorian terraced houses in Newark, Nottinghamshire, 20 miles from Cranwell. Lawrence was paying her two shillings a day while he was at Cranwell 1925-6. Bryant wrote to the Air Ministry at one stage querying a hiccup in the payments. Lawrence experts believe it was a request for overdue rent. Bryant was writing from 12 Friary Road, Newark, but added a postscript that she had moved to a new address at 31 Portland Street, Newark. Curiously, she does not appear on the electoral roll for either property. James Gregory, whose family owned the house in Friary Road from 1900-72, said she could have been a lodger who had let out her own property elsewhere.

Lawrence was in the habit of renting rooms near where he was based. The payments to Bryant, a spinster, started in September 1925, a month a after he arrived at Cranwell, and ended when he left in November 1926 to join a troopship headed for India and service on the Northwest Frontier. The amounts, 14 shillings a week, equate to the cost of room only rent at the time.

On the same day the payment was cancelled, Lawrence ordered a new set of payments to a WJ Ross in London. This was William James Ross, an assessor and collector of taxes who lived in Marsham Street, Westminster, near Lawrence's London home in Barton Street.

The war hero's biographers are convinced that the payments to Bryant were for rent of a room. Colin Simpson [*The Secret Lives of Lawrence of Arabia*] said, 'Lawrence was a writer first and foremost. You can't write a book and keep a manuscript in a barrack room. He frequently rented rooms to store his notes and textbooks. He reckoned he could get all writing material in the pannier of his motorcycle so he could just roar off to his bolt hole.'

This studious portrayal of Lawrence is at odds with last week's image of him having secret trysts with Bryan in Newark. Bryant was identified in one account as Ruby Ficklin Bryant who went on to become chief of the US Army School of Nursing and who died in January. This weekend both the Pentagon and her 80 year old sister poured scorn on the suggestion.

In the mid 1920s this Ruby Bryant was training at a teachers college in Fredericksburg, Virginia. 'If Lawrence of Arabia was chasing after Virginia school teachers in the 1920s he must have come across the Atlantic to give a class presentation,' said a spokesman for the US Centre of Military History. 'It's that unlikely.'

Chris Hastings and Charlotte Edwards, 'TE Lawrence's 'mistress' was an orphan', *The Sunday Telegraph*, 9 June 2002

The truth about Ruby Bryant, the woman who received secret payments from T E Lawrence, prompting suggestions that the pair had enjoyed a clandestine love affair, can now be revealed. Two weeks after Government documents disclosed that Miss Bryant had received money from Lawrence, this newspaper has established that far from being the First World War hero's lover, she was instead a timid orphan who was saved from destitution by his simple act of philanthropy. The revelation brings to an end a worldwide search for details of the identity and background of Miss Bryant.

After his exploits in Arabia, Lawrence, who was lionised across the British Empire, left the Army with the rank of colonel and later sought anonymity in the Royal Air Force during the 1920s, serving as a leading aircraftsman under the alias of Shaw. The files, opened by the Public Records Office at Kew, included a pay order allocating two shillings a day, two thirds of his pay, to Miss Bryant. They gave no information about her identity or why she had received the money and led to an army of reporters descending on her last known address in the small Nottinghamshire town of Newark.

The disclosure fuelled speculation that Lawrence, who has been widely portrayed as a homosexual with sado-masochistic tendencies, actually had a mistress or wife. Until now, no further details of Miss Bryant's life have emerged. *The Telegraph*, however, has been able to piece together a picture of Miss Bryant, who was born in Southwark, south London in 1904. Her descendants insist that the payments were an act of kindness motivated by Lawrence's friendship with her brother, Greyham. Mr Bryant was among Lawrence's closest friends, and is thought to have met him while serving at RAF Cranwell in Lincolnshire.

He and Mr Bryant shared a passionate interest in motorcycles and would tear around the countryside together. It was soon after he arrived at Cranwell that Lawrence, who first met Miss Bryant at an RAF dance, began sending her most of his pay. Although she later told her family that she was "unimpressed" by the war hero, he decided to help the 24-year-old after being alerted to her tragic circumstances: Miss Bryant had suffered an unhappy childhood following the death of her father, a private in the Essex Regiment who was shot in the back by a sniper on the battlefields of Flanders in 1915. His death proved to be too much for his widow, Florence, who died soon afterwards.

Miss Bryant and her four siblings were separated and sent to live with different families, most of whom were unsympathetic to their circumstances. She was treated cruelly and her prospects worsened after she took a job as a maid. The long hours had a severe impact upon her health, causing her weight to plummet. Mr Bryant became so concerned about her condition that, during a visit to her place of work, he insisted that she quit her job immediately and move with him to Newark.

Around this time, the payments from Lawrence began. They transformed Miss Bryant's life by enabling her to go to secretarial college. The payments stopped in 1926 and Miss Bryant subsequently married John Lyons, an accounts clerk, in 1933. She gave birth to twins, Sylvia and John, in 1935. Months later, Lawrence died in a motorcycle accident. Ruby Lyons died aged 76 in 1980 and her brother, who pursued his RAF career and reached the rank of wing commander, died seven years later.

Mr Bryant's friendship with Lawrence is well known to surviving members of his family. Until the recent disclosures, however, they had been unaware of the help that Miss Bryant had received. They believed instead that Mr Bryant and an uncle were the only people who had offered her financial assistance. Miss Bryant's daughter, now living in Western Australia, said: "It is so difficult to take all of this in. I was very close to my mother and she never mentioned anything about this money. She talked about Lawrence occasionally. She had met him at a dance but she didn't think much of him. In fact, she said he was quite a pathetic figure with a weak handshake."

Sylvia said that her quietly spoken mother and her fun-loving brother, Greyham, were like "chalk and cheese" but very close. She said that her mother had, up until her death, credited Mr Bryant, who was also a jazz musician, with rescuing her from poverty in the 1920s. She said: "It may be that Lawrence wanted my mother to keep these payments a secret. She was a committed Christian and the sort of person who always stood by her word. If she promised to keep something a secret she would have done."

Professor Greyham Bryant, who is Miss Bryant's nephew, said: "I have never heard about the payments myself, but everyone in the family knows about the friendship between Lawrence and Ruby's brother. He used to talk about it quite a lot, how they used to go tearing around the countryside together. Greyham was a bit of a character and knew how to enjoy himself. I think he and Lawrence would have got on very well."

The files released last month included a letter from Miss Bryant asking about a missing payment. Her letter, dated January 12 1925, shows that she knew that Lawrence was serving under an assumed identity. It said: "Kindly note, the allotment made out to me on behalf of Col Lawrence (going under the name of LAC Shaw) has not yet come to hand. This should have been due last Saturday.'

Lawrence attracted worldwide attention after leading an Arab rebellion against the Turks in the Middle East during the First World War. He later wrote about his exploits in the *The Seven Pillars of Wisdom* and *Mint*. He made other charitable donations. In 1935 it was revealed that he had donated £4,000 to a fund set up to help the children of RAF staff.

The Mint

Lawrence joined the Royal Airforce as 352087 Aircraftman John Hume Ross on 30 August 1922. During his basic training at Uxbridge he compiled the notes and observations which were to form the core of his second famous literary work, *The Mint*. Early in November he was sent to the RAF School of Photography at Farnborough. On 27 December the fact that a famous war hero was serving in the ranks under another name was the front page story in the *Daily Express*. This led to his dismissal from the RAF on 23 January 1923. By March he was back in the ranks as Private T.E. Shaw in the Army.

He was posted to the Tank Corps Training School at Bovington in Dorset, where he stayed for two years, and where he made some of his most important friendships, from fellow soldiers to Mr and Mrs Thomas Hardy. He moved into Clouds Hill a small cottage which became his home and sanctuary for the rest of his life. But he felt no affection for the Tank Corps and he pleaded with Chief of the Air Staff, Sir Hugh Trenchard, to be let back into the RAF. After veiled threats of suicide he was at last readmitted in August 1925 and was sent to the Cadet College at Cranwell in Lincolnshire – though not, of course, as a Cadet, but as an ordinary Aircraftman. He stayed there until late 1926, when he sailed by troopship for India.

The Mint, contains some of his finest writing. Among other things, some of his descriptions record - by common agreement accurately - the barrack-room language used by his fellow servicemen. Lawrence stipulated that the book should not be published until, at least, 1950. In 1955, when *The Mint* was first published in England, it appeared in two versions - a limited edition containing the full text, and an expurgated trade edition. More recent English editions, including the one available for some years in the 'Penguin Modern Classics' series, contained the full text, which is reproduced here.

<u>Note by A.W. Lawrence to the First Edition of *The Mint*</u>

'On 6 August 1928, answering a letter from E.M. Forster, he wrote the longest account of the genesis of the book; it should be compared with that on p. 189 [An Explanation – see below]:

'The Cranwell part is, of course, not a part, but scraps. I had no notes for it... any more than I am ever likely to have notes of any more of my R.A.F. life. I'm it, now, and the note season is over. The Cadet college part was vamped up, really, as you say, to take off the bitterness, if bitterness it is, of the Depot pages. The Air Force is not a man-crushing humiliating slavery, all its days. There is sun and decent treatment, and a very real measure of happiness, to those who do not look forward or back. I wanted to say this, not as propaganda, out of fairness, the phrase which pricked up your literary ears, but out of truthfulness. I set out to give a picture of the R.A.F., and my picture might be impressive and clever if I showed only the shadow of it... but I was not making a work of art, but a portrait. If it does surprisingly happen to be literature (I do not believe you there: you are partially kind) that will be because of its sincerity, and the Cadet college parts are as sincere as the rest, and an integral part of the R.A.F.

Of course I know and deplore the scrappiness of the last chapters: that is the draw-back of memory, of a memory which knew it was queerly happy then, but shrank from digging too deep into the happiness, for fear of puncturing it. Our contentments are so brittle, in the ranks. If I had thought too hard about Cranwell, perhaps I'd have found misery there too. Yet I assure you that it seems all sunny, in the back view.

Of Cadet College I had notes. Out of letters on Queen Alexandra's Funeral (Garnett praises that. Shaw says its the meanness of a guttersnipe laughing at old age. I was so sorry and sad at the poor old queen), for the hours on guard, for the parade in the early morning. The Dance, the Hangar, Work and the rest were written at Karachi. They are reproductions of scenes which I saw, or things which I felt and did... but two years old, all of them. In other words, they are technically on a par with the manner of *The Seven Pillars*; whereas the Notes were photographs, taken day by day, and reproduced complete, though not at all unchanged. There was not a line of the Uxbridge notes left out; but also not a line unchanged'.

Preface by J.M. Wilson to the Penguin Edition of *The Mint*

'At the end of August [1922], just after his 34th birthday, he arrived at the Uxbridge recruits' Training Depot. Following his dismissal from the RAF in January 1923, Lawrence enlisted in the Tank Corps, where he served at Bovington Camp. After much pleading and veiled threat of suicide he was eventually allowed to return to the RAF in August 1925. While in the Army he began the final detailed revision of *Seven Pillars*, which was not completed until the end of 1926, when a subscription edition had been printed. By then he had been back in the RAF for 16 months, which he spent serving contentedly at the Cranwell RAF Cadet College. In March 1927 a new abridgement of *Seven Pillars* was to be published, and to avoid press attention Lawrence was posted to India. There, in his spare time, he at last tackled the Uxbridge notes.

To follow the Uxbridge chapters he included some impressions of Cranwell. 'Obviously these notes libel our general RAF life by being too violently true to an odd and insignificant part of it. So out of my head and with no formal notes I attempted a Part III to show the happiness that came after the bullying. Only happiness is such a beast to put on paper' [letter to Noel Coward, 15 August 1930]. Much of the Cranwell section is based on descriptions of the Cadet College which he had sent at the time to Mrs Bernard Shaw, and which she now copied and sent out to him in India. 'They will correct the drabness of the Uxbridge tale; for Cranwell was a warm and happy place.' [letter to Charlotte Shaw, 8 December 1927].

Despite the dramatic relief provided by the Cranwell finale, the impact of *The Mint* unquestionably lies in its description of the brutalities at Uxbridge. Many [critics], however, have objected to the Cranwell chapters which are so unlike and irrelevant to the dramatic content of the Uxbridge notes. Lawrence himself recognised their inadequacy, but they were a 'political' and personal necessity, included through loyalty to the service in which he elected to pass ten years of his life.'

The Mint: a day book of the RAF Depot between August and December 1922 with later notes by 352087 A/C Ross

PART ONE: THE RAW MATERIAL

1. Recruiting Office
2. The Gate
3. In the Park
4. The Fear
5. First Day
6. Us
7. The New Skin
8. Officers' Mess
9. P.T.
10. Last Post
11. Fatigues
12. Reveille
13. Vanities
14. Holiday
15. Church
16. Mess-deck
17. Corporal Abner
18. Raper's Roll call
19. Shit-cart
20. Our Commanding Officer
21. The Social Code
22. Breaking or Making
23. Cook's Mate
24. Inspection
25. Humbugging About
26. China's Trouble
27. A Sermon
28. Our Mould of Form
29. The Last Fatigue

PART TWO: IN THE MILL

Nearly three days pass

1. Disciplines
2. The Four Senses
3. Officers, Please
4. Non-Commissioned Officers
5. My Hours
6. Intemperate
7. A Fresh Start
8. The Time-table
9. School
10. Our Instructor
11. Now and Then

PART THREE: SERVICE

Nearly three years pass

An Explanation

An Explanation

I had the ambition - before I turned back in 1923 and saw the inadequacy of my *Seven Pillars* in the cold light of revision to write a real book: and I thought to find its subject in the Royal Air Force.

The foregoing fifty chapters were noted down night by night in bed at the Depot, as foundations for the intended book: not exactly word for word: - in their natural state sentence was twisted over sentence like the entrails in a man's belly; and here I've pulled them out into one string, like a pound of sausages: - but essentially these are my depot notes.

Depot would have been a porch, a short porch of selected scenes, to the book I meant to write for the incomparable Hogarth upon Life in a Flying Flight, which is the veritable air force:

but my sudden dismissal from Farnborough knocked that experience on the head. When, three years too late, I was allowed back to what has since been my element and fellowship, things could not be the same as they had been in 1922.

Therefore I've rearranged for you (Hogarth is gone, so you must be Edward Garnett, to whose sense of form I owe so much) every single sentence of my Depot notes. Not a recorded word is missing, nor a word added, yet. But I cannot leave the tale at this point. The Depot I knew was a savage place. That is now changed: so for fairness' sake I've picked out the few following extracts, mainly from letters to my friends: in the hope that they may give an idea of how different, how humane, life in Cadet College was. There is no continuity in these last pages - and a painful inadequacy: but perhaps some glint of our contentment may shine from between my phrases into your eyes.

How can any man describe his happiness?

1. Rail Journey

Being dressed for my train-journey was like a dose of jankers: tunic, breeches and puttees: - that's a hot kit. Marching boots so hobbed that every pavement became a skating rink. My overcoat (mid-August). Complete equipment so thickly clayed that at any movement its brown powder rained like pollen on my clothes and neighbours. Full pack, weighing many pounds. A bayonet - for the Great Northern Railway, ye gods! Looped over the bayonet, a little haversack of cold beef and bread, balanced on the right side by a filled water-bottle. This poor man's camel had dumbly accepted its load so far: but at the two-and-a-half pounds of lukewarm water it found voice. Regulations. You're in the Depot still. Hold your blasted tongue or you'll go inside the guard-room.

At the station gate they threw on my shoulder (knocking my cap off) the kit-bag of all my spare goods: only eighty more pounds. For the 'stuffy airman' a porter would be a crime as capital as an umbrella. Before I reached the end of the platform, sweat was running like a hot bath down my arms and legs.

The trip slowly convinced me that this military equipment was not designed for peace-time trains. I had become too wide to advance frontally through any carriage door. In each queue or press I jabbed the next man with a buckle in the mouth, or browned the next woman with my equipment's clay. When I sat, the little sidebags and skirts of my clobber occupied two places. The pack fouled the back of the seat, so I had to perch all the while on the edge, and block the gangway.

The old lady next me in the underground wore a flippant skirt, all doo-dahs. My scabbard chape enlarged one of these. She rose up and went, more fretted even than the skirt. I bulged with relief into her extra space: but my water-bottle tilted nose-down on the arm rest, and filled the vacant seat with a secret lake. Then, fortunately, I changed trains.

It was all changing trains: and as I learnt how, I stood in the vestibule for the short trips, to lessen my unavoidable nuisance to the public: and took off my harness and overcoat for the long spells. That was much better, until water began to drip from the rack. So I disentangled the silly bottle from its straps, and emptied it out of the window (into the window next door, as we soon heard).

By Victoria I was fed up with changing trains, and funked the press of lunch-hour in the city. So I climbed into an empty bus for King's Cross, taking the seat nearest the door. The top, of course, was out of my power. We were past Russell Square and again empty, when the conductor came back, and looking down on my cap's polished peak said 'Ah, we didn't wear our marching order nicely blancoed in them days. You wouldn't think it, but I was one of the original four thousand in your mob. That was in '14; days of the war. Bit before your time, sonny.' 'Yes, dad,' I murmured, blandly.

At King's Cross a half-hour to wait: good, for the trains today were crowded. I got a corner and sat down. The scurrying crowds peered in and passed: people do not travel with service fellows if they can help it. We had a quiet long run all across the sunny fens. Another change was due at tea-time. I got up to resume my harness, for railway platforms abound with service police, who report airmen not wearing it properly.

To put on equipment in camp you hold it out in front, dart one arm suddenly through it and with a cast of the disengaged arm and a lively whirl of the body on the left foot, spin into the rest. This calls for eighty square feet of floor space. To attempt it in a crowded compartment would be to knock too many teeth out. For a while I tangled myself like a fly in a web, trying to slide into it quietly: but then a grown man in the carriage rose and held it for me silently and professionally, like a strait waistcoat. A minor effect of the war's military education of England had been notably to ease the lot of an airman travelling by rail.

Another change, another journey, dusk, detrainment, and a long road. The lights of the camp were like a town, east and west of the arrow-straight tarmac. Time I got serious. Positively that was a guard-room ahead. We feel these buildings by some instinct. My curiosity grew very keen. Here I would spend years: what was its first impression? Distinctly good. The sentry had only a cane, no belt or rifle. Inside, the dazzle of light showed me a mob of service police. Will have to look out for them. Their sergeant took my papers, and directed me to 83 hut, down the second path on the left. 83 hut, it seemed, was kept furnished with beds for chance arrivals. That sounds like consideration for the men. I peered into its not very bright corners, and guessed it empty: but someone in the bunk heard the scrape of my boots, for its door opened. Out came a solitary man: an A/C like myself.

'Hullo, where'd you spring from? Depot? Well, you're in luck here: this place is cushy. Any bed you like: there's no one but us two. I'm sort of hut orderly. Spot of grub in the canteen? Right O. . . . Roll call? Yes, they do have a sort of a one, I fancy, down in the lines: but the corp won't tool all the way up here. Your next stop'll be Adjutant tomorrow. I'll tool you along.' He was the runner at headquarters.

'What about a wash?' I asked, beginning to peel off the loathly clothes, all gummed to me by the hot trip. Barnard waved to the hut's entrance, through a shallow annexe. 'Help yerself: two baths, hot and cold.' After Depot it seemed too good: but it was true.

2. B. Flight

I woke up feeling easy. I shall like this place. Today is glorious with sunlight. The runner and I ate a slow breakfast, of service type, and I helped him sweep out the few rooms and passages of headquarters by half-past seven before the first officers showed up. I waited on till just after eleven, when they had leisure for me.

'I've seen you before' said the first adjutant. 'Were you at Depot three years ago?' I admitted it, in a tone which checked his asking more. 'You'll go to B Flight. Just book his particulars, Sergeant Major, and send him down.'

I spent the afternoon shifting kit into Hut 105, and in drawing bedding. There's a corporal in charge of the hut and its dozen fellows. The flight is only fourteen A/Cs, him, and a sergeant: and we all live together in this neat little hut of sixteen beds. It's holidays just now. Holidays sound queer to me: but it seems our reason of existence here is to maintain the machines on which the cadets learn flying, and in August the College shuts down. Most of the irks take their month's leave then. The others do odd fatigues to fill in the empty days

3. Manners

Up ever so early, but with this wonderful sunshine filling the hut from soon after five, it feels sticky lying abed. The place is country. I wandered across to the reception hut, where I'd spent the first night, and helped myself to a hot bath, quietly, not to wake Barnard. That had been his stipulation, in making me free of his water. The reason he's so favoured with it is that Hut 83 backs on the cadets' lines, and they must have hot water always. I thank them. So shall I.

Back, and everybody yet asleep. I made my bed up, Depot fashion, and went to breakfast. When I came in again, my neighbour was regarding the bed with disfavour. 'You bobbing, mate?' he queried. 'This here's not the fuckin' Depot, you know.' Out came the Corporal from the bunk. 'Where do you come from, anyhow?' 'Depot, Corporal,' I rejoined, bringing my heels together as I'd been taught. 'Well, just you forget it, see? And put your bed like this.' With three or four deft twists of the hand my bedding sprawled and poked its corners to the four airts, like a dissipated haycock. 'And you don't stand to attention in the Air Force when you talk to an N.C.O.'

'Right O, Corporal,' I laughed, daring a pounce at this new easy manner. In Depot 'Right O' to a strange corporal would have put me on a charge. The Corporal rounded on me like a trodden snake. 'And cut that right out, too, you and your "Corporal." Want to make a bloody cunt of me? My name's Geordie: get it? This is Cadet College. Wash out all that blarsted bull-shit you've bin taught. You're in the Air Force now. Fucking corporals in the Depot are bigger 'n wing commanders outside.'

He's right: it isn't the Depot. That assertion of manner has passed, with its boastful carriage, the abrupt heely stride, the clatter of boot-nails. These fellows can saunter as if no eye was on them: and when they want to hurry they nip along, quiet-footed, with a spring in it. Perhaps they're allowed rubbers on their soles. Their uniforms, too, seem *worn*: not so much badges of service, as the private clothing of their profession. Blue is a reducing agent. The modest colour and spare fit prompt its wearers to seem a handy size.

4. A First Note

I'm just going over to the hangar to continue valeting aeroplanes. We do it lazily, killing time for the new term to open and our cadets to come. They say we 'sweat like buggery' in term time. This life pleases me all over: the people not so much: but I'm a slow starter, always unfavourably impressed, whenever I'm dropped into a hut-full of strangers. It is only after their crudities have been well learned and forgiven that the more interesting core appears.

Their limited expression hides them at first: the monotony of their adjectives revolts me. Not so bad, pretty good, fucking good: - there are positive, comparative, superlative, for everything. Nothing's funny, or vivid, or familiar unless it travesties our sexuality. However, give them time. Some people get on terms directly: but in return give a great deal of themselves away, as fast.

5. Lodgings

I wonder how you would like our nights? The hut is so small for the sixteen of us: a row of beds down each long wall, a table and two forms in the narrow middle, a square stove. In the centre of each short wall, a door: one gives on the open air, one to a wash-house-shower-bath-lavatory annexe, which makes a porch to the eastern or wintry side of the hut.

We, as I said, are sixteen: fourteen men, a corporal, and a sergeant. Our beds are of iron sheeting, and slide in. Very hard they feel, for the first nights. The mattresses are three little square brown canvas cushions, rammed solid with coir. Biscuits they call them.

The next bed is only an arm's reach from mine. It is odd to have the other man's whispering breath so near my pillow all the night. His name is also Ross: a Scotchman from Devonshire, just married, a nice fellow: which is good fortune since a rough bedfellow is exhausting. Riches wholly deliver a man from bedfellows: - a privilege, and a loss, too: for the intimate jostling of like and like is often as fertile as it's disconcerting.

Airmen sleep very restlessly, always. Partly it may be due to the hard beds, on which a man cannot turn without a groan and half-waking up to lift the hip: yet turning is needful because the hardness cramps our bodies, if we do not constantly shift them. So the night to one who, like me, lies much awake is never fully quiet. There are groans and mutterings, and dream-words. They all dream, always: and sometimes they say beastlike things in their sleep.

I wonder how far I betray myself in the first part of the night, which is my sleeping time? In the Army, when on armoured car work I was being driven unskilfully by other fellows all day, my nervousness so increased that it turned to fever and delirium, and I talked like a river half one night. None of them would ever tell me what I said: but in the morning they looked at me strangely.

Our nights are white. The ten windows have been catching the moonlight, since I came, and the walls are lime washed a water colour: so that even starlight and the reflections of the distant lamps over there in the College make them gleam. It seems never dark, here in the north, for very soon after I wake up there comes the first touch of dawn. I feel like a fish in a still cistern, dreaming away these short hours. The sleep in my eyes is like water to dull them and the quietness is real, compared with the noise of day. If you could hear the iron hangar throbbing at this moment, with the running up of a 260 h.p. Rolls-Royce engine at nineteen hundred revs!

Yet the quiet does not last long. Its beginning is delayed by the late men not coming in till midnight or after: and they may come in stumbling, unsteadily knocking puttee-defended legs against bed-foot after bed-foot, swearing or chuckling inanely, the while. And the end of quiet is at reveille.

The reveille here is the most grateful of any camp I know. There are no whistles or bugle calls (how every serving soldier hates a bugle) and no orderly sergeant to bray hideously. Just we let the dawn rouse us. As the five tall windows each side the whitewashed hut brighten, the sleepers stir, more and more frequently, till they are completely awake. At this season that is yet too early to rise: for we have no unavoidable duty before breakfast, between half-past seven and eight. So the crowd lie dozing, or sleeping; or read or chat lowly to one another. This quiet prelude to the working day was the first and greatest beatitude of College.

I get up soonest of all, and nip over in the running vest and shorts which are my sleeping suit, to 83 hut, of the opposite lines, across a grass meadow. There I bath. Such a funny little bath, a square brown earthenware socket, like a drain, in the cement floor. Fortunately I'm little, too, and if I tuck up like a tailor I can just squat in it, as if I were a dirty dish in a sink, with six inches of warm water round me: and there I splash, and shave, and splash again. This is heaven on a cold morning: and Cadet College faces the North Sea and can be colder than any spot in England. Indeed we are particular to score the low temperature record every winter.

About seven I run back to the hut and enter noisily, for a signal to the others, who begin to exhort one another to get up. We make our beds, heaping the three biscuits in a column and wrapping four blankets in a fifth, with an intervening sandwich of sheets. Then boot-cleaning, button-polishing, sweeping out the bed-area and doing my weekly one of the fourteen jobs into which hut-maintenance is divided. If it's stove-black-leading, another wash. Then I grab knife, fork and mug and run over to the mess-deck for breakfast.

6. Body and Soul

The mess-deck is long and bare, chill as a vault, and moist smelling from its rows of white-scrubbed heavy tables and forms. On each table is a pile of twelve plates. As we come in we put our mugs on the end of a table. When he has counted twelve waiting mugs, the supervising corporal throws down a tin ticket: and the end men, the last comers, go to a serving hatch and draw their bucket of tea and an iron ration tin, holding twelve breakfasts.

The food in this camp is miserable: little and bad. Hence the flourishing canteen. Today's offer to our appetites was a scrap of cold ham, swimming for its desperate life in a flood of tinned tomato juice. Yesterday it was steak, stewed to a good imitation string. The irks grumble also at the tea, because it is not strong, and not sweet. I am thankful for both lacks: and wish, besides, that it was not hot. A pity that men strive to surpass water, that cheap, easy, affectionate and subtle drink.

A feature of Cadet College is that we have not to wash our plates. It is done for us (not well, but who looks a mercy in the mouth?) by a special squad whose utter greasiness of life and work is redeemed by unlimited pickings in food. All that we leave is theirs. So every belly-favouring man jumps at the job. I ran the risk of being put among them, when I enlisted as unskilled: but after my sorrows in Farnborough in 1923 I dared not try for photographer again. For the time, though, the risk of mess-orderly is past, with my enrolment in B. Flight.

After breakfast we go on parade: about two hundred of us men, and one hundred cadets, would-be officers. We form three sides of a hollow square. On the eastern, open face is a flagstaff. We face this, after some shifting back and forward. The R.A.F. colours are broken at the peak: the trumpeter (imported for the ceremony from East Camp) blows a royal salute: the cadets, who have rifles, present arms. We who have nothing, stand still.

The salute is the shrillest note a trumpet can sustain. It goes through us, however densely we close our pores. The thrill of exceeding sharpness conquers, in blades, sounds, tastes. Everything else upon the square, a huge asphalt place, hut-circled and echoing, is deadly still. Imagine a raw wind, and a wet early sunshine, making our shadows on the tarred ground the exact blue colour of our clothing.

After the salute Jews and Roman Catholics fall out: while the chaplain says prayers: we all bowing our heads meekly, standing at ease. Having been prayed over (a little ironical, it sounds, the petition that this day we fall into no sin, neither run into any kind of danger, when some of us will fly an hour later, and all of us have been misdoing and swearing obscenely since the dawn: however . . .), at last the Wing Commander dismisses us: and we march off by flights to the hangars and our day's work.

7. The Hangar

The hangar and our day's work.' That sounds an easy picture to draw. Now, for a year and more, it has been the staple of my life: but not yet can I see its truth in sober prose, though always I am thinking of it, always trying to see it.

The facts of course are there. Our hangar is a girder frame, sheathed in iron. The floor is of concrete, without one pillar or obstruction across its main expanse. The mere space of it is rewarding, to a daily dweller in low rooms. Too rewarding, perhaps. An airman alone in it feels puny and apprehensive. It is as great as most cathedrals, and echoes like all of them put together. We have parked fourteen aeroplanes within its central hall.

The southern face is wholly door: giant twenty-five foot leaves of iron, hanging on wheels from their top edge, and rolling back, leaf by leaf, with the roll of thunder when three or four of us put our shoulders to the work. Then, on every fine day, the sun streams in, gilds our kites, and plants fifty-yard ladders of dancing motes in the dingiest corners of the huge place. Also the sun evokes the private smell of B. hangar: something in which oil and acetone and hot metal have part.

I like the hangar well in storms. The darkness and its size conspire to make it formidable, ominous. The leaves of the closed doors tremble in the guides, and clap boomingly against the iron rails. Through their crevices, and the hundreds of other crevices, packs of wind hurtle, screaming on every high note of the scale, to raise devil-dances across the dusty floor. Screech, boom: and the rain after the squall is like all the rifle-fire of an army. That shivering moment Tim will choose to issue from the office, and set all our hands to sweep the half-acre of concrete.

At night it looks a palace. We switch on lamp after lamp, high in the roof, and a wedge of golden light pours through the open front across the illimitable aerodrome which runs up, saucer-like, to a horizon like the sea, and sea-coloured, of waving grey-green grass. In this stream of light puny figures, eight or ten of them, swim, at a game of push and pull around the glitter-winged Bristol Fighters or Nine Acks. They drag them one by one into the lighted cave: then the doors clang shut, the lights go out: and the dwarfs trickle out from a dwarf-door in rear, across grass and gravel, bedwards.

Tim is the Flight Commander. He's a jewel. We enjoy every massive inch of him. It's a sight to see him shaking with silent mirth when somebody is foolish. We can watch the smile coming, from behind him, by the slow widening of his jowl. It's another sight to see us scuttling with fright behind buses and round corners, when word goes forth that Tim has a weed on. Tim is our barometer; he sets the flight's weather. B. Flight has the most exciting climate in the world.

At Cadet College the R.A.F. officer comes back to his own, in the foreground of authority, with the flight commander as the absolute fore-head. Our fifteen-man flight has three or four officers. Can they help meeting us, speaking to us, knowing us? We are the hands who actually push their machines about: on our vigilance and duty the officers' lives depend, for hours every flying day.

Because officers take their proper places, sergeants and corporals take theirs. Gone is the Prussian N-c-ocracy of Depot. They become our representatives, not chosen by us perhaps, but nominated from our best with tacit approval. We accept them as useful creatures who intervene and parley for us with the government. If they do not function to our bidding, we can go behind their backs, informally, any day out on the drome where we have the officers to ourselves. The incumbent give-and-take makes us a family: a happy family if the grown-ups are good, an unhappy family when they do not pull together. Praise be to Tim that B. Flight can never suspect a meanness in its constitutional king.

We adopt the officers. Tim is flight-property, the general boast: but John belongs to the three who valet his kite, Crasher to those other three, while Ginger is the object of my gang's service. We match our poppets and swap their virtues and vices in the hut of nights, as the airmen out east match their fighting scorpions and tarantulae.

8. Work

Just as the roomy, sordid, clanging, momentous hangar is our cathedral, so our day's work in it is worship: and the one's as hard to rationalise as the other. There's a defiance of common-sense in every faith. We believe the job's worth every last lift of our arms and kick of our legs: and our belief, to outsiders, may well seem senseless as a Mass.

It's no slug's life we lead. Inside the hangar they keep us for the eight hours of an ordinary workshop: and before and after that there's our own cleaning, bed-making, hut-tidying: another hour and a half. Add, much grudged, an occasional hour wasted over equipment or bayonet for some posh parade: our monthly week on duty flight, when we stand by all the hundred and sixty-eight hours for emergency aerodrome occasions: firepicket at night: a rare police guard, when we relieve the service police of some special responsibility: and you get a full life of work. Wednesday afternoons, Saturday afternoons and the few Sundays not desecrated by a parade service are golden spots in our laboriousness.

So much work, even when the work is worship, dulls the devotees. I get out of bed, often, as tired as I was at Depot: but so gratefully tired. And it passes off, for we all muck in: - the keenness of whoever feels fresh that morning whips up the reluctant. When they fag us out, in Cadet College, it is at least upon the pith of life and not upon a surface adornment. We are greatly useful here in the eyes of all who accept our premiss, that the conquest of the air is the first duty of our generation.

The darling partiality of Nature, which has reserved across the ages her last element for us to dompt! By our handling of this, the one big new thing, will our time be judged. Incidentally, for the near-sighted or political, it has a national side: upon the start we give our successors in the arts of air will depend their redressing our eighteenth-century army and silly ships.

Don't imagine that we all feel this, or that this is all we feel. We face something whose scale towers out of our imaginations. Each of us knows that a hundred thousand men like him will work their hardest at it, for many lifetimes, and still not see an end. My loose loquacious mind gets so far in words. The extreme carefulness of our work gets further. It's not mercenary work, nor duty work. The Air Force and the pay are only fleas making our inspirations itch.

And don't fly away on the notion that I'd pretend us wonderful. We are everyday sinners, keyed to extreme action only because we're up against something bigger than ourselves: but we translate this into talk of nuts and bolts for the day's need. If one of our kites can't go up, for an avoidable reason, the flight hangs its head in disgrace. Suggest to Tug, there, that he's left something undone in his rigging: or tell Cap'n that his engine's not as well maintained as he can maintain it: - and then run for your life, if they think you serious.

When I passed from Depot to Cadet College I passed from appearance to reality. After two days I was saying I had found a home. At Depot we had soldiered so long and so harshly that soldiering had become second nature: sterility quickly beds down into habit, by use. Now at Cadet College I was to learn to be an airman, by unlearning that corporate effort which had been the sole spirituality of the square.

It was a stress, the being chucked a job, and just bluntly told to get on with it. Taffy Jenkins had given us the detail of every movement, by numbers, for a joint performance at the word of command. Here they take intelligence for granted and are impatient with those who ask to learn. If we don't do the thing our way, sincerely, quickly and well enough, we're thrown out to something else. There's a ruthlessness with their human material that braces us: and a refreshingly high standard among the survivors. Our machines fly when they're as good as it lies in our power to make them. If that is not good enough, we drift to mess-deck fatigues or to sanitary squad: forfeiting the technical esteem of our pals. That is a harsh penalty, which puts poor Stiffy's extra drills far in the shade. There is no judgment so beyond appeal as the judgment of peers: and B. Flight's a republic: - or would be, but for its willing obedience to King Tim.

9. Funeral

It was an odd morning, that on which we heard Queen Alexandra was dead. The fog which collects here on most autumn mornings was so shallow. Across the ground it lay like a veil: but when we looked up we could see a sparkle, which hinted at a sun almost shining upon the eaves and mast-heads. When we parade in fog, our figures go flat. There is no thickness, no shadows, no high-light of polished buttons. Instead the fellows are as if cut out of grey cardboard, with a darker tint drawn round the edges, where the shafts of refracted light slip round them.

We stood so, in our hollow square, this morning, while they hoisted colour, and played the daily salute for the King: but after the salute they held us at attention, ever so long in that dead shivering silence: for the air was very sharp. Then the ensign began to creep downward from the peak, while the massed drums of the band rolled. And they rolled and rolled all the minutes that the flag crept down. At half-mast the trumpets came out brazenly with the last

66

post. We all swallowed our spittle, chokingly, while our eyes smarted against our wills. A man hates to be moved to folly by a noise.

They would not let us off the worst of it. There had to be a parade service the day she was buried. Our distrusted chaplain preached one of his questionable sermons. He spoke of the dead Queen as a Saint, a Paragon: not as an unfortunate, a long-suffering doll. With luscious mouth he enlarged upon her beauty, the beauty which God, in a marvel of loving-kindness, had let her keep until her dying.

My thoughts fled back sharply to Marlborough House. The yellow, scaling portal: the white-haired footmen and door-keepers, whiter than the powder of their hair: the hushed great barn-like halls: the deep carpet in which our feet dragged unwillingly to the ceiling-high fireplace which dwarfed the whispering Miss Knollys and Sir Dighton. She incredibly old, wasted, sallow: he a once huge man, whose palsied neck had let down the great head on the breast, where its gaping mouth wagged almost unseen and unheard in the thicket of beard which overgrew the waistcoat. Sir Dighton had won the first V.C. in the Crimea: and he was so old, and Miss Knollys so old that this seemed a cruel duty which kept them always on their feet. We whispered with them: everybody whispered in that charnel-house.

We had to wait, of course: that is the prerogative of Queens. When we reached the presence, and I saw the mummied thing, the bird-like head cocked on one side, not artfully but by disease, the red-rimmed eyes, the enamelled face, which the famous smile scissored across all angular and heart-rending: - then I nearly ran away in pity. The body should not be kept alive after the lamp of sense has gone out. There were the ghosts of all her lovely airs, the little graces, the once-effective sway and movement of the figure which had been her consolation. Her bony fingers, clashing in the tunnel of their rings, fiddled with albums, penholders, photographs, toys upon the table: and the heart-rending appeal played on us like a hose, more and more terribly. She soon dismissed us.

These memories lost me much of the sermon. I listened in again to hear the chaplain telling the story of Prince Albert Edward in the House of Lords warning Lord Granville he must miss part of his speech, because he had promised to take his daughter to the circus. 'This,' declaimed the padre, 'this was the domestic picture and example which the Prince and Princess of Wales set their adoring people.' 'Balls!' hissed someone, savagely, from behind me. In its thirty-second minute the sermon ended. More rolling of drums and last posts, now firmly resisted by all of us in our rage: and then back to dinner. 'Fall in at two for work!' shouted the Orderly Sergeant. 'Not even a half-holiday for the old girl,' grumbled Tug.

10. Dance Night

Chick came in first, just after eleven: but the strangeness of the empty hut made it feel like no time at all. The floor flickered and vanished, white and dark, like a waving flag, as my logs blazed up momently, or guttered away in smoke. He came in quickly, but the rubbers on his walking-out boots hushed his step, and he was careful not to wake me. For a moment he hesitated by his bed: flung down cap and stick, unhooked the choking collar of his tunic: then again he hesitated.

The fire rose, and caught his notice. He walked over, and seemed to extinguish it for a while, behind the black screen of his solidity. After, he began with lithe springing strides to pad up and down the wood-blocked floor, not noisily, but as though he loved the striding. He swung his arms, and once or twice muttered something, half-aloud, as he turned on his toes.

I rolled over in my bed, to warn him of my notice: he walked across, nuzzled down on my blankets, and bending his face (a strange scent) down to mine whispered, 'You awake, Ross?' I whispered back in my normal voice, reassuring him. He began to talk about the intoxication of the moon-lit frosty night, which filled his legs with dancing-love, like gin.

Suddenly he bent down again, muttering very gently, 'Do you know what happened to me, tonight? I met a girl... or she wasn't a girl, really... and we... clicked and went off together. Remember that dollar I borrowed off you, Monday? Well that just did it.' He threw his hard weight flat along the narrow bed, whispering eagerly, 'You know blanket-drill, and what that feels like? Well, it's chalk to cheese. Made me jump, this did, like two hundred volts. I wondered if we'd go up in flames, like poor old Mouldy and his kite. I've come back in one run, without a breather. It's all of five miles, isn't it? Breeches and puttees: Christ, some run. Just you feel here and here: I'm sweating like a bull. You could wring my togs out. Don't think I can bug down tonight. Where's Tug? I can't ever do it the first time again: but Christ, it was bloody wonnerful. 'I say, what've I got to do now? Wash it, I s'pose. Got any dope?'

11. <u>On Parade</u>

The A.O.C., a very exalted person, strolled round our hollow square, half-hiding a yawn in his gloves, and scarcely letting the fact of us strike his withdrawn eye. Dolly (so we irreverently call him) has played his part in affairs: governed cities, planned battles, and conferred death on many hundreds of men. He enjoys the clash of idea, and such explorations of mind as go far and strangely. The set of another man's tunic seems to him mainly that man's affair. We like him, therefore, for our commanding officer: he is a type to picture; and to yarn of: also his aloof shyness allies itself to his memory of when things were real, to save us from over-much formality.

This inspection lasted only fifteen minutes. The wind blustered down our ranks, also inspecting us, but roughly. It brushed back the flap of the opposite flank's tunics (and of ours, no doubt, in their view), showing the lividly blue pocket-linings, underneath, and the top of each man's trousers. The sunlight caught the lifting or falling cloth at an angle, brightening it. So the still figures seemed to be all signalling together. This movement singularly destroyed the illusion we were set to give, of blue cylinders standing most stiffly, hardly breathing, eyes level and straight ahead.

The wind, taking no heed of our strain, blustered on, whipping sudden curves into the trouser-legs - long bows of curves, from groin to ankle, much deforming the semblance of legs inside. Meanwhile the Adjutant bear-led poor enduring Dolly down the three interminable lanes of us dressed ham-bones all tightly sewn up in bags of unvarying serge. Dolly was too civil to disappoint the Adjutant by saying No: and too decent-minded to scrutinise the reluctant flesh of his men, so paraded for judgment. Very soon came his famous final order, 'Cawwy on, Sergeant Major,' lisped with relief and a shy salute in our direction. Good old Dolly.

What a revenge that unwholesome Depot takes on its victims! Any drill-order, even on these jocose parades, brings me back the hot odour of our panting flight, and the sound of Stiffy ramping up and down. An instinctive twitch of every nerve follows: and I square myself to

68

hate drill with the hatred in which we hold the Depot. Stiffy's trying to hustle the young west has made the nascent R.A.F. unmilitary by deepest conviction. His square was an alien prelude. An airman at Depot was an airman being warped from nature. That unwholesome subjectitude, which he miscalled discipline, contained not even a root of the motives of service which enrich this place.

The Powers seem afraid to exploit this gravity, this devotion of a deadly purposefulness, which underlies our profession. Worse, they make themselves ridiculous by piping to us on the minor key of their panache. When five hundred airmen on parade see their officer march up to the Squadron Leader: (the two live together, as Ching and Alec, in the mess): see him halt with a click at the regulation distance, draw swellingly up, and salute like a pistolshot - then five hundred airmen titter gently. It is theatrical, and theatre in England spells circus, and circus spells clown.

Perhaps, in days of Chivalry, even the north took the parade of arms lovingly, and throbbed at the feel of swords, the sight of banners. Perhaps: though I've chased through mediaeval literature after the days of chivalry, and found their revivals, and legends or reminiscences or ridicule of them, but never the real thing. Today these modes are right out of tune with the social system, whose firm-seatedness makes one doubt if an Englishman's blood can ever have flowed hotly enough for him to swallow a tomfoolery divorced from alcohol.

12. Police Duty

Tonight, Saturday night, saw the end of summer time. So our tricks of sentry-go were an hour longer than military wont. It was strange to walk up and down, killing time, while time, or rather the clock, stood still. This camp is electric - clocked. At first the night was good, for the air (not too cold) was calm. All the camp slept, and there was no traffic on the roads. The transport-yard, our care, opens off the smoothly-tarred main road and is spacious. The moonlight filled it. Across the sky crept a thin haze, so transparent in the beginning that its translucency increased the brilliancy of the moon.

Gradually, as the mist thickened, the moon seemed to wane. Its rays struck upon the cliff of trees which bordered the far side of the road, rendering it more cliff-like, by flattening the planes of its height. The mist was yet dry, so that the light became dusty, and the trees were powdered grey with it. Grey trees, tied about their roots with a grey ribbon-wall of dry oolite slabs, well-fitted: and, shining through the copse (it not being thick enough to leaf over every chink) glowed the watch lamps of the power station, like beasts' eyes: while the transformer, which alone works at night, whined low or loud as it spun round.

The leaves, Autumn's first converts, were falling singly, rarely, sadly, as though the trees were conscious of each loss. The moon and myself counted their fall. By the yard-gate the ragged leaves of a plane-tree lay upturned, so ashy-pale on the black grass edging of the road that they gathered the moonlight: and at first I thought them torn pages from a note-book.

The moon looked on, while I fitted words to what we saw. My vacant eyesight normally sees little: so when anything does get through the mind's preoccupation, at once I try to fix its form in phrases. Tonight I was fortunate, for one end of my beat turned by the alarm-lamp of the fire-station. I used its glow-light to note down the word or group of words which my mind and boots had hammered out on the patrol.

Later the night grew very cold. The chill of the earth soaked into me through the leather under my feet. The mist rallied and altogether hid the moon. My clothes became grey-haired with its wetness: also a longing for sleep weighed upon me, almost uncontrollably. When the clock at last moved again, and the hands crept forward to the half-hour of my relief I was more than glad.

The hot air and light of the guard-room poisoned my face: even as the forced company of the service police, those vermin in the body of the R.A.F., poisoned my self-respect. They pushed free a seat for me on the form nearest the fire, and Shorty passed me his mug of cocoa, to thaw out my tongue. I had interrupted Corporal Payne, a sexual-smelling policeman, in the midst of retelling some adventures in London on last leave. So word-perfect was he (we do not ordinarily excel in fluency) that I suspected many previous tellings lay behind this tale.

The confusion of cold moonlight still weighed on me, and lost me much of his detail. I think his tart's bedroom must have been somewhere off Golden Square. She slept him on a couch, and would not let him into her bed, behind curtains in an alcove: so while she was washing he peeped between: to see a dead infant lying on the counterpane. 'It was three days ago he died,' sobbed the girl.

The Corporal urged upon her the need to lose the body promptly. They wrapped it in brown paper, and took it to a neighbouring court, whose precipitous tenement-walls pushed London's nightcap of smoke and mist almost sky-far away, so that its arc refulgence hardly modified the blackness of the pit.

In the court's centre was a large drain, trap-covered, to shoot surface water away to the sewers. Payne felt round the grating, discovered the hinges, and pulled it open. He began to stuff in the body: but there seemed some obstacle. He kneeled to thrust his arm right down, and clear it: when a hand fell on his neck, and a loud voice said 'Now what do you think you're doing in here?' It was the Orderly Sergeant, and he was asleep in his own bed in the police hut. 'My God, what a relief.'

13. The Way of a Bird

Airmen are so healthy and free of the joints, that they exult to fling their meat about. Activity does not remind them, yet, how man hangs in his body, crucified. So we drill hard, desperately hard, exercising our bodies. It is a kind of fun, just to pant them out. The raggedness of the mass-effort testifies that, after his own time, each man is caring to the utmost for his good health and muscularity.

Stiffy would have called it a rebellious caring, which tried more for movement than for combination, pretended towards individual benefit, and made his rhythms only a means to fitness. That centipede-lesson of a comity had been the occasional gold upon the slavery of Depot. Slavery? We now called it soldiering, a strumpet-exhibitionism. The airman at Cadet College who dared try for excellence at drill was a bull-shitter, a bobber, a creeping cunt.

Stiffy has been superseded by the new redeeming standard of a job to live by. In its virtue we resist the gas of militarism, which is breathed at us by our sergeants: - eight in ten of whom are old soldiers or old sailors, transferred in authority to the R.A.F. till the baby service has bred its own veterans. They do their best with us men-in-the-moon, do these old minds, which were set before ever they transferred: but we and they speak different languages: their traditional eyes cannot even see how far from their pasts we have diverged.

Airmen estimate in terms of their trades. The overwhelming responsibility our generation lays on us is that our kites and engines must always be airworthy, to take our masters and ourselves into the air. If these masters so interpret their duty as to break into work-hours with drill, then are they so much less our masters: but we must not complain except privily. It is for the public, which pays them and us, to see to it. Besides perhaps they are like cunning old Tim who vexes us with bull-shit if he sees a trace of dirt on the machines. After a minute on the square how excellent is work, how real!

A touch of punishment for slackness in duty: - yes, that's drill's reasonable function. Men will never work for long, unpunished: but punishment, for the thin-skinned, must be feather-light, only perceptible by the victim in its after-effects. But if the Powers blunder and ask that a drill be done well, for its own sake: or for a decoration, to smarten our bearing: - why then the body politic festers. We instinctively work canny, resisting within bounds to checkmate the enemy. At least so we intend: but all of us aren't saints enough or clever enough to stop in the right place. Our lightweights will go wicked and take their revenge out of the innocent work, identifying their splendid service with some trumpery drill-maniac.

The hard names show how we are moved. At Cadet College was an abortion (we called it the clockwork lobster) for whom the poetry and high feeling and zest in achievement of the irks were so many devils to be hammered out of them by discipline. When Dolly gave his lobster a yard of line, these complainants of ours would go slow in the workshop not merely on the day of drill (we all did that, in nausea. It is bitter to be betrayed by an officer of our own service) but on the day before and on the day after, too. Happily the greater part saw it was bad form so to betray that the atom could anger us.

Against these few bolshies, the fellows of my kidney would struggle fiercely, preaching submission: even, if necessary, as low as the Depot point of sterilising ourselves to await orders for everything. Let the militarists have their way to its *n*th of futility. Time played into our hands. If the technical men held together and, ruefully smiling, offered both cheeks and the conduct of their handicrafts to discipline, why in no time the whole freedom of the future would be forced on them, by the discovery that the soldier and the mechanic were mutually destructive ideals. As the art of flying grew richer, the trade must deepen in mystery, or go under - and there could be no failure for the R.A.F. with the material now accepting enlistment. It had grown bigger than its rank and file, bigger than its chiefs.

The officers might delay progress for a few years: no more. Even now the airmen called the tune, in work-hours. A spanner, a screwdriver, a scraper, a file - these are our insignia: not the plumed wings, the swords, the eagles. There compete for our respect the officers who order the public carriage of our canes, and those who design new aircraft, or authorise two extra thou of backlash in the planet pinions of an epi-gear. Which will win the suffrage of fellows as trade-proud as ourselves? Yet the first sort think to bully it with high chins over us on parade, while the others are round-shouldered, shy, and scruffy with oil-stains. A parting of the roads!

It is a real danger. In this new service there can be nothing more traditional than the immemorial crafts: nothing so human as the mechanic off duty: nothing sentimental except a rare pantomime at Wembley or Hendon. The working mechanic will not be gay, with the weight of the effort towards indefinite victory on his unguided head: - unguided, largely because the Officers' Mess achieves the public-school tone, and so dares not look beyond the concrete.

Those we regard as our natural aristocracy show three generations of artisan forbears by their mere grip of the tool-handle. Lacking this touch, though you're the best fellow in the world, you cannot be our leader. A pilot climbs into one of our buses, yanks the throttle open and flogs her into the air. Hear us curse his ham-fisted cruelty to machines. Our machines, please: the beloved created things whose every inmost bolt or outstretched spar has felt our caring fingers. Many officers know only the back and bottom cushions of their cockpit seats. 'Officers? I've shit 'em' rigger or fitter will choke out over there, angered nearly to tears.

14. <u>Classes</u>

The Air Ministry recognises a rightness in our worship of the technical engineer, by promoting sergeant or sergeant pilot the best men from the ranks: those who have understanding of the souls of engines, and find their poetry in the smooth tick-over.

They form our aristocracy of merit. Against them, over them, stand the lords spiritual, the commissioned: whose dignity comes extrinsically, from some fancied laying-on of hands. When they are forceful souls, Tims or Taffys, one to a squad, all is well. The basic lesion of character in every enlisted man makes him ready to laugh or cry, always, like a child: but seldom leaves him sober. So the hand of a father seems neither incongruous nor disagreeable to us. We earn force, by our root-folly.

Our conscious inferiority excludes Tim from comparison or challenge: but there is rising up a second category of airman, the boy apprentice. They disrupt us now: for the men don't like the boys: but this inevitable phase is a passing phase. Soon the ex-boy will be the majority, and the R.A.F. I knew will be superseded and forgotten. Meanwhile there is jealousy and carping.

The boys come fresh from school, glib in theory, essay writers, with the bench-tricks of workmen: but they have never done the real job on a real kite: and reality, carrying responsibility, has a different look and feel from a school lesson. So they are put for a year to work with men. An old rigger, with years of service, whose trade is in his fingers, finds himself in charge of a boy-beginner with twice his pay. The kid is clever with words, and has passed out L.A.C. from school: the old hand can hardly spell, and will be for ever an A.C.2. He teaches his better ever so grumpily.

Nor do all the ex-boys make the job easier for those they are about to replace. As a class they are cocky. Remember how we, the enlisted men, have all been cowed. Behind us, in our trial of civy life, is the shadow of failure. Bitterly we know, of experience, that we are not as good as the men outside. So officers, sergeants and corporals may browbeat us, and we'll lie down to it: even fawn on them the more for it. That sense of inferiority may not save us from the smart of discipline (your bully will always find his way to be severe, if it's merely to put the fear of God in us) but it gives us the humility of house-dogs, under discipline.

The airmen of the future will not be so owned, body and soul, by their service. Rather will they be the service, maintaining it, and their rights in it, as one with the officers. Whereas we have had no rights, except on paper, and few there. In the old days men had weekly to strip off boots and socks, and expose their feet for an officer's inspection. An ex-boy'd kick you in the mouth, as you bent down to look. So with the bath-rolls, a certificate from your N.C.O. that you'd had a bath during the week. One bath! And with the kit inspections, and room inspections, and equipment inspections, all excuses for the dogmatists among the officers to blunder, and for the nosy-parkers to make beasts of themselves. Oh, you require the gentlest touch to interfere with a poor man's person, and not give offence.

The ex-boys are professionally in the R.A.F. as a privilege, making it their home. Soon, when they have made their style felt, officers will only enter their airmen's rooms accompanied, by invitation, guest-like and bare-headed, like us in an officers' mess. Officers will not be allowed to slough their uniform for social functions, while airmen walk about branded everywhere. The era of a real partnership in our very difficult achievement must come, if progress is to be lasting.

15. Fugitive

My Cadet College notes shortened, grew occasional, stopped. Months and months flowed silently away. I think I had become happy. 'Why,' complained E.M.F., 'as the years pass, do I find that word harder and harder to write?' Because when we write we are not happy: we only recollect it: and a recollection of the exceeding subtlety of happiness has something of the infect, unlawful: it being an overdraft on life.

If happiness was vested in ourselves, we could make it our habit, by selfishly shutting ourselves away: though this complete peacefulness of the restricted circle is not to compare with the half-peace of a wider one: but happiness, while primarily dependent on our internal balance of desire and opportunity, lies also at the mercy of our external acquaintance. One jar in all the circumambient - and our day is out of tune.

We, in the service, if a good time comes, snatch at it: knowing that blind chance has overlooked us sports of circumstance for the moment. Cadet College, during my spell, was passing through such a golden weather: and B. Flight was probably the best of Cadet College. Look up from the bottom as high as we could, even to the A.O.C., and each degree of our commanders was benignant. We were fortunate in Tim, fortunate in our sergeant and corporal. Within the hut we were free and equal. Troops can exist in harmony by tolerating one another. In B. Flight we were luckier than that. We liked one another.

There was a quality of desperation about this liking. We knew our transience. The flight was as fugitive and feeble as a summer cloud. Every week some rumour of change would shake our trust. Every month or so a change would take effect. For the days before it we would go about - knowing that old Tug was posted, trying to estimate what we should specially miss in old Tug: and the new man? Who would he be? How would he muck-in?

I shall not forget the black despair which overwhelmed me as the day approached of my own going into self-appointed exile, to save my R.A.F. skin from the repercussion of a folly in 1918. I lost, then, the best home and companionship of my forty years' living. I wonder who took my place? In a society of twelve, each player has a solo importance, and a bad man will spoil the whole. For three weeks we had an unfitting sergeant, who turned the best pleased and best-working flight of Cadet College to rebellious misery. The fortune of an airman is gossamer, disordered by a single breath, and his life poignant, from its fragility.

Of course we strive to mitigate the evil. A first instinct of existence teaches us to sacrifice everything which might endanger our solidity. Twelve men in a constricted bedroom: - indeed we cannot afford the luxury of our own angles. The ideal of troops is to be as like and close-fitting as bee cells. If one dislikes another, and shows it, the flight will be out of joint: and the egg-shell of its comfort crack. We so cultivate the face of friendliness that from a mask it becomes a habit, from a habit conviction. To preserve it we jettison our realities... or cover them so deep that we fail to hear their voice. In the hut no point is put without qualification, no opinion pressed far enough to hurt. We run on half-throttle, in company.

This constriction within doors demands a venturesome outlet elsewhere. Out of it comes a degree of the heat and heart of our work. Out of it, too, comes our passion for games. In the practical argument of football a fellow can do his damnedest, giving and taking knocks; can be gloriously reckless of mud, and of his clothes and his body. To live as hard as we play would make life earnest. Those who do not play can find an escape in immoderate social exercise among the neighbouring towns and villages. A few find it in the wet bar of the canteen.

16. <u>The Road</u>

[Originally titled 'Ramping', this was written as one of a series of anonymous articles that Lawrence submitted unsuccessfully to the *Motor Cycle* magazine: 'I wrote a string of articles about bike rides: but the *Motor Cycle* would not take them' (letter to F. L. Lucas, 23 March 1929). He later incorporated this article in the Cranwell section of *The Mint*, which was assembled from a number of contemporary sources. It appears there under the title 'The Road' (*The Mint*, Part III, Chapter 16].

The extravagance in which my surplus emotion expressed itself lay on the road. So long as roads were tarred blue and straight; not hedged; and empty and dry, so long I was rich.

Nightly I'd run up from the hangar, upon the last stroke of work, spurring my tired feet to be nimble. The very movement refreshed them, after the day-long restraint of service. In five minutes my bed would be down, ready for the night: in four more I was in breeches and puttees, pulling on my gauntlets as I walked over to my bike, which lived in a garage-hut, opposite. Its tyres never wanted air, its engine had a habit of starting at second kick: a good habit, for only by frantic plunges upon the starting pedal could my puny weight force the engine over the seven atmospheres of its compression.

Boanerges' first glad roar at being alive again nightly jarred the huts of Cadet College into life. 'There he goes, the noisy bugger,' someone would say enviously in every flight. It is part of an airman's profession to be knowing with engines: and a thoroughbred engine is our undying satisfaction. The camp wore the virtue of my Brough like a flower in its cap. Tonight Tug and Dusty came to the step of our hut to see me off. 'Running down to Smoke, perhaps?' jeered Dusty; hitting at my regular game of London and back for tea on fine Wednesday afternoons.

Boa is a top-gear machine, as sweet in that as most single-cylinders in middle. I chug lordlily past the guard-room and through the speed limit at no more than sixteen. Round the bend, past the farm, and the way straightens. Now for it. The engine's final development is fifty-two horse-power. A miracle that all this docile strength waits behind one tiny lever for the pleasure of my hand.

Another bend: and I have the honour of one of England' straightest and fastest roads. The burble of my exhaust unwound like a long cord behind me. Soon my speed snapped it, and I heard only the cry of the wind which my battering head split and fended aside. The cry rose with my speed to a shriek: while the air's coldness streamed like two jets of iced water into my dissolving eyes. I screwed them to slits, and focused my sight two hundred yards ahead of me on the empty mosaic of the tar's gravelled undulations.

Like arrows the tiny flies pricked my cheeks: and sometimes a heavier body, some house-fly or beetle, would crash into face or lips like a spent bullet. A glance at the speedometer: seventy-eight. Boanerges is warming up. I pull the throttle right open, on the top of the slope, and we swoop flying across the dip, and up-down up-down the switchback beyond: the weighty machine launching itself like a projectile with a whirr of wheels into the air at the take-off of each rise, to land lurchingly with such a snatch of the driving chain as jerks my spine like a rictus.

Once we so fled across the evening light, with the yellow sun on my left, when a huge shadow roared just overhead. A Bristol Fighter, from Whitewash Villas, our neighbour aerodrome, was banking sharply round. I checked speed an instant to wave: and the slip-stream of my impetus snapped my arm and elbow astern, like a raised flail. The pilot pointed down the road towards Lincoln. I sat hard in the saddle, folded back my ears and went away after him, like a dog after a hare. Quickly we drew abreast, as the impulse of his dive to my level exhausted itself.

The next mile of road was rough. I braced my feet into the rests, thrust with my arms, and clenched my knees on the tank till its rubber grips goggled under my thighs. Over the first pot-hole Boanerges screamed in surprise, its mud-guard bottoming with a yawp upon the tyre. Through the plunges of the next ten seconds I clung on, wedging my gloved hand in the throttle lever so that no bump should close it and spoil our speed. Then the bicycle wrenched sideways into three long ruts: it swayed dizzily, wagging its tail for thirty awful yards. Out came the clutch, the engine raced freely: Boa checked and straightened his head with a shake, as a Brough should.

The bad ground was passed and on the new road our flight became birdlike. My head was blown out with air so that my ears had failed and we seemed to whirl soundlessly between the sun-gilt stubble fields. I dared, on a rise, to slow imperceptibly and glance sideways into the sky. There the Bif was, two hundred yards and more back. Play with the fellow? Why not? I slowed to ninety: signalled with my hand for him to overtake. Slowed ten more: sat up. Over he rattled. His passenger, a helmeted and goggled grin, hung out of the cock-pit to pass me the 'Up yer' Raf randy greeting.

They were hoping I was a flash in the pan, giving them best. Open went my throttle again. Boa crept level, fifty feet below: held them: sailed ahead into the clean and lonely country. An approaching car pulled nearly into its ditch at the sight of our race. The Bif was zooming among the trees and telegraph poles, with my scurrying spot only eighty yards ahead. I gained though, gained steadily: was perhaps five miles an hour the faster. Down went my left hand to give the engine two extra dollops of oil, for fear that something was running hot: but an overhead Jap twin, super-tuned like this one, would carry on to the moon and back, unfaltering.

We drew near the settlement. A long mile before the first houses I closed down and coasted to the cross-roads by the hospital. Bif caught up, banked, climbed and turned for home, waving to me as long as he was in sight. Fourteen miles from camp, we are, here: and fifteen minutes since I left Tug and Dusty at the hut door.

I let in the clutch again, and eased Boanerges down the hill along the tram-lines through the dirty streets and up-hill to the aloof cathedral, where it stood in frigid perfection above the cowering close. No message of mercy in Lincoln. Our God is a jealous God: and man's very best offering will fall disdainfully short of worthiness, in the sight of Saint Hugh and his angels.

Remigius, earthy old Remigius, looks with more charity on and Boanerges. I stabled the steel magnificence of strength and speed at his west door and went in: to find the organist practising something slow and rhythmical, like a multiplication table in notes on the organ. The fretted, unsatisfying and unsatisfied lace-work of choir screen and spandrels drank in the main sound. Its surplus spilled thoughtfully into my ears.

By then my belly had forgotten its lunch, my eyes smarted and streamed. Out again, to sluice my head under the White Hart's yard-pump. A cup of real chocolate and a muffin at the teashop: and Boa and I took the Newark road for the last hour of daylight. He ambles at forty-five and when roaring his utmost, surpasses the hundred. A skittish motor-bike with a touch of blood in it is better than all the riding animals on earth, because of its logical extension of our faculties, and the hint, the provocation, to excess conferred by its honeyed untiring smoothness. Because Boa loves me, he gives me five more miles of speed than a stranger would get from him.

At Nottingham I added sausages from my wholesaler to the bacon which I'd bought at Lincoln: bacon so nicely sliced that each rasher meant a penny. The solid pannier-bags behind the saddle took all this and at my next stop a (farm) took also a felt-hammocked box of fifteen eggs. Home by Sleaford, our squalid, purse-proud, local village. Its butcher had six penn'orth of dripping ready for me. For months have I been making my evening round a marketing, twice a week, riding a hundred miles for the joy of it and picking up the best food cheapest, over half the country side.

['Ramping' was sent to Rupert de la Bere on 8 October 1930, for publication in the *Journal of the Royal Air Force College* over the initials 'J.C.' Lawrence's covering letter suggests that the text was drawn from *The Mint*, but its true history is given in a letter to George Brough of 13 June 1933:

'I read the article in the *Motor Cycle* and was disappointed. That is no way to taste the merits of a B.S. By the way, did you ever see the note of a ride to Lincoln from Cranwell that I gave to the RAF College magazine a year or two ago? It was more my notion of what Broughing should be. Captain de la Bere, the Editor, would probably show you the article, if you asked him nicely. I did not keep a copy...Ten years ago (nearly) I wrote a set of articles on the joys of riding – but the *Motor Cycle* would not have them. This is the survivor.'

The title of the article refers to the nickname, the 'Ramper', given by cadets to a particular stretch of road near the RAF College at Cranwell. The article was first printed in *Journal of the Royal Air Force College, Cranwell,* Vol. XI, No.1, Spring 1931. It was signed pseudonymously with the initials J.C. It may be a coincidence that these were the initials of his parents' family names, Junner (or Jenner) and Chapman. It is difficult to understand why David Garnett, who had access to Lawrence's correspondence with de la Bere, should have included an inaccurate and critical footnote on page 781 of *The Letters of T.E. Lawrence* (1938), suggesting that the text printed in the Cranwell Journal had been copied from the much later *British Legion Journal* piracy.

'Ramping' was reprinted in the *Journal of the Royal Air Force College* in Autumn 1935: 'Ramping by Aircraftman T.E. Shaw. (A reprint of an article sent to an earlier issue of this *Journal* under an alias which some recognised as that of the late Col. Lawrence).'

An extract from 'The Road' was reprinted as 'Brough versus Biplane: a Chapter from the Lawrence of Arabia story' in *Motor Cycling* on 21 May 1959: 'Recently, several readers have suggested that we should reproduce a chapter headed "The Road" which appears in *The Mint*, a posthumously published book by T.E. Lawrence..."The Road" has been mentioned in *The Manchester Guardian* as "one of the most striking descriptions ever written of the experience of riding a powerful motorcycle at high speed" and, by kind permission of the publisher of *The Mint*, Jonathan Cape, we reprint it this week, 24 years after Lawrence of Arabia died on 19 May 1935.'

John Rennison, *The Digby Diary* (2003): 'It was towards the end of 1925 that a certain Aircraftsman Thomas Edward Shaw re-enlisted in the RAF and was posted to nearby Cranwell...Whilst stationed at the RAF College at Cranwell Shaw / Lawrence would often take the opportunity to escape the rigours of military life by taking to the local roads on his Brough Superior motorcycle. In his book The Mint he describes one particular instance when out on his motor cycle travelling north along the modern-day A15 towards Lincoln, he had what could be described as a "close encounter" with a Bristol Fighter from Cranwell's neighbouring aerodrome, which was known to the airmen as "Whitewash Villas". This can only be an allusion to Digby, which is Cranwell's nearest neighbour being only some six or so miles away. Indeed, the station's single story First World War barrack blocks had at that time been whitewashed, looking for all the world like holiday villas. The aircraft to which he refers in the book was almost certainly one of the Bristol F2B Fighters based at Digby. It was late afternoon when Lawrence suddenly became conscious of the shadow of an aircraft passing over him. The pilot of the aircraft banked over and waved to the speeding motorcyclist, pointing down the road to the north. The challenge was inherent in the gesture and the race was one. Lawrence opened up the Brough and started to edge up towards 80 mph as the aircraft flew low over the road ahead. Lawrence drew level with his hand wedged in the throttle lever to prevent the vibration causing it to close. He passed the fighter at well over 90 mph and then throttled back and impudently waved to the pilot to overtake him. As they approached Bracebridge Heath on the edge of Lincoln, her once again drew level with the speeding Bristol, which was only some 50 feet above him. Tweaking the super-tuned twin cylinder Jap engine, he put on sufficient speed to catch and pass the Bristol about a mile from the main cross roads at Bracebridge. He coasted to a halt as the pilot of the Bristol banked the aircraft and turned for home acknowledging defeat with a long waving salute. The trip from Cranwell to Bracebridge had taken only 15 minutes.']

17. A Thursday Night

The fire is a cooking fire, red between the stove-bars, all its flame and smoke burned off. Half-past eight. The other ten fellows are yarning in a blue haze of tobacco, two on the chairs, eight on the forms, waiting my return. After the clean night air their cigarette smoke gave me a coughing fit. Also the speed of my last whirling miles by lamplight (the severest test of riding) had unsteadied my legs, so that I staggered a little. 'Wo-ups, dearie' chortled Dusty. 'More split-arse work tonight?' It pleases them to imagine me wild on the road. To feed this flight-vanity I gladden them with details of my scrap against the Bif.

'Bring any grub?' at length enquires Nigger, whose pocket is too low, always, for canteen. I knew there was something lacking. The excitement of the final dash and my oncoming weariness had chased from my memory the stuffed panniers of the Brough. Out into the night again, steering across the black garage to the corner in which he is stabled by the fume of hot iron rising from his sturdy cylinders. Click, click, the bags are detached; and I pour out their contents before Dusty, the hut pantry-man. Tug brings out the frying pan, and has precedency. The fire is just right for it. A sizzle and a filling smell. I get ready my usual two slices of buttered toast.

Nigger turns over the possibilities. 'What are eggs?' he asks. I do a lightning calculation: penny ha'penny. Right: he chooses one egg. Rashers are a penny. Two of them and two dogs, at tuppence. He rolls me his sixpence along the table. 'Keep the odd 'un for fat,' he murmurs. The others choose and pay. Selling the stuff is no trouble: we have run this supper scandal among ourselves all the winter. The canteen food is dearer, though not dear; and much less tasteful than these fruits of our own fetching and cooking. And you have to queue up there, for ten minutes, to be pertly served.

Paddy, the last cooker of tonight, cleans the pan for tomorrow by wiping out its dripping on a huge doorstep of mess-deck bread. Later we'll see him put this bread to belly-use. 'Old grease-trap' Tug calls him, rallyingly. Meanwhile the gramophone plays jazz stuff to charm down the food. My brain is too dishevelled after a hard ride to be fit for string-music, its dope of a wet evening. For tonight I am drowsy-drunk on air. Lights out finds us all willing for sleep. Tomorrow the golden eagle moults on us.

18. Interlude

Service life in this way teaches a man to live largely on little. We belong to a big thing, which will exist forever and ever in unnumbered generations of standard airmen, like ourselves. Our outward samenesses of dress and type remind us of that. Also our segregation and concentration. The clusters of us widen out beyond Cadet College, beyond Whitewash Villas, beyond Depot, over hundreds of camps, over half the world. The habit of 'belonging to something or other' induces in us a sense of being one part of many things.

As we gain attachment, so we strip ourselves of personality. Mark the spiritual importance of such trifles as these overalls in which we shroud ourselves for work, like robots: to become drab shapes without comeliness or particularity, and careless, careless. The clothes for which a fellow has to pay are fetters to him, unless he is very rich and spendthrifty. This working dress provided us by the R.A.F. is not the least of our freedoms. When we put it on, oil, water, mud, paint, all such hazardous things, are instantly our friends.

A spell of warm weather has come back to us, as if summer feared to quit this bleak north. The wind keeps its bite; but our hangar shelters a calm crescent of tarmac and grass, and its open mouth is a veritable sun-trap. Through the afternoon eight of us lay there waiting for a kite which had gone away south, across country, and was overdue. Wonderful, to have it for our duty to do nothing but wait hour after hour in the warm sunshine, looking out southward.

We were too utterly content to speak, drugged with an absorption fathoms deeper than physical contentment. Just we lay there spread-eagled in a mesh of bodies, pillowed on one another and sighing in happy excess of relaxation. The sunlight poured from the sky and melted into our tissues. From the turf below our moist backs there came up a sister-heat which joined us to it. Our bones dissolved to become a part of this underlying indulgent earth, whose mysterious pulse throbbed in every tremor of our bodies. The scents of the thousand-acre drome mixed with the familiar oil-breath of our hangar, nature with art: while the pale sea of the grass bobbed in little waves before the wind raising a green surf which hissed and flowed by the slats of our heat-lidded eyes.

Such moments of absorption resolve the mail and plate of our personality back into the carbo-hydrate elements of being. They come to service men very often, because of our light surrender to the good or evil of the moment.

Airmen have no possessions, few ties, little daily care. For me, duty now orders only the brightness of these five buttons down my front.

And airmen are cared for as little as they care. Their simple eyes, out-turned; their natural living; the penurious imaginations which neither harrow nor reap their lowlands of mind: all these expose them, like fallows, to the processes of air. In the summer we are easily the sun's. In winter we struggle undefended along the roadway, and the rain and wind chivy us, till soon we are wind and rain. We race over in the first dawn to the College's translucent swimming pool, and dive into the elastic water which fits our bodies closely as a skin: - and we belong to that too. Every-where a relationship: no loneliness any more.

I can't write 'Finis' to this book, while I am
still serving. I hope, sometimes,
that I will never write it.

Letters

During his time at Cranwell (August 1925 – November 1926) Lawrence was working intermittently on *Seven Pillars of Wisdom*; by the time he left for India his lavishly printed and illustrated subscribers' edition was completed and the popular abridgement entitled *Revolt in the Desert* was awaiting publication. That this latter event would inevitably lead to another upsurge of publicity and myth-making led to his request to be posted abroad.

This is an important period for letters – the beginning of the high tide which was only to subside in the last weeks of his life. The main sources of letters by T.E. Lawrence are:

- *The Letters of T.E. Lawrence* edited by David Garnett (1938)
- *The Home Letters of T.E. Lawrence and his brothers* (1954)
- *T. E. Lawrence to his Biographers Robert Graves and Liddell Hart* (1963)
- *Solitary in the Ranks* by H. Montgomery Hyde (1977)
- *The Letters of T.E. Lawrence* selected and edited by Malcolm Brown (1988 & 2005)
- *T.E. Lawrence Letters Volume One: Correspondence with Bernard and Charlotte Shaw, 1922-26,* edited by Jeremy and Nicole Wilson (2000)
- *T.E. Lawrence Letters Volume Two: Correspondence with Bernard and Charlotte Shaw, 1927,* edited by Jeremy and Nicole Wilson (2003)

The country home of Bernard and Charlotte Shaw was close to the road between Cranwell and London and Lawrence soon began to visit them there. The Charlotte Shaw correspondence was candid, confessional, written with a sense of style and ranging widely over life and literature. Many years older than Lawrence, Charlotte was his principal confidante and confessor. Like Lawrence she was Anglo-Irish, had suffered under a formidable and domineering mother and had no intention of having children. He wrote over 300 letters to her between 1923 and 1935. They are remarkable pieces of writing and a most vivid portrait of a mind on the edge of despair. This includes a long letter (after his meeting with Lord Winterton and King Feisal of Iraq in September 1925) written in a mood of such unhappiness and disillusion that it has been described as the bitterest letter he ever composed: 'I've crashed my life and self and gone hopelessly wrong: and hopelessly it is, for I'm never coming back, and I want to. O dear O dear, what a coil.'

The verbatim letters in this chapter have been published and are now out of copyright. Also included are summaries of those letters which have been published, but are covered by copyright until 2040.

August 1925

[T.E. Lawrence was transferred in August 1925 to the RAF College at Cranwell.]

E. Palmer

RAF Cadets College, Cranwell, Lincs.

25.VIII.25

When I entered the R.A.F. station at West Drayton (a derelict misery-stricken unfinished factory-place) from its upper windows came 'The Lass of Richmond Hill', violently sung. At once I remembered Clouds Hill, and you, and H.H.B. and I hung my kit-bag on a willow-tree and wept.

They set me sums: which I solved as fast as they brought them. A flight-sergeant came along, 'Hullo Ross!'... and a dynamo-switch-board-attendant behind him said 'Garn... that ain't Ross. I was at Bovington when he came up, and he's Colonel Lawrence'. After that things got very complicated. Before lights out I was in charge of the recruits' hut.

Wednesday so passed. Thursday is a blank in my memory. On Friday early they sent me to a doctor. He said 'Have you ever had... ... .?' 'No Sir' 'Have you ever had... ... ...?' 'No' (less confidently).

'Have you ever - broken any bones?' This was my chance: I poured over him a heap of fractured fibulae, radii, metatarsals, phalanges, costes, clavicles, scapulae, till he yelled to me to stop. So I stopped, and he made clumsy efforts to write them all down.

Anyway it was all over by noon on Friday. At two o'clock they put me in a tender, and sent me to Uxbridge in charge of a corporal, who was charged to get a receipt for my body. Everyone at Uxbridge was willing to take delivery: but none would sign for me. At last I was dragged into the Headquarters' Adjutant, the last hope. (All the world else being at the Wembley Tattoo). He glared 'What are you?' I very stilly replied 'Yesterday I was a Pte in the R.T.C.' He snorted 'Today?' 'I think I'm an A.C. twice in the R.A.F.' Snort second. 'Will you be in the Navy tomorrow?' 'Perhaps,' said I. 'I can't sign for you. I don't want you'. 'I don't want anyone to sign for me.' 'Damned silly... who the hell are you?'

At this point my feeble patience broke. 'If your name was Buggins, and I called you Bill...' Then he yelled with joy, recognising my names for him (as I might all you Posh when you are very old and rich and important) and gave me tea.

Friday night, 6 p.m. I am handed into the recruits' hut. Messenger arrives. A.C.II Shaw to report to Flight Office at once. 'Sergeant take this man to the Q.M. stores, kit him at once, and put him into the first train for Cranwell. The Air Ministry have ordered his immediate posting.' Help: poor me: 8p.m.: two kit bags, a set of equipment, great coat, bayonet, like a plum tree too heavy with fruit. However 'last train gone'. Sergt. and self returned to recruits' hut. I slept: very wet. On Saturday squared tailors and got my stuff altered: polished bayonet: scrubbed equipment.

Sunday blancoed equipment: polished bayonet. Walked round Uxbridge very new in blue. Monday 11 a.m. started for Cranwell. Finished up in a taxi. Reception-hut: hot and cold laid on to hut: a bath. Heaven: sleep.

Tuesday, today. Reveille 7.30. Hot bath: Heaven: breakfast: H.Q. office: M.O.Adjutant: S.-M. very curious questions. Posted as aircraft hand to B. Flight. Fatigues when the cadets are on holiday: pulling their machines in and out of the sheds, filling up, starting, cleaning etc. when they are here. Sixteen men in flight. Sergt. a speed-demon on a twin N.U.T. Bath-furnace out of order. Cold: wet: not heaven.

Kit inspection once a month: hut inspection once a month: marching order parade once a month: no guards: church parade twice a month. Few other duties. Can do, I think. No P.T. Feel odd and strange: exhilarated: crazy sometimes. Is it going to meals does that? Haven't spent a shilling a day lately. Will you tell Clouds Hill that all is well so far? People who come to Cranwell often stay there for five years. I will go over to Nottingham on Saturday week, and try to see Brough, who has a 1926 S.S.110 waiting for me. After that I'll get a room in some near village, and begin work. Meanwhile - got to scrub that equipment again.

T.E.S.

R.A.F. issue three towels: Also one pair plain light boots, and one pair marching boots. Slippers of normal Bovington type. No other changes to note. If there is a bunch of letters please insert in a fresh large envelope, and address as above. Willis has envelopes.

Florence Hardy

[When Lawrence was in the Tank Corps at Bovington he was a frequent visitor to the Hardys at their home at Max Gate. Their parlour maid Nellie Titterington recalls that 'Visits by Col. Lawrence were always a very great source of pleasure to him and he was especially fond of them. I also liked Lawrence, and although he looked ordinary and unassuming, I could sense he was no ordinary being, but a man of great strength of character. He had a wonderful sense of humour, and I always saw and chatted with him when he came and I opened the door. When he called I always asked as a joke, "Is it Col. Lawrence, Mr Shaw or Mr Ross today?"; he would smile and say "Mr Shaw today".]

R.A.F. Cadets' College, Cranwell, Lincs.

26.VIII.25

Dear Mrs. Hardy,

You see, it has happened! Quite suddenly at the end: so that I was spared a visit of farewell. It is best to go off abruptly, if at all.

I never expected the move to be so drastic. Cranwell is not really near anywhere (nor is it anything in itself): and the disorder of falling into a new station is yet upon me. The R.A.F. is a home to me: but it is puzzling to find the home all full of strangers who look upon me as strange. My known past always rouses curiosity in a new station. Probably in a few days things will be comfortable.

Alas for Clouds Hill, and the Heath, and the people I had learned in the two years of Dorset!

Please remember me to Mr. Hardy, who is no doubt wholly taken up now in *Tess*. You have a good actress. I hope it will seem fitting both to you and the public. It is hard to please two masters.

You said to me that I might see that work of yours again, some time. Please don't forget that: though I can't seem either to read or to write in this noise!

Yours sincerely

T.E. Shaw

<u>John Buchan</u>

Cranwell, Lincs.

27.VIII.25

Dear Buchan,

Do not distress yourself to answer this. It's a letter of realised thanks, for the great difficulty is over. I feel like a person home at last - to find everyone else grown up, or changed, and the house open to all manner of other people beside myself. A new camp is always such a plunge into unknown.

This is a very comfortable, peaceful, cleanly camp, and will be glorious when I have settled into it. Indeed it is then I should have written to you, and not now, the first day of work, when I am tired. But you aren't in need of beautiful letters!

My thanks pile higher and higher.

Yours sincerely

T.E. Shaw

<u>A.P. Wavell</u>

RAF Cadets College, Cranwell, Lincs.

29.VIII.25

Lawrence said that he had changed his skin and loved the new one. The job was less good and the pay was less and the Lincolnshire countryside was very bleak, but he felt content. The book he was writing had staggered and halted but when he had settled in it would move on again.

<u>Robert Graves</u>

338171 A.C.II Shaw
Hut 105

RAF Cadets College
Cranwell
Lincs.

29.VIII.25

What a long address. I begin the letter exhausted.

No, I have not seen the *Marmosite*: have not seen it yet: for I write as soon as it arrives to let you know that I am no longer an inhabitant of Dorset. The RAF had its arms prized open unwillingly again for my entry: and thanks be to all the Gods I'm now in a flight, my ambition of seven years. I pull aeroplanes into and out from their stables.

Dorsetshire was a very good two years. Max Gate, Clouds Hill, and the perfection of English country round them.

I'm very sorry that your life has been ragged of late months. Illness of one's own is exasperating, because humiliating...and I get angry at the downfall of others when I see them as I would despise myself.

However...

I'm very glad to hear that S.S. is all right. He is rather like a Miltonic archangel: no doubt all right in the archangels' mess: but rather terrifying to the rank and file.

But are we even rank and file angels? Most of the RAF are not angelic, except in the faculty of flight.

au revoir

T.E.S.

S.C. Cockerell

29.VIII.25

No bicycle here yet: but I live in hopes of one next spring when that book [*Seven Pillars*] is finished.

[T.E.L. did not take his Brough motorcycle ('George IV') with him to RAF Cranwell in August 1925. In reality he was hoping for a replacement. His letter to E. Palmer on 25 August had mentioned his intention to 'go over to Nottingham on Saturday week, and try to see Brough, who has a 1926 SS.100 waiting for me.' In fact it was October before George IV was exchanged, and letters suggest that he fetched it in late September to be ready for this purpose].

September 1925

[On 1 September Charlotte Shaw received a note from Lawrence giving his new address as the RAF College, Cranwell. She wrote to him there the following day. On 4 September Charlotte Shaw received proofs of Book III of *Seven Pillars*. On 9 September she returned proofs of Book VI 'twice read'. She wrote about these on the 19 September and on 23 September sent a parcel containing John Masefield's *Lost Endeavour*; *Highways and Byways of Lincolnshire*; two issues of *L'Illustration*, and two of the *Times Literary Supplement*. Three days later she sent a further postcard about Book VI.]

E. Palmer

Cranwell

7.IX.25

How difficult writing is. I have been facing the need of it for some days.

Haven't written to E.M.F. either. He asked for as long notice as you could give him of your visit to London. Tell me too: so if there is a chance...

Seen Dick twice. There is a great gap between the Boys' Camp and ours (a metaphorical gap). Hard to cross.

The kitchen table I bought from Knowles last year.

I have some books to go to you: to-night's parcel will only be a beret, conveying the remains of my Tank Corps period: also 3 keys.

(i) Skeleton, presumably for Jeffrey. Anyone you please.
(ii) Clouds Hill... for the babes in it.
(iii) Kit bag: for the brown locked bag in the bathroom. Will you dig out of this my *black* helmet (motorcycling). There is a brown one: but I want the black one with a fur edging to the forehead.

I also want the black toe-capped leggings, which I left in the bath room. A nearly new pair, like those I used to wear.

I also want a pair of army boots, 5.6 which I remember flinging at you as I left.

I also want (from the canteen) a housewife: long pattern, stamped 338171. Can you arrange this?'

Does Willis wear sixes in boots? I want someone with feet that size to break in a pair of boots for me, till the soles are nearly done: and then to have them soled with rubber by Tangay. This is a reasonable trouble for you: but time does not press me: so wait till the staff is working in full strength again and then think of it.

The cadets are back now, and term has started. This has increased our work to a respectable point. Our six machines have been out all the morning. I have been, in a sense, lucky. The flight's clerk (an aircraft hand, unskilled, like me) has just been posted. So I am book-keeper, and runner for our little group: a 'Willis', so to speak.

We are 'B' flight. A sergt: a corporal, and fifteen men. Of them five are fitters, five are riggers, five are A.C.H's. We have a hangar of our own: and six machines. To these are four officers, who teach the actual flying to the fifteen cadets who are 'on' Bristols and D.H.9 A's this term.

There are no bugles in camp, and no reveille. I get up at 6.40, go over to a near hut for a hot bath and shave (hot water out of action in our lines, till November): breakfast 7.30 to 8. You walk in at your own time. 8.10 a parade, colour-hoisting. All of us together on the square while the cadets (with rifles) present arms. This takes 20 minutes. 8.30 down to the hangar: till 12.30, when we return to the hut. Dinner 12.45. Work again at 2. P.M. till 4.15 or 4.30. Canteen practically no food. No shops within 1½ miles. So we all go to meals, which are much like Bovington, but more systematic, and so quiet. I find them good enough.

On Sat. and Sunday lights out 11 P.M. Alternate week-end passes. A.D. Sat. -M.N. Sunday. No duty-hour passes. Church Parade every Sunday in camp. I went yesterday. Belt and bayonet. Skin inspection weekly, in the hut at 1.15 p.m. Breeches and puttees only for police-duty (once in three months, 24-hour) and church, or Jankers. Great plenty of these last. The Squadron Leader is hot on punishment.

Equipment inspected once a month in the hut, and once a month on parade (full pack). ½ hours drill every Saturday. Monthly kit inspection.

I miss very much

(a) The quietude of the office for working in
(b) Music
(c) Colour. Lincolnshire is only green.

and I wish there was someone like yourself in camp. The fellows in my hut are all right: but none of them tuned exactly to my pitch.

Yet, it's the R.A.F. and the fact fills me with a perverse, brittle, and nevertheless complete satisfaction. Odd that a man should be so ungrateful, for the R.T.C. was very good to me, and I've jilted her without a regret.

TES

I'm due for a week-end this week. If it is very fine I shall try and reach Bovington. Sleep in Coy stores or some hut: but don't put yourself about, expecting me, for I'm a doubtful starter.

Many thanks for letters and parcels. I hope they are not troubling you. Remember always there is no urgency therewith.

TES

E. Candler

[22 September 1925]

[Lawrence wrote to E. Candler about the last pages of *Seven Pillars*:]

I cut it off at the end like a knife: since that was how I cut myself off the Arabian adventure.'

Charlotte Shaw

[On 28 September Charlotte Shaw wrote Lawrence a short letter which crossed with the one below.]

Cranwell

28.IX.25

Lawrence described how he rode down to London and spent a night in a solitary bed. The next day he called in on Feisal who was lively and happy to see him. They had lunch at the house of Lord Winterton, who Lawrence had served with in the war. Lawrence regarded himself as a stranger who he once knew and he wanted to degrade himself. But he was too shy to go looking for dirt and that is why he could not go off stewing into the Lincoln or Navenby brothels. Lawrence felt fearful because he had crashed his life and self and gone hopelessly wrong.

[This letter reached Charlotte Shaw on 1 October. She answered it the following day, and wrote again on 12 October. Three days later she sent two books: *Dostoevsky* by Andre Gide (1925) and *Christina Alberta's Father* (1925) by H.G. Wells, as well as two issues of *L'Illustration* and a *Times Literary Supplement*.]

October 1925

Charlotte Shaw

[Cranwell]

17.X.25

Lawrence advised Charlotte to not spend much time on the proofs of Books VIII and IX as they were only incidentals. Book X was important. He did not keep in touch with H.G. Wells.

[On 20 October Charlotte returned the proofs of Book VIII. On the 27th she sent a card enclosing an issue of *L'Illustration*, two issues of the *Times Literary Supplement*, various pamphlets and cuttings, and a book: *Suspense, a Napoleonic Novel* (1925) by Joseph Conrad.]

[T.E.L. had been at Cranwell less than two months when he took delivery of his latest Brough motorcycle (George V) on 17 October 1925. This was the Brough which Lawrence described in his gripping account of a race against a Bristol Fighter].

Robert Graves

[Robert Graves, *T.E. Lawrence to his Biographer*: 'In October 1925 Arnold Bennett, whom the Foreign Office (apparently at Lawrence's instigation) had asked to approach me, wrote to know whether I would care to apply for the position of Professor of English Literature at the newly founded Egyptian University at Cairo. I asked Lawrence for his advice. He answered:]

21.X.25

Dear R.G.

Your letter about Cairo has broken the slow digestion of your new book: whose work is far and away your poetic best. Yet it gives me a feeling that you have nearly seen through this form of self-expression.

More on this subject later. I had meant to write you about a month hence.

The Cairo job...Yes, I'm partly responsible for that. Chance and the War made George Lloyd a friend of mine. I hope, if you go, that you will like him. Like the man in the Psalms 'He enlargeth his mouth over his enemies': and there is a snarl in it. Yet underneath he is diffident, kindly, considerate, generous, cultivated, careful. He reads: not always well and wisely, (few of us do) but is grateful for news of a good book. A very English Welshman.

I know nothing about the job. Egypt, being so very near Europe, is not a savage country. The Egyptians are very bestial, very savage: but you need not dwell among them. Indeed it will be a miracle if an Englishman can get to know them. The bureaucrat society is exclusive, and lives smilingly unaware of the people. Partly because so many foreigners come there for pleasure, in the winter; and the other women, who live there, must be butterflies too, if they would consort with the visitors.

I thought the salary attractive. It has just been raised. The work may be interesting, or may be terrible, according to whether you get ken on it, like Hearn, or hate it like Nichols. Even if you hate it, there will be no harm done. The climate is good, the country beautiful, the things admirable, the beings curious: and you are stable enough not to be caught broadside by a mere dislike for your job. Execute it decently, so long as you draw the pay, and enjoy your free hours (plentiful in Egypt, God's laziest country) more fully. Roam about. Yet possibly you will not dislike the job. I think the coin spins evenly. And you can get away by choosing a successor, and persuading Lloyd that he is better than yourself.

So altogether I hope that you will take it. The harm to you is little, for the family will benefit by a stay in the warm (Cairo isn't warm in winter) and the job won't drive you into frantic excesses of rage.

And the money will be useful. You should save a good bit of your pay after the expense of the first six months. And George Lloyd, if you like him, will be a good help to the family.

And so my blessing.

God help you about the assistant. I never heard of such a one. 'Knows Arabic and English' forsooth. God help you again. I couldn't recommend even myself on those grounds. Even myself. Even:..

Oh Lord.

T.E.S.

[Graves: 'George Llloyd is of course, Lord Lloyd, who had been with Lawrence in Egypt and in Arabia. Lafcadio Hearn and Robert Nichols held university appointments in Japan.

I applied for and was given the job. I then wrote to Lawrence asking whether he thought I should try to get the assistant professorship (which was vacant) for a poet of my acquaintance who had a rather poor teaching job elsewhere at the time and was interested in Egyptology. And, if so, could he mention the matter in the right quarter. He wired back from Cranwell:]

Can do but not knowing -------- weakens my case and doubt if assistant job good enough for him so suggest your asking authorities keep appointment open till you arrive Cairo and investigate conditions personally Shaw.'

[Graves: 'I don't remember what I wrote back, but the next letter says':]

[Undated]

You didn't quite 'get' my hesitation: not that ---------- isn't an excellent poet, and most worthy person: but clearly he is sensitive (that poem about the old homestead) and the consequences of taking an assistant-ship might worry him. Englishmen in these small colonies abroad are snobbish to a degree: the smallness of their colony makes them smaller. I don't know what it's like in Cairo now: but in the Sudan people with pay below £500 join a junior club, and above £500 a senior club – and God hath put them asunder. Anyway they can't meet ever, except at official places: and probably even then the lawn is roped into Senior and Junior pens.

 Let it comfort you that I spent three magnificent years in Cairo, and only went twice into a club – and then as some fellow's guest. Try the clubs: and if they are mess-like places – then do without 'em.

The important thing is GROPPI's, the Tea-garden shop: and the drink is iced coffee. Straws the process. 2 piastres the means. The children will love Groppi's. Chocolates all right, too: but not in summer.

You will, I think, really enjoy Egypt. Nancy too, I hope: but she is more difficult. You want a sense of the past to enjoy fully: and she is rather bleak upon ancestors.

The mouth organ amused me [which Graves had sent him as a Christmas joke]: and went further and mightily amused the RAF. God knows where it is now.

The very best wishes for that show out East. I think you have been very wise. The Morris-Oxford also is suitable, until the children swell: and then a char-a-banc (obtainable locally) will succeed it.

If I can I'll come down next week. But can't promise. They have made me char-man in the accounts section over the holiday, and the job holds me tightly here.

I would like to have your second impression of Cairo, after you have got over the first idea of squalor.

November 1925

[Lisa Porter, *Sleaford Target*, 26 May 2010: A lost letter from Lawrence of Arabia describing his experiences at RAF Cranwell is to be sold at auction. The letter from TE Lawrence to Francis Rennell was found inside a rare copy of his book *The Seven Pillars of Wisdom*. One of 170 written by the author in 1926, the letter dated 3 November 1925, talks of his recent move to cadet college at RAF Cranwell. He describes the county as "a picture of dead earth in green and grey", although he was upbeat about his time there. He wrote: "The camp is good. Also the fellows, also the life. Mark me down for a further spell of quite happy existence". The author also attempts to persuade his friend not to buy *The Seven Pillars of Wisdom* book, telling him it was too expensive. The letter reads, "You don't really want one, you know. Thirty guineas is an absurd price. Wash out the idea".

The letter and the book are valued at £28,000 [they sold for £33,000] and will be auctioned at Lyon & Turnbull in Edinburgh. The auctioneer's book specialist Simon Vickers said, "The book, a signed copy of Lawrence's *Seven Pillars of Wisdom*, was brought in by the vendor, which is exciting enough as they are very rare, but it was when I was leafing through the book I noticed the letter. It is a wonderful everyday letter from Lawrence discussing his move to RAF cadet college Cranwell, as well as trying to dissuade Lord Rennell from buying the very copy of *Seven Pillars* we are selling".]

Francis Rodd

Cranwell, Lincs

3.11.25

Yes, I'm here now. A queer change from the richness and beauty and colour of Dorset. Lincolnshire is like a picture of a dead earth in green and grey. You feel the curve of the great ball in the wideness of all the local views.

The camp is good. Also the fellows: also the life. Mark me down for a further spell of quite happy existence. That also is an odd change, for I had made up my mind, in Bovington, to come to a natural end about Xmas, when the reprint of my book would have been finished. Here I am too content to work so hard, so it will not be ready much before March.

You don't really want one, you know. Thirty guineas is an absurd price. Wash out the idea. In return I'll put Haslam down for one. Rich men are fair game. He will have to send a cheque for £15.15.0. marked *7 Pillars* Account: payable to T.E. Lawrence: to Manager, Bank of Liverpool and Martins, 68, Lombard Street, E.C.3.

I've got too many subscribers, so am very sticky over these last copies.

I'd like to turn up at your place, but I come to London so rarely. Lincolnshire is very far away.

Yours

T.E.S.

Edward Garnett

[Cranwell, 3 November 1925]

I'm in the RAF. Absurdly happy. Such content feels *brittle*, in the light of my past histories. Perhaps it will last. The Seven Pillars are at Book VIII. The joy of living is hindering its road. People only work when profoundly miserable. Profoundly but not hopelessly. In March perhaps it will be ready for issue. The poor subscribers...Have read again: *War and Peace, The House of the Dead, The Brothers Karamazov.*

Charlotte Shaw

[Charlotte Shaw wrote to Lawrence on 3 November, telling him about a lunch with H.G. Wells on 30 October.]

Cranwell

5.XI.25

Lawrence had tried to persuade Sir Herbert Samuel (British High Commissioner in Palestine, who Lawrence had worked with in 1921) to not buy a copy of his book. Lawrence speculated on how H.G. Wells and G.B. Shaw regarded 'the beastly book.' An RAF sauce completely hid a pudding from the men' palates but their bellies later found out. The hut groaned or shouted in the early hours but his stomach held firm.

Francis Rodd

Cranwell

6.XI.25

Lawrence thanked Rodd (who he met while serving in Egypt and Palestine) for the offer of a flat in London but he would not be able to use it much because weekends at Cranwell were only alternate Saturday nights. Concerning his book, Lawrence told Rodd that the reprint differed in many ways from the 'Oxford' text and, to avoid confusion in the future, he intended to make the six copies of the Oxford edition disappear. Lawrence was going to give the plain text version to people who he served with in Arabia and who could not spend thirty guineas on the subscriber's edition.

Florence Hardy

9.XI.25

Lawrence described how he was in Lincolnshire which was very cold, very bare and the land all brown or green fields with low dry walls dividing them. There were no hedges, trees or hills. It felt almost like a fen country but Cranwell was high up. The churches all had spires and were very beautiful and large. He described a visit to Bovington in Dorset and enquired about a stage version of *Tess*.

[On 10 November Charlotte sent Lawrence some papers and a card.]

Charlotte Shaw

[Cranwell]

17.XI.25

Lawrence thought that the epilogue was not finished and may be changed. Something was needed at the end of the book to leave people with a bad taste in their mouths. The book was nearly finished. He had to revise Book IX and X and page proof VI, VII, VIII, IX and X, followed by index, map and binding. He offered to show Charlotte the Cape abridgement ('a silly little job').

[Charlotte persuaded GBS to work on the *Seven Pillars* epilogue on Sunday 22 November.]

Francis Rodd

Cranwell

21.XI.25

 Lawrence described how life had been a rush at Cranwell for the last week and would be a rush until 15 December when the Cadets term ended. Lawrence thanked Rodd for the keys to his flat in London and wished Rodd good luck in the USA.

Edward Marsh

21.XI.25

Lawrence described how Prime Minister Stanley Baldwin put him suddenly back into the RAF when he had completely lost hope. Lawrence was now a ludicrously contented airman.

Lionel Curtis

R.A.F. Cadet College Cranwell

24.XI.25

Lawrence described how he was an Aircraftman, 2nd class. He was foolishly happy and proposed to stay at Cranwell until he was 90 years old. He said that A.C.II's were, as a class, almost immeasurably humble. They had to beg leave each morning of their flight sergeants just to live. He was the most junior A.C.II in Cranwell.

[On 28 November Charlotte Shaw sent Lawrence three books.]

E.M. Forster

Sunday 29.XI.25

 Lawrence described how he had been to church on the last four Sundays. He was looking forward to his planned visit to Cambridge to meet Forster and some of his literary friends. He estimated that if the road was dirty it would take him two hours to get back to Cranwell and 9.30pm was the camp limit. If the road was still snow-bound and ice-coated he would come by train which on Sundays could be a slow journey. Lawrence noted how the snow and frost in Lincolnshire had been unbroken for days and he was dying of it. The weather seemed to close up every pore of activity. He had a gramophone to play classical music but the rest of the hut played dance music, some of which was good fun.

December 1925

[On 1 December Charlotte Shaw sent Lawrence some newspapers and a book._She wrote again on 7 December and the next day sent a book. This may have been accompanied by a letter describing her meeting that day with Ernst Toller.]

Charlotte Shaw

[Cranwell]

[9 December 1925]

Lawrence described how his nature had been (like Nature) frozen for a fortnight. The cold had been dreadful. He liked Toller's poems. He wanted to see Charlotte and GBS about Book X. He would run down to see them one afternoon on Boanerges.

E. Palmer

[Lawrence regularly used his latest Brough motor cycle (George V) for weekend visits to London from Cranwell but in December 1925, the day after he paid a visit to EM. Forster in Cambridge, TEL skidded on a patch of ice at 55 mph and fell off the Brough. The repairs to his arm, knee and leg took longer than the repairs to Boa. Lawrence often referred to his Broughs by the name 'Boanerges', meaning 'Sons of Thunder'].

10.XII.25

News for you. Clouds Hill is to be evacuated in the early spring. April or May perhaps. You will be warned in ample time, and Robinson may help you in the taking-over board. There will still be a gramophone and some records there.

Our hut now has a little musical box: and E.M.F. advised me to the ownership of a new German firm's records (complete) of the Kreutzer and Spring Sonatas. They are magnificent. You will laugh with satisfaction to hear that nobody in B. Flight likes them... barring of course the last-joined A.C.II. However, his taste is the only one which concerns me. When I hear that you are my tenant they will be sent you for preserving.

I went down to Cambridge last Sunday, and there E.M.F. sat, large as life, but sad-looking, wasted almost, in another man's rooms in King's, the splendiferous college with the extra-splendiferous (and rather horrible) chapel. We talked about you and Middleton, and the world generally. M. writes more letters to him than you do. Then M. always was talkative.

I didn't dare ask about the Scarlatti piano scrap. Have you given it him? I don't want it sent by post, for it might break, and the Brunswick people will not be able to make any more, having lost the matrix. Do let him have it before Xmas, with our best regards. How is your new C.O.? Has B.B. gone, and is the R.Q. troubled? Any news of Jeffrey? He sent me a letter, which was as cold and correct as a fishes' kisses. (? a fish's kiss, a fish-kiss: fishes-kisses?...) Your Xmas plans? I had a great idea of some time in London, and was given the keys of a flat in Brook Street, off Berkeley Square. 'Very posh.' Unfortunately no leave was offered me. So I'm at Cranwell instead, general fatigues... Crashed off the Brough last Monday: knee: ankle; elbow: being repaired. Tunic and breeches being replaced. Front mudguard, name-plate, handlebars, footrest, renewed. Skid on ice at 55 m.p.h. Dark: wet: most miserable. Hobble like a cripple now.

S.

Your posting? a false alarm? presumably.

I've asked A.W.L. to plant trees round the hill-top... calling on you for Edkin's help if necessary, unless his own market gardener at Bournemouth plays up.

My respectful salutations to L/C Willis.

William Roberts

[10 December 1925]

[As the typesetting of *Seven Pillars* progressed there were more opportunities to use tailpieces, many of which were drawn by William Roberts. Lawrence sent him a batch of proofs:]

I don't suggest your reading all this, but the pages [indicated] would do with tail-pieces and if your imagination prompts you to anything fitting – why fire away! Designs needn't be *illustrations*. Abstract designs will do. Ditto remote things, like vegetables or trees, hills, sunsets, clouds: dead fishes, apples on a plate. *Not* Pierrots a la Beardsley. *Not* Ballet dancers a la Laura Knight. *Not* cafe scenes a la Sickert.

Lionel Curtis

Cranwell

14.XII.25

I am aweary, aweary,

I would that I were dead.

This completes the quotation referred to. It freezes: it snows: it blows. I'm cold as cold. The running rivers of my brain are all a-frozen. Don't expect coherence till a thaw sets in.

The sweater: the Canadian sweater? I'm almost sure it's there. I can feel it, by hooking a finger between the third and fourth buttons (next above the belt) of my tunic. But this is sense-evidence only. To make sure, I should have to unbutton my tunic, and look: and the wind is howling so terribly about this hangar that I don't dare.

You said something, when you sent the royal thing, about motorcycling, and Canada: but it must have been made for work in the Flights at Cranwell. They offer me huge prices here, for it: packets and packets of woodbines: spare pairs of boots, a 'civie suit'.... I refuse them all, frozenly waving one frozen hand, in icy refusal. Of course I should have written and told you: but... but... but...

It's cold.

Your envelope is perfectly addressed.

T.E.S.

[On 15 December Charlotte Shaw, who had been shopping at Maggs Bros., the London antiquarian booksellers, sent Lawrence a box of books as a Christmas present. The following day Charlotte ordered a hamper from Gunters, to be sent to Lawrence as an anonymous gift. Shortly afterwards the Shaws left for Cornwall, where they were to remain until mid January while GBS worked on *The Intelligent Woman's Guide to Socialism and Capitalism* (1928). Charlotte wrote to Lawrence on 22 December.]

Charlotte Shaw

[Cranwell]

26.xii.25

Lawrence described how he did not have any ink in the hut which was empty except for himself. He was working on book proofs and Book VI had been sent off. This was the 'bad' book with the Deraa chapter and working on it always made him sick. At Christmas the camp at Cranwell had come down to 40 men who lived in the wet bar mostly. The hangars were locked up. Lawrence had been transferred as runner (i.e. orderly and charman) to the Accounting Section which comprised a row of eight dirty offices in a corridor. The old charman did not do them very well so Lawrence had been down there in the holidays, when the place was empty, to scrub and sweep and clean the windows. It passed the time and he could lock himself in. The other fellows were happy and friendly but the drunks wore his patience thin. It was only bad at night and he would call it a happy Christmas on the whole.

His book was too ambitious, he wrote it too huge and big, printed it too elaborately and illustrated it too richly. The final effect would be like a scrofulous peacock.

The world was dripping outside, a thaw at last. The roads had been icebound and his motorcycle Boanerges rusted in its stall. Lawrence had damaged Boanerges, and himself, three weeks previously when the first snow fell. Boanerges was mended and Lawrence's arm was cured, his knee nearly so. But he could not ride Boanerges until his leg could bend, and he liked to ride because it chased off the broody feeling. As a boy he ran away from home and joined the Royal Garrison Artillery at St Mawes Castle, which was close to where the Shaw's stayed at Falmouth.

His Mother

28.xii.25

It's almost the end of the year: so I'm writing again, though there is nothing to say. A letter of yours (October) came lately. I've given up trying to send locks. Clearly someone on the road likes such things. I'm tired of supplying his needs. Let him buy them.

Arnie is leaving Clouds Hill almost at once. Just now he has Florence there with him. It's a bad place to ask a visitor: and a bad time of year. The winter this year is sharp.

No thanks: no money. I am quite right that way just now. How I'll stand a year or so hence, when all the bills of the reprint of my book come in, I don't know. The subscribers (about 100) have paid £15 each, to date. That is £1,500 more due from them. The expenses to date are £4,500. The Bank has loaned the rest, against security from me. To meet the deficit I have sold Cape (for £3,000 cash + a royalty) the right to publish 1/3 of the book after Jan. 1. 1927. And there will be American serial and other receipts, too. Probably I'll come out of it well enough off. Arnie is to have a copy of the subscribers' edition. Would you like one? I propose to buy the liability of Clouds Hill off him. So that will be £400 more for his pocket. Clouds Hill is very beautiful and suits me. Though I will not live there till I have been as long in the Air Force as pleases me. You know I always wanted to be in the R.A.F.

I've sent you a *Blackwood* article, in which Candler, an Indian journalist, has written some butter & sugar stuff about me. Don't worry about that - or me - or anything. People are solitary things (myself especially so) and as long as it isn't true, I don't care what praise or blame I get.

You talk of 'sharing my life' in letters: but that I won't allow. It is only my own business. Nor can anybody turn on or off the tap of 'love' so called. I haven't any in me, for anything. Once I used to like things (not people) and ideas. Now I don't care for anything at all.

My present name & address are A/C II Shaw, 338171, Hut 105, RAF Cadet College, Cranwell, Lincs but I may change to Ross in a month or two, so you had better continue to write to Clouds Hill, under any name. The Tank Corps Fellows will forward letters. Everybody up here knows who I used to be. I told them when I arrived. So all the wonder is over. Three years and a half now, my service. So I fit in well enough.

Yes I still have Boanerges: and ride it whenever the weather is good enough. Much snow lately. Arnie has a tiny car: not a good one.

N.

Sydney Cockerell

29.xii.25

There, Christmas is safely over, without my running down to Cambridge. The road is a tempting one, which explains my thinking of it; but the snow and ice made riding impossible. I hate going to people's houses on Christmas day, because it's a family festival, if a festival at all, and merely a false sentiment for single people. In camp they make it an excuse for eating a lot, and drinking too much, the usual police regulations being lifted, so that drunkenness goes unpunished. Yet at Cranwell this year I have been very fortunate. The rest of 'B' Flight went on leave, so that I have the hut to myself. Sixteen beds at choice. Sometimes I feel like the last survivor of a sinking doss-house. Still it is very pleasant to have a solitary bedroom, and quiet, and lack of talk. I even lent away the gramophone, so that there should be no disturbance, and passed my spare time reading T. S. Eliot's collected poems (he is the most important poet alive) and correcting the proofs of an old-fashioned book you can guess the name of. It's odd, you know, to be reading these poems, so full of the future, so far ahead of our time; and then to turn back to my book, whose prose stinks of coffins and ancestors and armorial hatchments. Yet people have the nerve to tell me it's a good book! It would have been, if written a hundred years ago: but to bring it out after *Ulysses* is an insult to modern letters - an insult I never meant of course, but ignorance is no defence in the army!

It was very good of you to ask me down: and I would have looked in at tea-time if the road-conditions had been possible. I have no fear of mud or rain: but ice-ruts, with a blizzard continuing on top - No, that's not motor-biking weather. Lincolnshire is a very wintry country: the weather is still awful.

Sometime next year I'll try to turn up again for a moment.

Yours

T.E.S.

I didn't tell you about Lucas, did I? E. M. Forster had him in a room at Kings for me to look at. The man is magnificent, a mental athlete. If he is ever sent down or divorced he will write glorious books. Well worth your knowing.

S.

Alec Dixon

29.XII.25

The weather barometer points to 'stormy'. My private indicator is set at 'calm'. Cranwell is the coldest place on earth, and the windiest: but all the wind is actual. In the metaphorical sense it is one great rest. As soon as I reached here I told everybody whom I used to be. It gave me an uncomfortable month. The back of every chair in the canteen used to sprout a face whenever I entered: and the airmen generally held their breaths waiting for a sign. A month that was. After it their strained lungs expired and inspired air in gulps, and then settled down to normal rate. When a new man comes to the station he is brought to see me: otherwise everything is the same as ever it was. God be praised. The R.A.F. is very good. My discharge date is August 1932. When I wake up suddenly at night it feels close, and frightens me: but six years is yet a long time. God be praised as I said before.

Savage has told me of you and Picton. Well, I go on hoping. My own ignorance of authorship is so profound, so immense, so absolute, that I dare not give a verdict in either of your cases. Authors make themselves by going on writing. Did you ever read *Martin Eden*, by Jack London? No, it's not like the rest of his work.

The Mesopotamian rebellion of 1920? Didn't Miss Gertrude Bell put together the only account of it in her annual report? It used to be a sort of blue-book thing, published at Bagdad. Try a big Public Library: or the British Museum. There was also a woman (Buchanan?) who wrote a blank book about herself in Arab hands. They were gentle with her but killed her husband.

Leachman was a thin jumpy nervous long fellow, with a plucked face and neck. He was full of courage, and hard as French nails. He had an abiding contempt for everything native (an attitude picked up in India). Now this contempt may be a conviction, an opinion, a point of view. It is inevitable perhaps, and therefore neither to be praised nor blamed. Leachman allowed it to be a rule of conduct. This made him inconsiderate, harsh, overbearing towards his servants and subjects: and there was, I stake my oath, no justification for the airs he took. Leachman was an ordinary mind, but a character of no ordinary hardness. I do not say a great character, for I think it made its impression more by its tough skin and unyielding texture than by any great spread or degree. I should call him a man too little sensitive to be aware of other points of view than his own: too little fine to see degrees of greatness, degrees of rightness in others.

He was blunt and outspoken to a degree. Such is a good point in a preacher, a bad point in a diplomat. It makes a bullying judge, too. I think he was first and foremost a bully: but not a fleshy bully. He had no meat or bulk on him: a sinewy, wasted man, very yellow and dissatisfied in face. He was jealous of other people's being praised.

For his few days with us in Hejaz we were not prepared. 'Leachman', it was a great name and repute in Mesopotamia (a land of fourth-raters) and we thought to find a colleague in him. After less than a week we had to return him on board ship, not for anything he said, though he spoke sourly always, but because he used to chase his servant so unmercifully that our camp took scandal at it. The servant was a worm, a long worm, who never turned or showed a spark of spirit. Any decent servant would have shot him.

Leachman lasted a long time after that: but one day he spat in a sheikh's face at a time when the veil of terror under which we had worked in Mespot had worn thin. The chief upped and shot him in the back, as he was running out of the tent. Both insult and reprisal were almost unprecedented in the history of the desert. Then Leachman wasn't quite what you call a decent fellow, and the sheikh (whom I met a year later) was febrile. As L. died tragically we must hide his fault. Don't make him a hero in your book. He was too shrill, too hot-tempered, too little generous.

Yours

T.E.S.

News of me, when you want it, from Posh.

Raymond Savage

[30 December 1925]

[Lawrence wrote to his agent regarding *Seven Pillars*:]

The book. It crawls. The distractions are too many, and I hate the beastly thing.

January 1926

[During 1926 Lawrence made regular visits on Boanerges to the Shaw's country home at Ayot St Lawrence in Hertfordshire (once late on a Wednesday afternoon after duty at Cranwell). Charlotte Shaw wrote to Lawrence on 1 January, enclosing some photographs.]

Charlotte Shaw

Cranwell

4 January 1926

Lawrence discussed the work of James Stephens, Irish poet and novelist. It was not possible to pretend in poetry but with prose you could 'swindle half the people half the time.' Stephens needed cold water, exposure to wind and rain and low company. Lawrence also discussed the work of Jonathan Swift, GBS and James Joyce. Lawrence wanted to spend an afternoon or evening with the Shaws to talk over his last two chapters. Charlotte's New Year letter, which he read three times, gave him great pleasure.

[Charlotte received this letter on 6 January and replied the following day.]

R.V. Buxton

[4 January 1926]

[Lawrence wrote to R.V. Buxton regarding the subscribers edition of *Seven Pillars*, explaining that he didn't:]

want to make the number exactly a hundred, for one of my many dislikes is the bibliophile, and that sort of man makes a fetish of numbers. To defeat him I am not numbering my copies, nor disclosing to anyone quite how many have been printed, nor making any two just alike.

D.G. Hogarth

14.1.26

Some illegible name has written me for a gratis copy of my book, the owner of it having been with me in Arabia. United Services Club. Mentions you. Is it Dowsett, of the Armoured Cars?

Encyc. Brit. Yes by all means. Let me try my hand... (*The red ink is not for publication*).

'L's family, though (*Leicestershire*) not Irish in origin, had been settled for some while (*Queen Elizabeth*) near Dublin (60 miles N.W.) His only recent ancestor (*since Sir W. Raleigh*) with oriental interests appears to have been that (*rogue*) Vansittart who worked in India beside Clive and Warren Hastings, but not always in harmony with them.'

Does that ring with the right loftiness of the *D.N.B.*?

At it again....

'L. the second of five brothers, was educated privately (*yes*), at the City of Oxford School (*very little, very reluctantly, very badly*), and at Jesus College, Oxford (*not at all*). After passing the first examinations for the Honour School of Modern History he was elected to a Demyship of Magdalen College Oxford, which he held (*in absence*) till 1919. In 1919 he was elected to a research fellowship at All Souls College.' (*which he held for three years*)

'L. was interested in the history of the Crusades, and explored Syria from 1910 onwards studying their records on the ground. At this time he picked up some colloquial Arabic, which supported his request to be attached (*D.G.H. did this for him*) to the British Museum Expedition about to excavate Carchemish, on the upper Euphrates. He worked for the British Museum for some years, and for the P.E.F. for some weeks in 1914. On the outbreak of war he was appointed (*by D.G.H.*) to the Geographical Section of the General Staff, in the W.O.'

After the War.

'L was attached (*with regret*) to the British Delegation during the Peace Conference. Afterwards he resided for a (*constipated*) year in All Souls. In 1921 he was made Adviser to the Colonial Secretary (Mr. Winston Churchill) upon Arab affairs, and as such (*silently*) attended the Cairo Conference, and passed some (*uncomfortable*) later months in Palestine. In 1922 he resigned this appointment to enlist in the R.A.F. in which (*after some interim misfortunes*) he was still serving in 1926.'

I'm sorry. It's the *Encyc.* not the *D.N.B.* and they probably want only four lines. Don't over-stress the war period. As it fades into distance, the war becomes a small affair.

T.E.S.

J.B. Acres

15.1.26

Dear Acres,

Your letter upon Dostoevsky was most excellent. I've always believed him the greatest of the Russians: though he never achieved an epic like *War and Peace*. He never aimed at the epic manner. When I'm forced to describe *The [Brothers] Karamazov* in a word I say 'A fifth gospel'. It is that intense preoccupation with supra-moral goodness, Christ-like-ness, which marks him so strongly. An epileptic and ex-convict, he drew always from his own experience and feelings. That's why his books are full of neuroses: and his characters so often criminal. There is a sameness too: for D. lived over-much within himself. Not many people are happy enough to strike the balance between inside and outside, and achieve a harmony.

André Gide's book on Dostoevsky was not good. He tried to make him into a Protestant (Gide is a French Protestant) and didn't get to grips with his real powers and depths. Few Frenchmen could. They are too dapper to feel as untidily and recklessly as the Russians. Here ended Friday's letter. A wire intervenes. A week-end.

I must send you more of D. but take a rest between whiles. Have you read *Lost Souls*? (Gogol). I think you spoke of it to me once. This was written on Monday. I give up trying to write.

There are two or three books here waiting for fine weather, brown paper, and string, before venturing to Oxford. Nothing earth-shaking or portentous, like *The Karamazovs*: but man cannot live entirely on either dynamite or beef.

Not this week-end at Oxford. I'm for Welwyn, on business, if the roads clear. Zero here on Sat. Night. My mind is frozen. Good luck.

T.E.S.

Charlotte Shaw

[Cranwell]

15.I.26

Lawrence described how it had snowed for two days, six inches deep, windless and warm. He advised her to stay in Falmouth until the Spring as England was no joke in winter. He had read a number of books and *The Informer* and *Krakatit* had been a great success in B. Flight who wanted more of the same. His RAF character had been assessed (for 1925) as 'exceptional', the highest grade. This showed how he could behave for four months.

[Charlotte had written to Lawrence on the same day.]

Charlotte Shaw

[Cranwell]

19.I.26

Lawrence described how Cranwell had surpassed itself. On Friday it held the English record for cold (31 degrees of frost) and on Saturday it achieved two degrees below zero. The men were proud of the place as they cowered under blankets round the stove. All the pipes froze so they could not wash which made them warmer. He was glad it was over and the thaw had begun. There was a foot of snow all round so it would take some time to run away. Charlotte was unwise to leave Cornwall so soon, Ayot would be perishing. Boanerges could not be ridden because the snow bound roads would cause a crash and bend the machine. It was too cold to work at Seven Pillars as his brain stood still in frosty weather.

[Charlotte wrote on 20 January after returning from Cornwall. On 23 January Lawrence arrived at Ayot in the evening and talked to Charlotte while GBS read. The following day they lunched with Cherry-Garrard, who returned with them for tea. Afterwards, Lawrence and Charlotte talked again. Lawrence left at about 11am on Monday morning 25 January to attend Charles Doughty's funeral at Golders Green Crematorium. Charlotte wrote on 27 January. The following day, Lawrence visited the Shaws in London.]

Florence Hardy

[Bertie Stephens became gardener at Max Gate in 1926, and recorded his memories of Lawrence's visits. 'Lawrence: Short and thick set. He would arrive like a thunderbolt on his large motorcycle and, after his visit to Mr Hardy, would leave as quickly as he came. He would arrive on his powerful motorcycle at great speed and brake hard in the drive. I remember once saying to him when I was working near the front door, "Good morning, Sir". Lawrence replied: "I'm just plain mister to you, gardener." He appeared to be very likeable and quite ordinary man. He had no side or swank about him for a man as famous as he was']

[20 January 1926]

I'm glad Mr Hardy is overcoming the winter. Up here the temperatures below zero. It is better today (and was yesterday): but there is no doubt that cold like this takes the strength away. Also it seems to freeze my wits, so that I can't do anything decent.

Francis Rodd

28.1.26

Dear F.R.,

The 23rd, so Haslam said, was your day of return. I left my keys with him: and he was going to leave them with his housekeeper, if he went to Mexico. All this going is terrible.

I hope you are back, & over the first emptiness of return. I've got to thank you for four exceedingly good nights in London. Four, you will say, is too few to justify my holding those keys all the weeks: but consider the quality of those nights. The place so quiet, so absolutely mine, and the door locked downstairs, so that it was really mine. Why there isn't a lock in my power at Cranwell, not even on the shit-house door! The happiness & security of those nights were very keen.

I didn't read many books: but I worked the bath-machine over-time. The best of thanks possible.

Yours ever

T.E.S.

H.J. Cape

[28 January 1928]

[A letter written to H.J. Cape on 28 January 1926 shows that Lawrence had already given a good deal of time to the abridgement of *Seven Pillars*:]

I'm not pleased with the abridgement...as now in my hands; I've done the first 500 pages, and it reads queer. The details are too large for the body. How would you view my dictating a more colloquial contracted narrative to some shorthand scribe? I'd take the subscriber version, page by page, and miss out or boil down rapidly in my mind each sentence as it came to the eye. The result would be unceremonious, swift moving, rough perhaps.

February 1926

Charlotte Shaw

[Cranwell]

8.2.26

Lawrence described how Charles Doughty's funeral had made him miserable because of its impact on Mrs Doughty. The ride back to Cranwell was also miserable and it rained all the way. The previous day he had a worse ride, up from a village near Oxford. The land was flooded and rivers ran across the roads. Cranwell was not a good winter station but it was so peaceful that he hoped to stay there for a long time.

[Charlotte sent Lawrence a parcel of books on 9 February and a batch of proofs on the 10th. She wrote on the 15th and received a letter from Lawrence on the 17th that appear not to have survived. She replied the following day.]

Florence Hardy

[13 February 1926]

[As work on *Seven Pillars* drew to a close, Lawrence began to consider further literary projects. The scheme to edit Hardy's early autobiography was especially attractive. He told Mrs Hardy:]

I had been reading it deliberately, tasting it all over: and I swear that it's a very good thing. There is a strange *individual* taste about the story of those old days. . It's very beautiful. Rarely so...I was seeing, every page I read, little things which might be done to polish the jewel more excellently. I do hope you will send it me back. I'll tackle it most humbly and honestly.

C.E. Wilson

R.A.F. Cadet College Cranwell

19.2.26

Lawrence described how he had shortened the new edition of *Seven Pillars of Wonder* by letting out wind and making two words do for six. He apologised for the print of the Oxford text which was not meant to circulate. Proof correcting was not a suitable activity for the barrack.

H.J. Cape

[22 February 1926]

[Cape thought that Lawrence should start some new project. CM Doughty had died in January (Lawrence had taken a day's leave in order to attend the funeral in Golders Green). Shortly afterwards Cape suggested a biography to Lawrence, who replied:]

I've thought of that "life" idea, up and down: and I'm sorry that I can't touch it. I would not have delayed so in considering the life of anyone else: but for CMD I have a very real regard.

Charlotte Shaw

[Cranwell]

22.2.26

Lawrence hoped that Mrs Shaw was better after her illness. His fellows at Cranwell got chills on top of the flu and then became wholly sick. *Mrs Warren's Profession*, Bernard Shaw's third play, was welcomed by B. Flight. Three had already finished it and praised it. A fourth was dealing with it.

Lawrence described measles as a gift, although it left him very tired and heavy headed. Everybody in camp was getting it and Church parade was cancelled, which obliterated the one real grudge an airman had against the weekend in Cranwell. On Saturday Lawrence went on a hard ride to Barton on Humber: the road, from Lincoln, included a stretch of 17 miles which he covered in 17 minutes and felt better for. On Sunday morning he sat in the hut and played bits of gramophone records to himself. The others were sky larking, and playing rummy, a noisy card game.

On Sunday afternoon the weather was fine with grey heavy clouds and windy so he took Boanerges over to Nottingham, his birthplace, for a stroll. The roads were not fit for going fast, so he turned into by-roads and sidled through Newark and Southwell. Nottingham was one of those 'Sunday' places with a deserted market square and dust and fog blew unchecked along the empty streets. The crowds went to a Weslyan Mission in their Albert hall. Lawrence went to a Lyons shop and ordered tea. The other people were amusing. The only friendly person was a black cat who sat beside Lawrence and insisted on food. Lawrence bought an éclair and shared it with the cat who the licked his face clean. A man sitting opposite also had cream on his face and tried to lick it off but failed. The cat was excellent but the humans were gross, noisy and vulgar.

[Charlotte received this letter on 23 February and replied the following day.]

March 1926

[On 2 March Charlotte Shaw sent a parcel and on 4 March a theatre program for Mrs Warren's Profession, which had opened in London the previous evening. On 9 March she sent another parcel.]

Lionel Curtis

8.3.26

Lawrence described how he had finished correcting the text of the Seven Pillars of Wisdom. He suggested that Lowell Thomas' book, *With Lawrence in Arabia*, should be burned or used to strengthen the embankment on the river front at Halescroft. Lawrence was nearly over the measles and was very sorry to hear about Curtis' health and long period of convalescence.

S.L. Newcombe

10.3.26

My Lord Duke,

It is time for you to change your name once more. In 1920 Lawrence was current. In 1921 our names became Ross. In 1923 we changed to Shaw. What shall we become next year?

Hurry up and learn to read. I have written a book: a long book. One copy is to go to your father, since it says rude things about his face and character. One copy is to go to you: so that you shall know what your father is like. Your mother is not to have a copy. She knows more than that already. It is time for me to stop writing.

Your worm

Shaw

This letter is intended for S. L. Newcombe, Esq. though I don't believe he can yet read writing.

[Note. S.L. Newcombe, Lawrence's godson, was then aged six. The letter is written entirely in capitals apart from the postscript.]

F.L. Lucas

R.A.F. Cadet College, Cranwell, Lincs

14.3.26

Lawrence told Lucas that his opinion of *Seven Pillars of Wisdom* would be important as he was the best of critics. Lawrence described his book as a builders' yard of second hand materials and could not understand why Lucas thought that it was good. This puzzled Lawrence and shook his conviction that it was rotten and based on writing 'tricks'. Lawrence always had the ambition to write something good and when the Revolt gave him a subject he tried to make up for a lack of instinct by studying how others got their effects and using their experience. So he built an enormous mass of second hand ornaments into his skeleton and completely hid the skeleton under them.

Lawrence thought that it sounded very conceited that he should continue to believe the book rotten when Lucas had praised it. Siegfried Sassoon had also called it epical.

[Lawrence had been impressed by articles and poems written by F.L. Lucas who, like E.M. Forster was a fellow of King's College, Cambridge. Forster had arranged for them to meet and Lucas had then read Seven Pillars. He had sent his comments to Lawrence, who now forwarded them to Charlotte.]

Whittingham & Griggs

[15 March 1926]

[Lawrence finished correcting the last proofs of the *Seven Pillars* text, but the illustrations were still well behind. Whittingham & Griggs told him they could not complete their part of the work before July, and he replied that this was too late:]

Will you let me know which are the laggard plates? And I'll cancel them, if possible...I want all the illustrations completed by the first week in June.

Charlotte Shaw

Cranwell

15.3.26

Lawrence described himself as a squeezed sponge and this letter was merely to report his husk present and correct. He was sorry about GBS who had measles and a temperature of 100 degrees. Lawrence's measles kept him at 102 degrees for some while. They were completely gone and there were only 90 cases in camp. He would send Charlotte the abridgement, or part of it, which was great fun and very easy.

[Lawrence was now working on the abridgement of *Seven Pillars* that Jonathan Cape was to publish in March 1927 as *Revolt in the Desert*. He roughed-out the cuts in pencil on a set of proof sheets which is now at the Harry Ransom Humanities Research Centre, University of Texas. The result was then fair copied for Cape in black ink on a second set of proofs, now on deposit in the Bodleian Library.]

Charlotte Shaw

[Cranwell]

18.3.26

Lawrence explained that he had broken his right arm, hence the drunken script. A car backfired and hit his wrist. Lawrence was glad to hear that GBS was better. Lawrence would send Charlotte the first nine books of abridgement and he wanted them back before Easter as by contract they needed to reach Cape by 31 March. The abridgement was a story, fit for boy scouts and not so good as the whole book. Two of B Flight had enjoyed reading *The Worst Journey In the World: Antarctic, 1910-1913* by Apsley Cherry-Garrard.

[The following account of how Lawrence broke his right arm was written by Sergeant Pugh of the same Flight at Cranwell as Lawrence. Here printed from the original manuscript. It differs materially from the version printed by Graves in *Lawrence and the Arabs* (p.430):

'Out riding one summer evening, he came across a smash up between a car (driven by an oldish man) and a pedestrian. When the pedestrian had been safely disposed of, S[haw] was asked to swing the car for the old boy. Nervousness and excitement caused him to leave the ignition fully advanced and on S. swinging, the starting handle flew back and broke S's right arm. Without so much as a sign to show what had taken place, S. asked if he would mind retarding the offending lever, and swung the car with his left hand. After the car was at a safe distance S. got a man to 'kick over' his Brough, and with his right arm dangling and changing gear with his foot, S. got his bus home and parked without a word to a soul of the pain he was suffering. Through some unknown reason the M.O. was away for over an hour before his arm could be 'done'. That is a man – S., I mean.']

[Charlotte replied on 25 March, and wrote again on the 27th. When Lawrence finished making the Cape abridgement in late March he decided to keep the pencil working draft. With help from two friends, another proof of *Seven Pillars* was marked up with all the cuts and linking passages for the abridgement. This operation, which consisted mainly of blacking out the deleted passages with Indian ink, provided the basis for a deliberately misleading statement Lawrence later gave to Cape's house journal *Now and Then*: 'The abridgement...was made by him in seven hours at Cranwell in Lincolnshire on March 26 and March 27 1926, with the assistance of two airman friends, A/A Knowles and A/c Miller'. The text they produced was submitted to Cape on 30 March 1926.]

April 1926

Edward Garnett

Tuesday 6.4.26

Your letter has interested me much: though you vitiate your thinking by the assumption that books are meant to be read. They are to be written only.

The abridgement is better than the complete text. Half a calamity is better than a whole one. By excising heights and depths I have made a balanced thing: yet I share your difficulty of seeing the shorter version's real shape across the gaps.

Specific points.

(i) The ending. I was overpersuaded to stop on page 644. The natural place is after 'sun', on line 35 of page 635. It fulfils your demands for balance and reflection and sordidness among the triumphs. Pages 632 and 633 are the philosophic climax of the narrative.

If you will consider anew, and approve this new FINIS, will you then please so amend your text, and also cross out 'a' before 'pearl' in the last line of the revised version.

Your statement that the hospital passage would be a wipe in the eye for 19 readers out of 20 puts it out of court, as I put it. This abridgement is to be fit for girl guides.

(ii) To include the death of Farraj meant the restoration of many pages, to explain it. The 'private delectation' of 115 people is better than the public delectation of 10,000 My men are not to walk the common street.

Me to write again? God forbid. I do not bear another misshaped child. C'est fini. If only I'd had the courage to destroy this one in time.

Yours ever

T.E.S.

Left handwriting constrains to brevity.

[Note: This letter refers to Lawrence's draft abridgement of the subscribers' text of *Seven Pillars*, to be published in 1927 as *Revolt in the Desert*.]

Charlotte Shaw

[Cranwell]

6.4.26

Lawrence wrote this with his right hand which was much better but which hurt and so he could not spell properly. Last week end was a service holiday so he went off to Clouds Hill on Boanerges which took 10 hours. He came home by easy stages and with his self respect much improved. He was sorry to hear that GBS was not well again and thought that it could be 'an overdose of Socialism'.

His Mother

Cranwell

20.4.26

It is a long time since I wrote: for two months ago I broke my radius and the right arm has not been very fit for paper-work since. I was starting a car, and the starting handle flew back and hit my wrist on the second turn. The tip of the radius was cracked off, and the wrist dislocated. Now they have put it nearly straight again: but it still cramps me badly after a few minutes in one position holding anything small like a pen or knife. They say that in another month it will be quite fit; though I have lost the power of twisting my hand round very far. It goes about half way now.

Otherwise there is little to tell you, which I have not already said. I'm still very pleased with Cranwell, and am doing exactly what I was doing before. So that's well. My bicycle is rejuvenated, and runs splendidly. I had it overhauled while I was in splints, and it is very fast now: though I do not yet feel inclined to ride more than a hundred or so in the day. Your hot weather will be starting soon (and ours, I hope!): I'm sorry you do not like it. I used to find that the heat gave a delicious sense of weary peace to everything within my reach.

My private book is not finished yet. August probably. It has stood still lately, but I hope to start now. Cape is to publish a fraction of the story in March, 1927. His extra money has enabled me to put more pictures and luxury into the private edition.

Nothing else.

N.

A letter - illegible - from Menon!

I will reply when I can: but have over 80 letters to write before I'm up to date.

Charlotte Shaw

[On 20 April Charlotte sent Lawrence a letter which crossed with the following:]

[Cranwell]

20.IV.26

Lawrence's handwriting had improved as his right hand was restored apart from a little cramp. After writing for a while he had to walk out into the hangar for a change of air and rest. GBS was back to normal. The Wing Commander had read his abridgement. He lit a candle after 11.20pm when the electric was cut off, to carry on reading it. Whittingham & Griggs, the colour printers, would not finish his work until August causing more delay. Lawrence was catching up on his letters, and would then work on an index and the maps.

E.M. Forster

26.4.26

I broke my right arm and wrist trying to start someone's car. It has been a source of discomfort since, and is not perfectly cured. In fact it's twisted a bit. No matter: but it takes away my last hope of being admitted some day to a beauty chorus.

At last, after weeks, I have found Lucas' letter, somewhat crumpled, for I carried it about with me for a while. His sentence about 'a supernatural background' startled me. Perhaps he meant unworldly: or unearthly. Surely not supernatural? I do not believe in that. There is no more rational being than myself alive. It's excess of reason which makes me seem mad to people. Otherwise I've now digested the letter, and can read it coldly, unblushingly. Odd that my confidence in my critical sense should let me condemn as rotten what so many excellent artists praise. I may see Lucas on May 9: and will then try to pin him down to particularities.

Your letter after Lincoln stares me reproachfully in the face. What can I say or do? I have a shell on me like a crab's: so I can't show what I think. It's my opinion that you will yet write (or have written and not yet shown) something very big: bigger than the *Passage*, which deliberately was bigger than any of the previous novels. Greatness lies in the eye that contemplates not in the subject: and your eye has grown very slowly. All the more lasting, thereby. Of course it's a bore being famous. You have cracked the crib, and the swag isn't any longer up to your standard. Consequently you feel empty, for the while: as if the profession was exhausted. But it isn't. Just wait a bit. Ten more years if necessary. You aren't wasting your time: everybody likes seeing you. Your present emotions span themselves into articles for the *Labour Leader*. Very well. There are sparks and flames: affairs of degree. Yours are the most sporting and fiery sparks. They are so good that someone will someday collect a shower of them. You needn't do that. Let the *Passage* represent you for the moment.

Do you remember little Smith, the bearded bookseller of Lincoln? He asked who you were. I told him, feeling pretty pleased with myself. He ordered a dozen assorted E.M.F's. (5/- brand) on the strength of your visit. Sold them. Ordered 20. Is selling them. I told him *The Omnibus* was a book. He ordered two. A Yank came in: guessed he wanted something to read. Saw *The Omnibus*. Said 'That's the best set of short stories ever printed'... and took the two.

I don't endorse the Y's opinion. V.G. yes... but the best? No, I don't agree. However my critical judgement, though dogmatic and dictatorial, is (according to Lucas) bad. Hoots. I congratulate you, anyway.

This letter must stop. Pen-holding is a small scale business, and makes my wrist ache: and there are many letters to write.

Writing is a mean snivelling business. It fails to convey anything bigger than its own scrawling miserable pot-hooks.

Hoots

T.E.

[E.M. Forster (*T.E. Lawrence By His Friends*): 'Excluding Clouds Hill and Plymouth, we must have met about a dozen times. There was a weekend at Lincoln when he talked brilliantly about medieval sculpture in the lounge of the hotel, with the result that after he had left people said to me, 'That airman friend of your must have been Colonel Lawrence, wasn't he?', and I had to tell a lie.]

Charlotte Shaw

[On 27 April Charlotte wrote a letter which crossed with the following, received the next day:]

[Cranwell]

26.4.26

It was raining and so Lawrence could not go to Lincoln to bring back a post card of the Queen [Queen Margaret, second wife of Edward I]. She stood on the south wall of the cathedral in a niche above the chantry, a very beautiful and rare 13th century portrait. His arm had improved and he could ride nearly as of old. He would send Charlotte his 'foreword-flyleaf thing'. GBS was sick again and Lawrence distrusted sudden recoveries.

[On 29 April Lawrence visited Lincoln. He bought two postcards showing different views of the statue and sent them to Charlotte. Both are postmarked Cranwell, 10.45 am, 30 April 1926].

Charlotte Shaw

29.4.26

Lawrence said that the Queen was lovely and just the sort of woman you met at tea. Interested in church work and had a pet dog.

Lawrence described James Stephens (author of The Charwoman's Daughter) as curious and puzzling. Stephens had been poor but derived no benefit from it.

[On the morning of 30 April the Shaws were in Stratford, returning from Malvern. GBS was unwell. After lunch they drove to Hammels, a house on Boar's Hill outside Oxford, which was the home of Sir Frederic Keeble, an Oxford professor, and his wife the actress Lillah McCarthy. The following day Charlotte and Lillah went to the Ashmolean, hoping to see D.G. Hogarth, but he was away in Italy. They then went to the Bodleian Library where they saw Dr Crowley, who showed them the manuscript of *Seven Pillars of Wisdom*, one of the rare events that Charlotte underlined in her diary.]

May 1926

[Charlotte Shaw received Lawrence's postcards on 3 May and replied the next day. A general strike began in England on 3 May, and lasted until the 12th. On the 10th Charlotte sent a long letter, which crossed with the following, received on the 13th:]

Charlotte Shaw

[Cranwell]

10.5.26

Lawrence described how all leave was cancelled and they were waiting in camp until the government wanted to use them. In B Flight there was an Irish man who would not fight, not even in self defence. On Saturday he had rushed down to London for a meeting, stayed one hour, and rushed back. He had been tempted to stop off at the Shaw's but did not have a pass and so had to be back by 9.30 pm. He was so glad to be back in the RAF and did not want to spoil his character. He was also tired, dizzy sore eyed and half deaf with speed and movement. The road was busy, it rained and he had only half a right wrist. He also feared that the Shaw's would be very political and full of judgement about the General Strike. Service men could only endure a civil war if they clung deafly and blindly to their passive duty. It took him two hours and a quarter from Welwyn to Cranwell at 60 mph when the road was open.

[Charlotte replied on 18 May, inviting Lawrence to Ayot.]

Charlotte Shaw

[Cranwell]

20.5.26

Lawrence felt very sorry for a small troop which acted as his personal body guard during the Arab Revolt. They were worked too hard and too constantly hurt. Lawrence was a spasmodic inconsiderate chief, too busy with his own problems to be kind to them. So they didn't love him.

Florence Hardy

[20 May 1926]

[Distance restricted Lawrence in his visits to Max Gate. He wrote to Florence Hardy on the subject of the now long overdue publication of the *Seven Pillars*:]

Yes, by all means: take Mr Lemperly's [Paul Lemperly was an Ohio bookseller] copy, if it is worth its money to you: and sell it or give it away at your discretion. I'd suggest you selling it. I have a waiting list as long as my arm (or could have, if I kept all their letters) and lots of other outside people & libraries (all of which have been refused) want copies. The booksellers tells me it will go to £50 a month or two after publication, which I now expect will be in September.

H.H. Banbury

[25 May 1926]

[In late May he learned that he was to be posted to India that autumn. This seemed to be for the best, because it meant that he would be out of reach of the publicity surrounding Cape's issue of the abridgement. But the posting did not please him personally; he wrote to H.H. Banbury, a Tank Corps friend then serving at Quetta, on 25 May 1926:]

I will be low in India. Living on my pay, and trying to be an airman. The *Seven Pillars* will have been built by then, and my hybrid existence ended. In some way it will be a relief. So long as I am in England I cannot avoid sometimes bridging the classes. The writers and artists are intoxicating to meet and talk to. For a while with them I imagine myself to be an artist: they feel somehow (presumptuous it sounds) to be of my own sort. With these fellows in the service I'm very happy; but the play times are rather a strain. I don't play – not at anything: so that the more hours work they give us the better life goes.

J.G. Wilson

25.5.26

Dear Wilson,

The Windsor copy will be duly sent: but I'm an old-fashioned person, to whom it seems improper that Kings should buy and sell among their subjects. You told me that the advance cheque was Fortescue: and I mean to return it gently to him with the book when it is ready. F. is decent, and will not tell his owner: for I should prefer Him to think He is paying for it, since that is His notion of propriety.

Whittingham and Griggs, the printers of the colour plates, had promised August as their finishing date, before the strike. Now, I suppose, one cannot say. After them there is only the binding. Text is ready, index in hand, map begun. I begin to see light through the back cover, at last.

Yours

T.E.S.

Me for India in November: so it must end before that.

Charlotte Shaw

[Charlotte Shaw must have sent Lawrence an account of something that had happened during her stay in Hammels. This was written in the style of a play, as is a surviving letter that she sent to him on 19 December 1927.]

[Cranwell]

26.5.26

Lawrence was horrified that Charlotte had endangered the chance of a visit to HGW because Lawrence might turn up. Wells was one of the really excellent and important people and Lawrence was just an A/c in the RAF. B Flight cheered when Charlotte sent him a book by Storm Jameson. They liked the *Three Kingdoms*. Lawrence heard the groaning of engines, 18 machines which were 'uneasy guests' that flew off for manoeuvres at 9 am (he spent a sweating early day pushing them out, and filling them up) and return at 6 pm. It was drizzling and he was 'bound stiff' (RAF for constipated) with them.

Francis Yeats Brown

[26 May 1926]

June 1926

[On 1 June Charlotte sent Lawrence a parcel].

Charlotte Shaw

[Cranwell]

3.6.26

Lawrence described how he would fall in on parade in his 'best blue' at 9.30 am on 5 June to celebrate the King's birthday. The RAF flag would be broken at the masthead and he would 'remove headgear' and give three cheers. This would affect him in the wrong place because of natural perversity. After cheering HM he would have the rest of the day off and, if given a pass, would rush down the London Road on Boanerges. He would stop off at the Shaws, if they were at home, or continue to London and work with Roberts, Kennington and others on his book. He has been four years in the ranks for 360 days of each year. Charlotte only saw him on the odd days. For the rest of the time he was one of the fellows and felt with them and of them. His first day in uniform taught him that there was a gulf between him and ordinary people. He was treated differently. Only 'Colonel Lawrence' opened doors but he did not value them being opened that way. He often resented the doubleness of his shape. He was essentially uncertain and small, unlike the Shaws. Lawrence and his book were incurably amateur. The RAF recorded that as an AC he was first class. The book was only a by product. Two of B Flight had approved Storm Jameson. They read such odd stuff. Four had read Cherry-Garrard. The third was fighting his way through Wyndham Lewis. They praised *Bliss* and *Odtaa*. They called G.A. Birmingham 'a bind' and Lawrence's book 'a binder' and

Eliot's poems, and Doughty, and Peacock. All binds. O'Casey was tolerated without much ordeal.

[In addition to this letter, Lawrence sent a telegram on Friday 4 June to say that he would visit Ayot the following day. He arrived at about 3.30 pm on Saturday 5 June and left at 5.30 pm on Sunday 6 June, having joined the Shaws for lunch with Cherry-Garrard. Charlotte wrote to Lawrence on 7 June and the next day she sent him a parcel, which crossed with the following:]

Charlotte Shaw

[Cranwell]

8.6.26

Lawrence described rain at Buckden and the road surface became greasy so the very fast bit from Biggleswade to Stamford was not as fast as usual. He reached Cranwell at 8pm and Hut 105 felt happy and comfortable like a worn coat. The other fellows were broke and waiting for him to lend them enough for supper in the canteen. He liked his visit to Ayot. Two machines had just run into each other. One of these was from Cranwell which meant overtime clearing away the wreck.

[On 9 June Charlotte sent a parcel and notes on the *Seven Pillars* flyleaf.]

Charlotte Shaw

[Cranwell]

11.6.26

Lawrence thanked her for the flyleaf notes. He enclosed some diaries to amuse her. When read they could go in the bin as their last drop of juice had been extracted. He had lost his later notes, observations on the road, written at random in the saddle, including sketch maps, tribal notes, personal thumb nails and complaints. He wrote them on blocks of Army telegraph forms which were limp and easily crushed into the fold of his belt. He still had three or four at Clouds Hill but many were lost. These notes, like the diary, were nearer a bunch of thorns than a flower but he would give her a sample some day. If he had made proper maps and notes he would have written a better book, more actual, but he had been too busy for side lines.

[Lawrence is referring to two pencilled pocket diaries for 1917 and 1918. These contain, principally, the names of the places where he had slept each night. He had used them as a basis for Appendix II of *Seven Pillars*. Lawrence later gave Charlotte two of his note pads. Charlotte bequeathed the diary and note pads with her other Lawrence papers to the British Museum Library.

Charlotte wrote to Lawrence on 12 June. The following day, Sunday 13 June, he arrived at Ayot unexpectedly for tea. She wrote to him again on the 14th.]

Charlotte Shaw

[Cranwell]

17.6.26

Lawrence described how he could only keep happy in the RAF by holding himself a little bit below par. If this happened too much – if he got hurt or was crazed overmuch by some NCO with a grievance to hand on - he would feel sorry for himself. If he grew excited then he chafed at the tightness of uniformed life. When he visited the Shaws at Ayot he felt intellectually intoxicated but then he went back to Cranwell where the policeman in the guard room made him stand to attention during an inspection of his clothes and attitude. This made Lawrence flustered and sorrowful but Hut 105 was a balm to this: for there all were on the same footing, there was compulsory intimacy, not of mind but of existence. Everybody saw everybody in his shirt daily. Equality existed only under compulsion, among the bullied.

Lawrence had tried to live with decent people at All Souls and elsewhere and could not. He was able to avoid people all day and there was no goodness in being a recluse. So he declared himself a failure socially and he had failed in his ambition to become an artist, at book writing. So he backed out of the race and sat down among the people who were not racing.

In the Tank Corps he did not take leave in case he could not return but at Cranwell he was not afraid of the temptations to desert. The equilibrium between conditions and expectations of life was so fine that he shunned all disturbances. Happiness lay in maintaining this balance of opportunity and desire.

Like a cat he loved firesides and rugs and quietude but these things were outside the power of a serviceman. People only felt little things (like the throb of his right wrist) when their bodies were at rest, and there was a world of importance in the little things.

Florence Hardy

Cranwell

21.6.26

Dear Mrs. Hardy,

I'm very sorry about that MS. Always I feared that something of the sort might happen to it. Of course Mr. Hardy can't see it as outsiders will. His life matters so much to him, and he is 80: and he resents other people fussing over something of his own which he cannot himself keep. Especially as he has been reticent always. However you still have the other copies, and they are good. The early, formative, life is so beautifully done. The middle-age is not so important, for the novels cover that. I would have liked a documented, intimate study of his old age, since its reality would be worth a great deal to everyone old, or growing old. Only you could hardly detach yourself cruelly enough to write that.

There: it doesn't matter. You have done a most excellent thing.

The Greek Play will escape me. We are very busily flying just now, and I am not feeling energetic, when we do get a day off. The inclination is to lie in the grass and watch its greenness turning slowly into yellow. Lincolnshire has a severe winter, and a severe summer: a county of extremes and suddennesses.

The R.A.F. are sending me to India this autumn: in November probably. Did I tell you? I am not sorry to miss the campaign of publicity in which Cape will try to sell my abridged book next spring: but sorry to be abroad for so long. England is the only place fit to live in.

I've told the Bank to transfer the Lemperly copy to you: and despite your 'maid of all work' I've no doubt that the extra expense will not be crushing to you. For myself I haven't given any libraries any copies, though British Museum and Bodleian wanted them. Somehow they feel dehumanised, those places. Do with the extra book just what you please. I wish it was finished. The colour printer is held up for lack of power to move his presses. It may be August or September before he is finished. Everything else is printed and ready, and I'll send the copies out before I go abroad, whether all the possible pictures are finished or not.

The booksellers confirm to me that it is a good investment. They will pay £50 now for a copy, and it will rise yet further after publication. Why not sell Copy No. II and share the profit with the maid:- of whom I have the pleasantest recollection. Your house, your dog, your servants, are all of them individualities!

What a sprawling silly letter. There are engines roaring through the corrugated iron partition, and people questioning me upon flight business every moment. There goes a rocket. Rain coming, I suppose.

T.E.S.

[In the foregoing letter of 21 June, Lawrence had announced that the RAF authorities were sending him to India in the autumn, and that he was glad he was going to be out of the country when *Revolt in the Desert* was published. The RAF authorities in India however do not appear to have been informed of his impending arrival until 23 November.]

Charlotte Shaw

[With the letter below, Lawrence enclosed a draft of the preface for *Revolt in the Desert*, Jonathan Cape's abridgement of *Seven Pillars*.]

[Cranwell]

24.6.26

Lawrence explained that Cape's abridgement had to begin with a word written specially for it. There was so much that might be said, but it was best to say next to nothing. In the preface he explained that the abridgement was not more drastic because to carry through so big a job in the barrack rooms which had been his home since 1922. He was disillusioned to see how far the finished book fell short of his ambitious aim.

[Charlotte noted that GBS worked on the preface in the morning of 27 June. She sent it off the following day.]

July 1926

Charlotte Shaw

[The first part of this letter has been torn away.]

[Cranwell]

[1.7.26]

Lawrence described how he went 'officially' to the annual RAF air display at Hendon in a wheeled vehicle of the most inferior type. And they bought him back, so the weekend was what the RAF called a wash out.

[It is possible that Lawrence did not entirely accept Shaw's amendments to the draft preface, and that his comments were contained in the part of the letter that is missing. On 6 July Charlotte noted that she wrote to him about the Foreword. In the version finally printed in *Revolt in the Desert* he explained that he chose to abridge an unsatisfactory book instead of recasting it as a history because to do so would need a degree of concentration amounting in an airman to moroseness, and an interest in the subject which was exhausted long ago in the actual experience of it.]

His Mother

Cranwell

6.7.26

I've been waiting for sure news before writing to you: but the Air Force authorities drag too slowly. So here it is. I'm to go to India this winter: perhaps in September, perhaps in November, perhaps in February. It's the ordinary overseas draft, of the R.A.F. pattern. Most airmen do a turn abroad in their seven years' service. The Mesopotamian term is 2 years, the climate being bad. Egypt is 5 years: India is 5 years. I'm glad I'm not going to Egypt, for there is the risk of trouble there.

In a way I'd rather have stayed in England: but the warmth, if there is any, will be welcome: and it is good to be out of England when Cape brings out that abridgement of my Arabian book. I made the abridgement myself, and it is a severely plain one, but to sell it Cape must advertise it, and his best way of doing that will be to rake up all the old silly stories about me. I shall be glad this autumn when the real book is finished and distributed. All the work of the little book is done, already: a good thing, for with this uncertainty about going abroad I do not want more liabilities than I can help. Your cheque turned up: many thanks for it: but it is bigger, I fancy, than the money I have spent.

Florence wrote to me some while ago that you might come home with Bob in 1929. I hope so: and not go out again!

They wanted me to go out on a Commission of Enquiry to China, the other day! I told them I was happily engaged in the R.A.F.

N.

[On Sunday 11 July Lawrence arrived unexpectedly at Cherry-Goddard's, and afterwards joined the Shaws for tea. On 13 July Charlotte sent him a book by James Joyce and a letter.

On 16 July Christies, the London auctioneers, sold more than 30 portraits by Sir William Orpen. Among them was one of Lawrence from a series that Orpen had painted during the Peace Conference in 1919. Lawrence thought little of the portrait. When Blanche Patch, Shaw's secretary, sent him a reproduction of it in 1933, asking him to sign it for her, he wrote on it: 'Painted in Paris in two sittings of 90 minutes, which being done by Orpen was the then fashionable pastime.'

Charlotte viewed the Orpen sale, and may have stayed for the bidding. Afterwards, she sent the catalogue to Lawrence.

The letter below crossed with a letter from Charlotte, sent on the same day together with a parcel containing a book.]

Charlotte Shaw

[Cranwell]

20.7.26

Lawrence described Orpen as someone who did not paint with all his soul and strength and mind, unlike Augustus John. Orpen was clever, sly and witty and had been offended by something which Lawrence said of his popularity. Lawrence had not seen the Orpen portrait since 1919 and he asked Charlotte to forget it. E.M. Forster had lent his Seven Pillars to one of his friends. Afterwards Charlotte could have it.

[On the afternoon of Friday 23 July Virginia Woolf and her husband visited the Hardys, which was subsequently recorded in Volume 3 of *The Diary of Virginia Woolf*. She recalls how Thomas Hardy was 'very active minded; liking to describe people; not to talk in an abstract way: for example Col. Lawrence, bicycling with a broken arm "held like that" from Lincoln..."I hope he won't commit suicide" said Mrs Hardy pensively...He often says things like it, though he has never said quite that perhaps. But he has blue lines round his eyes. He calls himself Shaw in the army. No one is to know where he is. But it got into the papers. "He promised me (to give up fly-) not to go into the air" said Hardy. "My husband doesn't like anything to do with the air' said Mrs Hardy.'

Lawrence visited the Shaws at Ayot in the afternoon of Sunday 25 July. Charlotte sent a letter to him on 27 July.]

August 1926

[Charlotte sent letters to Lawrence on 1 and 3 August. On 4 August she and GBS left for Stresa in Italy, where they stayed for some weeks, returning to London on 6 October. Charlotte wrote to Lawrence on 5 August, and on 12 August sent two postcards.]

Air Commodore Borton

Cranwell

15 August 1926

Mr Geoffrey Dawson persuaded All Souls College to give me leisure, in 1919-20, to write about the Arab Revolt. Sir Herbert Baker let me live and work in his Westminster houses.

The book so written passed in 1921 into proof: where it was fortunate in the friends who criticised it. Particularly it owes its thanks to Mr and Mrs Bernard Shaw for countless suggestions of great value and diversity: and for all the present semi-colons.

It does not pretend to be impartial. I was fighting for my hand, upon my own midden. Please take it as a personal narrative pieced out of memory. I could not make proper notes: indeed it would have been a breach of my duty to the Arabs if I had picked such flowers while they fought. My superior officer, Wilson, Joyce, Dawnay, Newcombe, and Davenport, could each tell a like tale. The same is true of Sterling, Young, Lloyd, and Maynard: of Buxton and Winterton: of Ross, Stent, and Siddons; of Peake, Hornby, Scott-Higgins, and Garland: of Wordie, Bennett, and MacIndoe: of Bassett, Scott, Goslett, Wood, and Gray: of Hinde, Spence, and Bright; of Brodie, and Pascoe, Gilman and Grisenthwaite, Greenhill, Dowsett, and Wade: of Henderson, Leeson, Makins, and Nunan.

And there were many other leaders or lonely fighters to whom this self-regardant picture is not fair. It is still less fair, of course, like all war-stories, to the unnamed rank and file, who miss their share of credit, as they must do, until they can write the despatches.

T.E.S.

[The proof copy of *Seven Pillars of Wisdom* at Cranwell College library was described in the catalogue of the Lawrence exhibition at the National Portrait Gallery in 1998:

'The working reference copy of the subscribers' edition assembled by Lawrence as the sections were printed. It was widely read by officers and fellow aircraftmen at Cranwell, where he served from August 1925 until November 1926. The proof was originally bound-up roughly by Lawrence himself, and titled mischievously 'The complete aircrafthand.' Before leaving Cranwell he presented it to the College Library, which commissioned the present binding.

It was inscribed by Lawrence: 'Copy placed at disposal of Air Commodore Borton. This is a spoiled set of proofs of the complete text of my book *Seven Pillars of Wisdom*. It includes two pages in their original form – pages which have been modified for the edition as distributed. This copy lacks title page and fly-leaves, table of contents, table of illustrations, nine 'argume4nts' prefaced to sections, many woodcuts and line blocks, all the plates, and two appendices; these, being trimmings of the text, are supplied only to subscribers / 18.x.26 T.E.S.']

Rupert de la Bere

[Letter from Lawrence written in the summer of 1926 to the editor of The Journal of the Royal Air Force College giving permission to quote from *Revolt in the Desert*, the forthcoming abridgement of *The Seven Pillars of Wisdom*, and also pointing out that he was never 'Prince of Mecca'. From the original in the library of the RAF College at Cranwell].

Thank you very much. I hope you will cut out 'Prince of Mecca', for that is an American invention and impossible in fact. 'Emir Mekky' = Prince of Mecca and denotes actual temporal overlordship. It could not be an honorific – and King Hussein was never in the mood to honour me. We did not get on together.

Alas I was not among the first to enter Damascus; indeed my position there was very equivocal. I found an empty will amongst our leaders, when they got there – and knowing there were things urgently required I compelled them to do as I wanted. That was all.

Otherwise there is nothing which is not a fair expression of opinion. Of course I do not share your view of the literary merit of the book. It seems too literary for a memoir, and too truthful for literature. However that doesn't much matter.

The AOC asked me for a copy for the C.C. library, and this I've sent him. So you will be able to look at it, when you wish.

The facts about publication are that this full text will not be published in my lifetime: but about 150 copies are going to friends of mine, without reservations: so knowledge of it will soon get about. They will be distributed in the end of November. An abridgement is to be published by Cape in March 1927 and the serial publication of 40,000 words of this abridgement can be begun by the *Daily Telegraph* after Dec. 15 next. So your long quotation shouldn't appear before the D.T. has had its whack. After that do anything you please. Other people will be doing the same.

TES

Charlotte Shaw

[In August 1926 George V made a seven and a half hour journey from Cranwell to Edinburgh where TEL visited the map making firm of Bartholomew who were adapting a map for *Seven Pillars*].

The George Hotel, Edinburgh

22.8.1926

Lawrence explained that he wanted to make books but using his surname was impossible because of DH Lawrence who was a very great but very strange man who also wrote books. Lawrence could smell the genius in DHL and this might burst through the darkness of his prose and take the world by the throat. DHL was very violent and dark with a darkness which only grew deeper as he wrote on. The revelation of his darkness might come if the public began to think dark thoughts as well. To avoid confusion Lawrence adopted the name Ross but then lost the hope of writing.

Lawrence went to Edinburgh to see Bartholomew, the map making firm which adapted a War Office map as an illustration in *Seven Pillars of Wisdom*. He planned to see them the following morning and he would be back in Cranwell in the afternoon. It would take him seven and a half hours if Boernerges went respectably. Boanerges would go madly if Lawrence would. He was growing old. Again and again that morning when he came to a piece of road which invited 90 mph he patted the tank and murmured 'Seventy only, old thing', and kept to it. His excuse was the distance to Edinburgh and that there should be no full open throttle on a long journey. That was once his maxim which he now kept without vexation which was significant. Or was it only that he had ridden too many hundreds of miles that last week. His time in England drew short and he was not yet surfeited but wanted to be. He had the appetite of the well fed for more food.

The colour printers were proving their last three prints. One had 23 colours on it and cost ten shillings a print. The planned timetable was bookbinding in October, distribution in November and deportation to India [to India] in December. He was tired and his head was swaying round corners and listening for the engine beat.

[Lawrence took the name John Hume Ross when he first enlisted in 1922, but had occasionally used it before to disguise his identity. He retained a bank account as JH Ross for many years.]

Charlotte Shaw

[14 Barton Street, Westminster]

24 Aug. 1926

It was nearly midnight and Lawrence had just returned from an evening at the annual series of Promenade Concerts, held at the Queen's Hall in London, and started in 1895 by Henry Wood. He had woken up in Durham, left the sleeping hotel and walked around the river edge, gaping at the place. The rough walls of the castle and the bulk of the cathedral rose beautifully from the trees and surrounding houses. The morning light made the colours very vivid and glorified the weir. He had ham and eggs for breakfast as every pub in England started every guest upon his journey with that 'loathsome, sticky, discordant mess' in his belly. He put Boanerges (B.) upon the London Road and continued his journey back from Edinburgh. After a mile or two he said to B. 'We are going to hurry', laid back his ears like a rabbit and galloped down the road to Cranwell (160 miles) in 2 hours 58 minutes. It seemed to him that 65 mph was a fitting pace, so he kept down to that when the road was not fit for more. But often he was at 90 mph for two or three miles on end with B. trumpeting like a war horse.

The rest of the North of England did not seem to love him and B. The Great North Road ('what a dream, what a drunkenness of delight of a name!') was very wide and smooth and straight. So you can biff along it safely without any tactics in meeting or overtaking traffic, which was mainly Morris Oxfords doing 30 mph. He and B. were pioneers of the new order, which will do 70 or more between point and point. Like all pioneers they incurred odium. The Morris Oxfords calculated on other traffic doing the same speed. While they were thinking about swinging off the crown of the road to let him pass, he had leaped past them, a rattle and roar and glitter of polished nickel, with a blue button on top. They waved their arms wildly, or their sticks, in protest. Boa was round the next corner, or over the next hill but two while they were spluttering. Never had Boa gone better. Lawrence kept on patting him and opening his throttle, knowing that in a month or two he would belong to someone else, and Lawrence would be in a land without roads or speed. If Lawrence were rich Boa would have a warm dry garage and no work in his old age. He was an almost human machine, a real prolongation of Lawrence's faculties, and so handsome and efficient. Lawrence had never had anything like him.

At Cranwell he got Charlotte's letter. He posted her a note from Edinburgh and went onto Durham, wondering how he was to answer her. He looked forward to her letters and enjoyed them but could not answer them in kind. It was easy when they were working together on a book as that gave him a peg to hang a letter on, but upon thin air he could not. Candler had said that he was essentially an unclubbable man, meaning one who took everything and returned nothing. Lawrence liked receiving letters from Charlotte but he could not send the same sort of thing back any more than he could play any game on earth. He had never played any game through to the end. At school he would be placed into football or cricket teams and he would always trickle away from the field before the match ended.

It was the same with letters, not because of any convictions or disbeliefs, except the one that there is no 'is'. He could not be interested in things for their own sake. He could not be interested in Durham or Boanerges unless he wished to interest another person in them. He hated to talk about the involutions and convolutions of his insanely rational mind. On his ride up to Edinburgh he had taken a 30 mile return around because his road came to a toll bridge and he never paid tolls. The *Seven Pillars* had said 'when a thing is inevitable, provoke it as instantly and fully as possible.' His matter of fact ancestry compelled him to carry his impulses into action. He was utterly lacking in common sense but with every other quality normal.

At Cranwell he greeted B Flight who came out and stroked Boanerges lovingly. He then fled wildly down the Great North Road to London but roared through Codicote. He looked forward to dropping in suddenly on Charlotte – a night was too long, he just wanted one short sharp drink so that he could travel back soberly in the saddle to Cranwell. Westminster had just struck half past one in the morning and it was only after midnight that he could write such rubbish. Charlotte had been unwell and GBS was not yet perfect. Mountain air could be quite trying. People who lived in Addis Ababa went mad in 8 years.

[Candler had written 'In appearance he is academic and aloof, not a comfortable or clubbable person.' Lawrence believed that without the stimulus of the Seven Pillars proofs that had passed between them, his correspondence with Charlotte would greatly diminish. Seven weeks earlier (6 July) he had written to his mother: 'I have now been four years in the ranks, and have not as many means of contact with people as I used to have. A good thing, that. It is always difficult to get away, and I've been long drawing in my horns, inch by inch like a snail. India will let me finish the business. I propose not to write any letters to outsiders from there. Arnie [A.W. Lawrence] and myself correspond at 6 monthly intervals, and you are about the only other person to whom I write regularly.'

Even making allowances for the complicated relationship between Lawrence and his mother, this would have been an absurd lie if he had thought that the correspondence with Charlotte would continue as before. In the event, the correspondence did continue, and his weekly letters to Charlotte from India form a remarkable series. Within a few months he would arrange for his mother to meet her. Charlotte wrote on 24 August, 26 August (postcard) and 31 August.]

September 1926

[On 12 September Charlotte sent a postcard of Mussolini, and on the 19th two postcards].

Robert Graves

[16 September 1926]

[Graves (*T.E. Lawrence to His Biographer*): 'I went to Egypt and did not like it; I resigned at the end of the academic year. The letters I had from Lawrence while I was there have since gone astray. The only letter I have of 1926 is about a private matter which does not affect the story. It is dated September 16th, and in it occurs the phrase: 'We are all intact and intangible and separate in the end.' It ends:]

I'm looking forward to letting go all the possessions I have before going aboard the *Assaye* about the middle of November. The advantage of a solitary man is his completeness. This should have been a reply to your glorious letter: but I can't do it. You know you have my help and fellowship whenever you need it, in any direction I can reach.

Yours ever

T.E.S.

Charlotte Shaw

[With the letter below, Lawrence enclosed a proof of an article by Hubert Young to be published in the October and November issues of *Cornhill Magazine*. This described Young's adventures during the later stages of the Arab Revolt. The material was later used in Young's book *The Independent Arab*, which Lawrence also read in proof. Charlotte kept the *Cornhill Magazine* page proof, which carries a brief note to Lawrence from Young dated 1 September 1926.]

[Cranwell]

24.9.26

Lawrence described Young as one of the best of his crowd in Arabia. Young's article told an honest an straight forward story and the conclusions ran strongly to Lawrence's credit. England had a few fine days but had sunk away again into chills. Lawrence was sorry that the Shaw's had to return.

[Charlotte wrote to Lawrence on 25 September and again on the 28th, having received the Young proof the previous day.]

George Brough

[This is the first recorded letter from Lawrence to George Brough, the Nottingham motor cycle maker].

Cranwell

27.9.26

Dear Mr. Brough,

I'm very much in your debt for four years solid pleasure. Would the enclosed be any use to you? I don't want to sign it Ross, since that only makes the newspapers sit up and take notice: whereas they have already made beasts of themselves over the 'Lawrence' name, and can keep it, so far as I'm concerned.

I don't mind your showing it to people (or sticking it up on your stand, if that is a practice at Olympia) but I'd rather you did not print it in a newspaper till after December 15, when I'll have gone abroad. This is supposing it's of use, as a chit. What I really meant it for is best thanks, for a hundred thousand very jolly miles.

Yours ever

J.H.Ross

[Enclosed testimonial:]

27.9.26

Dear Mr. Brough,

Yesterday I completed 100,000 miles, since 1922, on five successive Brough Superiors, and I'm going abroad very soon, so that I think I must make an end, and thank you for the road-pleasure I have got out of them. In 1922 I found George I (your old Mark I) the best thing I'd ridden, but George V (the 1922 SS 100) is incomparably better. In 1925 and 1926 (George IV & V) I have not had an involuntary stop, and so have not been able to test your spares service, on which I drew so heavily in 1922 and 1923. Your present machines are as fast and reliable as express trains, and the greatest fun in the world to drive:- and I say this after twenty years experience of cycles and cars.

They are very expensive to buy, but light in upkeep (50-65 m.p.g. of petrol, 4000 m.p.g. oil, 5000-6000 miles per outer cover, in my case) and in the four years I have made only one insurance claim (for less than £5) which is a testimony to the safety of your controls and designs. The S.S. 100 holds the road extraordinarily. It's my great game on a really pot-holed road to open up to 70 m.p.h. or so and feel the machine gallop: and though only a touring machine it will do 90 m.p.h. at full throttle.

I'm not a speed merchant, but ride fairly far in the day (occasionally 700 miles, often 500) and at a fair average, for the machine's speed in the open lets one crawl through the towns, and still average 40-42 miles in the hour. The riding position and the slow powerful turn-over of the engine at speeds of 50 odd give one a very restful feeling.

There, it is no good telling you all you knew before I did: they are the jolliest things on wheels.

Yours very sincerely

T E Lawrence

[George Brough (*T.E. Lawrence By His Friends*): 'It is very difficult for me to adequately express my feelings in regard to a man I admired above all others. His enthusiastic playfulness in the sport of motor cycling could easily have cloaked the genius of the man behind the boyish smile. I built him eight motor bicycles during the period of our friendship; he called them George I, George II, George III, George IV, George V, George VI, George VII – George VIII was never delivered, and in remembrance of the man for whom it was built, this machine is now ridden by me.

I have never met a more unassuming man, he would talk motorcycling to the biggest tyro at the game, and from his conversation, a stranger would probably form the opinion that T.E.L. himself was that tyro. As a matter of fact, not only was T.E.L. extremely clever in anything technical concerning a motor cycle but he was one of the finest riders I have ever met. In the several runs I took with him, I am able to state with conviction that T.E.L. was most considerate to every other road user. I never saw him take a single risk nor put any other rider or driver to the slightest inconvenience – but when the road was clear ahead, it required a very good and experienced rider to keep anywhere near T.E.L.

An article in a certain paper was once brought to my notice which stated that T.E.L. always rode racing motor bicycles. This article must have been written by some irresponsible person who had 'little knowledge which is a dangerous thing', and I was so incensed at the time, that such ridiculous piffle, so absolutely untrue, should be published that I insisted on the paper in question publishing a public apology for their misstatement.

His suggestive hints as to where details might be altered or improved were very helpful to me. The most outstanding characteristic of the man was his charming nature at all times and to all people. When I heard the Seven Pillars of Wisdom was going to be published I asked him on the occasion of one of his visits if it would be possible to see a copy. This was long before the book was officially published, and he sent along, by special messenger, his original MSS., telling me he would be pleased if I would let my works foreman, for whom he had great regard, look at it; also he would like Mrs. Brough to see it. We appreciated this thoughtful gesture of his very much and you can imagine my horror when a few days after the MSS. had been returned to TEL, Mrs. Brough showed me a pencil sketch of TEL himself that she had copied from the book. On the very next visit to my works he came to my house for lunch and Mrs. Brough, summoning all her courage, produced the evidence of her guilt. In a way that only TEL could do it, he not only told my wife that she had not done wrong but he congratulated her on what is a wonderful sketch, and duly signed it for her.

Another instance of his thoughtfulness concerns a visit to my works one day with a very dirty motor bicycle, and it was an invariable custom in my works for his machine to be cleaned immediately on his arrival because one never knew whether we should have his machine for an hour or a day. A few minutes later, I was walking through the shops with TEL, and a boy, who had only been in my employ for a few days, was very laboriously brushing and polishing away at the hubs and spokes of the bicycle's wheels. TEL spoke to the boy and said, 'I do like to see a boy set about the difficult parts. It is quite easy for me to clean the easy parts like the handlebars and tank, isn't it?' Imagine that boy's feelings, being spoken to in such a kindly manner by the one rider, above all others, of the machine he had helped to make. Immediately TEL had left the works, the boy asked permission to leave and run home to tell the good news to his parents.

These little instances were typical of the man's beautiful nature and the reason for him being loved and respected by everyone with whom he came in contact.']

October 1926

Charlotte Shaw

[Cranwell]

2.X.26

Lawrence described Charlotte's letters as sunny spots in the blue of every-day. The little black and white drawing of Lawrence by Augustus John was ready for Charlotte. Dates were all over the Seven Pillars, in the margin, where they showed most and did not uglify the page. Lawrence did not want the proofs of Young's book back. His ship was to sale on 5 December which would make most of November his private property. There was much good music threatening in London about that time. The autumn was golden in colour of sunlight and woolliness of air. He revelled in it, and walked to taste it. Boa was getting rusty, but was going to London that day, to hear the *Planets* at Queen's Hall. He had read a great book, *The Plumed Serpent* by D.H. Lawrence.

[The best known of Augustus John's sketches of Lawrence was drawn in Paris in 1919 and reproduced in the subscribers' edition of *Seven Pillars*. Charlotte Shaw bequeathed the original to the National Portrait Gallery.

During their holiday, the Shaws visited the Rosmini College near Stresa. Charlotte had sent Lawrence a photograph of the statue there of the Italian philosopher Antonio Rosmini Serbati.]

Charlotte Shaw

[Cranwell]

5.X.26

Lawrence had never heard of Rosmini. He was in London last Saturday but took the Baldock road, to avoid the temptation of Codicote. He was glad that GBS had rested to some extent. Boanerges rested in his stall but ran furiously once on the road. And GBS when not writing hard or talking hard was swimming hard or amusing someone or other. Lawrence was like his bicycle in his capacity for sitting or lying down, vacantly and happily, for weeks on end. It was the difference between a man of action and a dreamer. Sir Henry Wood could not make anything of the *Planets*. His book was not at the binders yet. Kennington had found fault with two plates. It would be three weeks before it was ready.

[Charlotte wrote to Lawrence on 6 October, the day of her return to London, and the following day she sent him a gift of chocolates. On 13 October she sent another parcel.]

Charlotte Shaw

[Cranwell]

14.X.1926

Lawrence was sorry that he could not visit on Saturday. He was on fire picquet which confined him to camp like a criminal. So he could not visit next Saturday and probably not the Saturday after but he would try to get away. As Flight Clerk he kept the roster of weekends and made out the passes and this made it difficult for him to get a fair share of what was going. The married men had good reasons for going home every week.

The wood fuel was the jolliest thing. They had none in the flight and he had to contrive a fire for the Flight Commander. The best he could do was to mix coal dust, sawdust and lubricating oil (old oil from aeroplane engines) and do them up in packets for the fire. They burned well but were messy. He did not advise a similar approach in Hertfordshire but in Lincolnshire there was no wood.

On 4 November at noon he will go on leave until 2 December. He planned to visit Charlotte occasionally during that time, which will pass quickly, like the condemned man's breakfast. The whole idea of exile for years was horrible. The autumn had been perfect and he will walk around India swearing that England's climate was all gold. The Augustus John drawing, 'a jolly little thing', was at Kenningtons home at Morton House, Chiswick Malll. Lawrence would collect it or Charlotte could phone and arrange for it to be sent.

B. Flight was in Charlotte's debt again. Gunter's chocolates were better than the canteen sweets. They were reading the American Geographical magazines and interrupting his letter writing so he had to give it up.

Mrs Friedlow

[14 October 1926]

Lawrence wrote that Cranwell had become his 'home for lost dogs'.

Dick Knowles

[18 October 1926]

Lawrence wrote about his plans for the leave he would get prior to going to India. 'Then I'll be free for ten days to say goodbye to everyone: then a week distributing the bound volumes.'

Manning Pike

[18 October 1926]

[The printer of the subscriber's edition, Manning Pike, had premises in London at 44 Westbourne Terrace North, WC2, which he leased from George H. Noble at £1 a week. Lawrence would ride his motorcycle from Cranwell to check on progress and sometimes would stay overnight, sleeping on a make shift bed on the hot water pipes in the basement.]

Keep at it. We are really last lapping. Get the Table of Contents done: make a title page which pleases you, and don't send it me: and then print and print and print.

Charlotte Shaw

[Charlotte sent Lawrence a parcel on 19 October. On the following evening, Wednesday 20 October, he called in unexpectedly at the Shaw's London home. On the 26th she sent another parcel with a note, which crossed with the letter below.]

[Cranwell]

26.X.26

Lawrence had been right about the weekends: the last two had been used to inoculate him (which gave him 48 hours fever) and the next he was to attend church. After that 28 days of freedom except for the packing of that book off to the binders and back. It was still not ready. He stole in suddenly on Wednesday evening and found GBS just back from a prize fighting film and looking so happy.

[Charlotte received this note on 28 October and replied the same day.]

T.B. Marson

[T.B. Marson had just retired from the Air Ministry, where he had been Trenchard's tactful Personal Assistant and Private Secretary. He had a son John who was a cadet at Cranwell, but Lawrence had not seen much of him as he was in another squadron.]

[26 October 1926]

The RAF is still my spiritual home, and I'm awfully sorry to leave Cranwell, where I've had the best year I ever remember to have had...However parts of that book of mine are to come out with Cape & Co. in the spring and people sort of agree that I'd better dodge out of reach of the daily press before that happens.

Birds are wiser than us, in their habits of ruling their young ones out of the nest, so soon as they have done their first solo! We make the weaning too slow. I hope he will like the RAF. From my point of view it is the perfect existence: but then I've been battered so much elsewhere.

November 1926

[On 1 November Charlotte Shaw sent Lawrence a parcel, which crossed with the letter below. Some days earlier she had met Winston Churchill at a luncheon where he was a fellow guest. She must have recounted their conversation in one of her letters.]

Charlotte Shaw

[Cranwell]

1.XI.26

Lawrence should have written on Saturday but instead he went to Lincoln and roamed all over it, saying goodbye. Yesterday he went to Southwell and said goodbye to the beautiful old church. Two miserable occasions.

Charlotte had tackled Churchill but Lawrence felt sorry for his most considerate chief for whom he had personal affection and admiration. Churchill had so much zest, will and courage and he enjoyed his successes and his food, drink, exercises, painting and writing. He lived life at full throttle and yet he was 50, without a follower and fighting alone. Living dangerously was fine when a man was strong but Churchill was on the down grade. Lawrence would not have supported Charlotte's attack on Churchill. The RAF was Lawrence's deliberate and very happy choice, he would not leave it to become Prime Minister. Churchill would have given him Egypt in 1922 when Allenby came home. But this was a social job with much entertaining, a large house, silk hat and dignity.

There was nothing the Cabinet could do for him except leave him in the RAF. They had rows in 1919 and 1920 but since 1922 all had been well. Lawrence's settlement of the Middle East, which he put to Wilson, had successfully stood the test of four years and was still going well. Lawrence liked Churchill's pictures better than his budgets: they were atmospheric, courageous, ill-drawn visions. Churchill was very honest but sometimes deliberately wicked. He hoped to see Charlotte in little more than a week. He discussed prize fighting with GBS.

[This was the last letter which Lawrence wrote to Lawrence from Cranwell. Charlotte wrote to Lawrence on 2 November. Lawrence left Cranwell on 3 November and took a month's leave to prepare his departure to India. On 4 November Charlotte had tea with Lawrence and E.M. Forster in London. During much of his leave, Lawrence had to work in London on *Seven Pillars*, collating the printed sheets and plates ready for dispatch to the binders. The work took far longer than he expected.

On Sunday 7 November he called in at Ayot, where he found Beatrice and Sidney Webb. The Webbs, industrious social reformers, neither understood nor sympathised with Lawrence's choice of living in the ranks, so the encounter cannot have been very successful. They left in mid-afternoon, and Lawrence shortly afterwards.

On 11 November he took Augustus John's portrait sketch to the Shaw's London home. This was a generous response to Charlotte's gifts and help with *Seven Pillars*, especially when added to the *Oxford Times* proof, which the Shaw's had now recovered, and a copy of the subscribers' edition. By nature, Lawrence preferred to give than to receive. Throughout his friendship with Charlotte, the financial value of his gifts to her always exceeded the cost of her gifts to him.

On Armistice Day she gave him lunch. Afterwards they went to the Tate Gallery, and then walked together through the Westminster streets. The following weekend, 13- 14 November, he arrived at Ayot around midday on Saturday, and spent the afternoon and evening listening to music. He then accompanied the Shaws to their usual Sunday lunch with Cherry-Garrard.

The following Friday, 19 November, Eric Kennington and Lawrence called for Charlotte and drove her to Kennington's house in Chiswick. Lawrence left them at Shepherd's Bush, but later rejoined Charlotte for lunch at Adelphi Terrace.]

Lord Trenchard

[20 November 1926]

Lawrence thanked Trenchard for giving him the option of going overseas or staying at home. Lawrence had volunteered to go abroad because *Revolt in the Desert* was to be published in March 1927 and this would cause a problem for the RAF when the press got involved. Lawrence could dodge them abroad and after a few years the bubble would either burst or be deflated and he could serve again at home. Lawrence was sorry to have troubled Trenchard as he hoped to be no trouble after joining the RAF. He was perfectly happy in the RAF but if B Flight found that he used to know Trenchard his character would be ruined.

Lord Trenchard

[Lord Trenchard's specially bound copy (of the *Seven Pillars*) in air force blue was sent direct to its recipient with a covering letter, in which Lawrence wrote:]

[22 November 1926]

It is not the right blue of course: but then what is the right blue? No two airmen are alike: indeed it is a miracle if the top and bottom halves of one airman are the same colour. So perhaps you are not particular.

I told the binder (ex-RAF) who it was for. 'Then,' said he, 'it must be quite plain and very well done.' And it really isn't badly done. Of course it's the first copy, and the later ones will profit by its experience.

You will see it marked 'Incomplete copy'. There are three plates missing: that's all. They make a tremendous difference in value, as you will find out if you try to sell it. Complete copies cost thirty guineas, and it would not be seemly (or financially possible) for me to give any of them away. This is the best I can do.

As I told you, it isn't given you to read: but merely as a sign that all is well...

Let's hope this is my last letter till March 1930, when you are to be asked to prolong my engagement.

Lord Trenchard

[29 November 1926]

[Trenchard's copy of *Seven Pillars* was inscribed by the author: 'Sir Hugh Trenchard from a contented, admiring and, whenever possible, obedient servant. 5.XII.26. T.E.S.' This gratified and amused the Chief of the Air Staff as 'being a delightful touch from the most disobedient mortal I have ever met'. In the same letter, in which he acknowledged the gift of the book, Trenchard wrote kindly and considerately:

'I hope you keep fit but if you get seedy you may get sad and *if you* do, do write and *let me know*, so that if necessary I can bring you home.

You say you hope I shall not receive a letter from you until March 1930. By then I shall have gone and others will be here, but I will promise you that as far as possible I will see that you can get out if you want to.

I would very much like to have seen you before you actually sailed, but I suppose that is not possible, and perhaps it would be inadvisable from your point of view: but if you want to be put up for a night, my wife and children would be delighted to see you before you went out at Dancers Hill. Let me know'. Lawrence replied:]

Many thanks, but I will not trouble Lady Trenchard. It wouldn't do in uniform: and I've no other clothes fit to wear. Also the last four or five years of low life have reduced my never very high social sense.

I'm always obedient when things go well. They have gone very well the last 18 months.

You say "I shall have gone (by 1930) but so far as possible I will see that you can get out of it if you want to." You have misread me. Getting out is easy. They would send the band to play me to the station. All my efforts are to stay in. If you can do anything to persuade your successor to prolong me, I'll be grateful to both.

This has been a hard-working, rushed month for me: and yesterday I had a crash on my bicycle. Broke the poor thing, and scratched my knee! First crash for 11 months. Hard luck'.

[H. Montgomery Hyde, *Solitary in the Ranks*: 'A former telegraph boy, who worked in the station post office at Cranwell fifty years ago and is still there, was asked by the present writer what he remembered about Lawrence. "The large number of telegrams addressed to A/c Shaw which I had to deliver to him at his hut," was the reply. "He would give me a shilling for each one – and that means a lot to me as my wages then were only half-a-crown a week!"'].

Charlotte Shaw

[Charlotte Shaw met Lawrence for lunch on 24 November in London. Lawrence planned to spend his last free Sunday with the Shaws, but that morning he crashed his motorcycle and had to telephone to say that he could not come. Charlotte then suggested meeting him for lunch on Wednesday 1 December.]

[London]

[Dated 30 November 1926, 9.46 am]

Lawrence agreed that Charlotte's suggestion that they meet for lunch was an excellent idea. He would pick her up at one fifteen on Wednesday wherever convenient.

T.E.S.

[Lawrence made a final visit to the Hardys at Max Gate during November. When this visit took place is not definitely known, but it must have been before Sunday 28 November, for on that day he was to have ridden down to Dorset again but had a motor cycle accident, which badly damaged the machine as well as giving him a limp. Lawrence's visit was recorded in *The Life of Thomas Hardy* by Florence Hardy:

'During this month, November, his friend Colonel T.E. Lawrence called to say goodbye, before starting for India. Hardy was much affected by this parting, as T.E. Lawrence was one of his most valued friends. He went into the little porch and stood at the front door to see the departure of Lawrence on his motor cycle. This machine was difficult to start, and, thinking he might have to wait some time Hardy turned into the house to fetch a shawl to wrap around him. In the meantime, fearing that Hardy might take a chill, Lawrence started the motorbike and hurried away. Returning a few minutes later, Hardy was grieved that he had not seen the actual departure, and said that he had particularly wished to see Lawrence go.']

December 1926

His Mother

[14 Barton Street]

I.xii.26

This is my last free night in England, & I'm writing to you, very late, in the top of Barton Street, where [Sir Herbert] Baker has let me stay during this month. It should have been leave, preparatory to going overseas: but for me it has been a very hard month of work on that book of mine...

Thank you for suggesting my leaving the RAF and living quietly somewhere: but I cannot be quiet, and so the bustle and enforced duty of the RAF is good for me. I wish it was not India – an experiment which has lasted too long and where we are failing...

I cannot tell you where I'm going. Tomorrow it is to Uxbridge. Our ship should sail on Sunday, from Southampton perhaps. We disembark at Karachi, about a month later...

There: this is not a cheerful letter. The last four weeks I have been wandering about seeing my time drawing to an end, & so I am not able to settle to anything, or rest myself in anything. Once off, it will be all right.

Charlotte Shaw

[Charlotte travelled up to London alone for her last meeting with Lawrence on 1 December. As a gift, she brought with her a manuscript commonplace-book of mystical passages that she had copied from various sources. Lawrence sailed for India a week later, expecting to remain overseas for five years.]

[RAF Barracks]

2.XII.26

He was to sail on the *S.S. Derbyshire* on Tuesday 7 December. Lawrence thought that he and Charlotte had managed their goodbye occasion very well. Lord Burnham of the *Daily Telegraph* thought better of his refusal to serial rights of *Revolt in the Desert*. There would be no more letters from Lawrence until something definite like Suez or Karachi happened.

[Extracts from *Revolt in the Desert* were serialised in the *Daily Telegraph* from 15 December 1926 to 10 January 1927.]

Robert Graves

[Robert Graves, *T.E. Lawrence to his Biographer*: 'There was a little more before he sailed:]

[Undated]

I've had the L.R. book [Laura Riding's *Close Chaplet*]. It puzzles me. Either she is very deep or very different-minded – another way for saying that her poems slide out of my grip. I cannot remember them, after I have read them. This is not criticism, but a personal statement.

Your work affects some people that way: whereas my mind seems tuned exactly to them, so that what you say is what I'd say, if I had your power.

Off to India, or to Uxbridge for India, tomorrow. The leaving England is a very bitter thing. I wish I could stay always here in London.

Don't fail to send me word of yourself, and of how things, even material things, are with you. There needn't be any reserve between us. I'm going to ask you for help any time I need it!

Yours

TES

Francis Rodd

[3 December 1926]

I had an awful month, real hard labour upon my old man of the sea: final printings, plates, collection, collation, issue to binders, correction of subscribers' lists, allotment of copies. Yet though I sweated it at every possible hour of the day and night, seeing no one and doing nothing else, even now it is not finished. About 20 copies have gone out, and most of the rest will go out about Christmas time ['my Christmas pudding' he called it in another letter] but the very special copies will hang on till the New Year. I think my experience is almost a conclusive demonstration that publishing is not a suitable hobby for an airman.

Dick Knowles

[Uxbridge Depot]

3.XII.26

Dear Dick,

I'm sitting in a very poor hut at Uxbridge... I spent the whole of my leave, seeing no one, and going to no concerts: not one single scrap of public music all that while: though by the goodness of my dentist I twice heard Harold Samuel play in his house.

I managed to squeeze out ½ an hour in Clouds Hill: and ½ an hour at the Hardys. I had meant to come to you last Sunday, and started about 7.30 A.M. but Islington streets were greasy (I had to see G.B.S. on the way) and I got into a trough in the wood paving, and fell heavily, doing in the off footrest, kickstart, brake levers, ½ handlebar, and oil pump. Also my experienced knee-cap learnt another little trick. Alb Bennett took the wreck for £100. I limp rather picturesquely....

Yours

T.E.S

[Lawrence told Knowles that he was sending him a set of the largest possible proofs of his book: the dirty old B Flight Manual which circulated to so many people at Cranwell. Some squadron leader or other re-covered it. The final book came out not so badly. It was very large and not quite enough copies were produced to give away. He had a strangely empty feeling to have finished with it after nine years. He was to go on a voyage to India on the *Derbyshire*.]

[Lawrence sailed for India from Southampton on 7 December 1926].

[Robert Graves, *TE Lawrence to his Biographer*: 'The day after he sailed came my gift copy of the *Seven Pillars* in heavy morocco binding. In it was a tiny card: "Please sell when read." I was in money difficulties again and, after reading the book and writing at length to Lawrence about it, finally sold it for £330: once more my fortunes were restored.']

John Buchan

[December 1926]

[On 14 December John Buchan forwarded to the Prime Minister a copy of *Seven Pillars of Wisdom* and quoted from a letter of Lawrence's, which he had received with it.]

This copy [*The Seven Pillars*] is one of those which I am giving to the fellows who did the Arab Revolt with me. They are incomplete in the sense that many plates are missing. I want you to ask Mr Baldwin if he would care to accept it. He did me the best turn I have ever had done to me, and I think gratefully of him as often as I have leisure to think about my contentment. It is no great return (incomplete copies have no future in the second hand market) but I am hardly in the position to make any great return, and if he likes books, as I am told, he may prefer a broken copy to none at all. The thing is, anyhow, a rarity.

[David Garnett, *The Letters of TE Lawrence*, 1938: 'The voyage out to India in the troopship Derbyshire was, as far as Suez, an unpleasant ordeal. It is described in some pages of pencil manuscript found at Clouds Hill after Lawrence's death which appear to be notes for a final section of *The Mint*, to be called *Leaves in the Wind*. I have divided the four notes so that each appears chronologically according to the date of its subject. For I cannot tell exactly when they were written, though on the analogy of The Mint I believe them to have been noted shortly after the events they describe. Both in subject and style these notes belong to The Mint, of which they will give some general idea to the general reader.]

From *Leaves in the Wind*

Final section Leaves in the Wind, snatches of life and letters, misarranged, from 2 lines to pages. M.Q. [Married Quarters] sentry – the shabby haversack that denoted my office. The wash of the water, the *Derbyshire* swaying in a long slow swell, going over so far, swinging back: ever and again going further, with a muffled musical clash of crockery far away in her depths, oscillating back again – now and then an upward heave, and the slow sinking back. My eyes began to swim, and to see gassy clouds in the corridor, between the blobs of the dim safety lamps. They twinkled to electric blue. Wave upon wave of the smell of stabled humanity: the furtive creeping by rushes along the alleyway of the women to their latrine, fending themselves from wall to wall with the right arm, while the left held the loosened dress across their body. Belches of gas come back up my throat – hullo, I'll be sick if I stay here forever – yet I promised the guard commander that I'd do two tricks: my poor little ex-apprentice relief got so bad down here after fifteen minutes that they had to help him up to the air. *Swish swish* the water goes against the walls of the ship – sounds nearer. Where on earth is that splashing. I tittup along the alley and peep into the lavatory space, at a moment when no woman is there. It's awash with foul drainage. Tactless posting a sentry over the wives' defecations, I think. Tactless and useless all our duties aboard. Hullo here's the O.O. [Orderly Officer] visiting. May as well tell him. The grimy folded face, the hard jaw, toil-hardened hands, bowed and ungainly figure. An ex-naval warrant, I'll bet. No gentleman. He strides boldly to the latrine: "Excuse me" unshyly to two shrinking women. "God", he jerked out, "flooded with shit – where's the trap?" He pulled off his tunic and threw it to me to hold, and with a plumber's quick glance strode over to the far side, bent down, and ripped out a grating. Gazed for a moment, while the ordure rippled over his boots. Up his right sleeve, baring a forearm hairy as a mastiff's grey leg, knotted with veins, and a gnarled hand: thrust it deep in, groped, pulled out a moist white bundle. "Open that port" and out it splashed into the night. "You'd think they'd have had some other place for their sanitary towels. Bloody awful show, not having anything fixed up." He shook his sleeve down as it was over his slowly drying arm, and huddled on his tunic, while the released liquid gurgled contentedly down its re-opened drain.'

Charlotte Shaw

[Troopship *Derbyshire*]

16.XII.26

Lawrence was ten days at sea and was due in Port Said the next day. The ship would then go to Basra (Dec 29) and Karachi (Jan 7). He would be thankful when the journey ended. His expectations were not good but he was surprised at the badness of the accommodation and the misery of the crowd on board. Nature had been kinder than mankind and gave calm seas and moderate temperatures.

He did not wish to write anything and he only wanted to sit and drizzle softly to himself. Tomorrow nearly three hundred would go ashore for Egypt and Palestine. Their going will improve conditions for the 900 left on board. He will not write again until he gets to India and is in his proper place on say Jan 15.

Sergeant Pugh

[On board the troopship *Derbyshire*]

16.XII.26

Lawrence described how he had been at sea for 10 days and was about to arrive in Port Said. He had squatted on deck with Smith, C.J. lamenting Cranwell and England and all good things. Smith had asked Pugh to send his best wishes to the Flight. Lawrence asked to be remembered to Mrs Pugh and to tell the fellows at Cranwell that he would write when he was settled in India.

[Lawrence went east without enthusiasm. When the long unpleasant voyage was over he found himself in an RAF camp at Drigh Road just outside Karachi.]

January 1927

J.S. Hollings

[11 January 1927]

[The journey by troopship was worse than anything Lawrence had expected. Afterwards he wrote to J.S. Hollings, a friend at Cranwell:]

This worm dares to advise any airmen of B Flight who may be posted overseas to make up their minds to suffer every human misery during the trooping voyage. If they expect hell they may be merry to find themselves treated little worse than cattle, packed little tighter than sardines, fed worse than charity. The best training for a trooper is to haunt a Tube Station during the rush hour. This worm, being old and hardened and wicked did not spew out its guts into the sea. The fishes were sufficiently fed by other airmen, however. Better food would have been wasted on the airmen; and wasted on the fishes.'

March 1927

[On 16 March Charlotte sent a packet of press cuttings. She wrote on the 22 March sending some books and an article. The letter below was written on the back of a review of Seven Pillars by Rupert de la Bere, from the *Royal Air Force College Journal, Cranwell* (Vol. 7, No. 1, Spring 1927, pp 27-9).]

Charlotte Shaw

[Karachi]

23.III.27

Capt. De la Bere (English master at the Cadet College, and Editor of the Cadets' magazine) had read *Seven Pillars* minutely. Lawrence gave a proof of it to the AOC at Cranwell (Borton) who gave it to the Cadet Library. De la B. asked Lawrence's permission to review it.

April 1927

Charlotte Shaw

[Karachi]

7.IV.27

It had been weeks since Lawrence had sent Charlotte a decent letter and it was his only stamp. It was rather fun, being always broke, with everybody envying him for rolling in money. At Cranwell where the food was not good, a broke man went hungry. Here, the food was plenty and so he sat and laughed at himself.

[Charlotte sent a letter and press cuttings on 13 April].

Sergeant Pugh

[Karachi]

[27 April 1927]

Lawrence gave Pugh a copy of *Revolt in the Desert*. Pasted in this copy is a letter from Lawrence, written from Karachi, dated 27 April 1927.

May 1927

Jonathan Cape

[Karachi]

25.V.27

Dear Cape,

I've been sent wild stories of the genesis of *Revolt in the Desert*. If you like, make a 'third person' note in your *Now and Then* booklet saying:-

The abridgement of Mr. T. E. Shaw's *Seven Pillars of Wisdom* which we were able to publish by arrangement with him on March 10 last, under title *Revolt in the Desert* by 'T E Lawrence', was made by him in seven hours at Cranwell in Lincolnshire on March 26 and March 27 1926, with the assistance of two airman friends, A/A Knowles and A/c Miller. It was received by us (in the form of cut-down proofs of *The Seven Pillars*) on March 30, three days later, and reprinted immediately as we received it. There were no author's corrections, nor was this text ever submitted to anyone for advice or criticism. The only subsequent alterations were the division into chapters and the writing in (at the publisher's request) of three paragraphs to justify the inclusion of two much-desired illustrations from the many in *The Seven Pillars*.

The author has promised the subscribers to *Seven Pillars of Wisdom* that no further copies of this shall be published during his lifetime: and he will make no additions to the issued text of *Revolt in the Desert*.

Revolt was sold to us in order that our advance on its royalties might enable the author to commission extra drawings for *The Seven Pillars:* and the author's contract with us gives him the option of terminating our sale of the book when this advance is fully met.

There: short and sweet! Any good? I think so.

T.E.S.

June 1927

<u>John Buchan</u>

Drigh Road Karachi India

20.vi.27

Lawrence explained how he had made his abridgement of *Seven Pillars*, unaided except by two airmen from Cranwell. They did the whole thing in two evenings.

[John Buchan wrote the introduction to the American edition of *Revolt in the Desert*].

<u>Robert Graves</u>

28.VI.27

[Lawrence gave Graves some sources and notes for his biography *Lawrence and the Arabs*]

For Modern Period only useful sources might be Lionel Curtis and Mrs Bernard Shaw. Letters. Pte. Palmer (for the Royal Tank Corps). Sgt. Pugh for RAF period. A lot of people will give you yarns: but the above are reasonable truthful people, and not dullards. You'll have to persuade them I've given you their names.

The abridgement, Revolt in the Desert, was made entirely at Cranwell, in two evening's work, by myself with the help of two airmen, Miller and Knowles.

<u>Sergeant Pugh</u>

Karachi

30.VI.27

Lawrence recalled how they would light the stove at Cranwell and burn the letters which he did not have time to reply to. It was easy in B Flight. In Karachi he had to do all his letters in his own time. Terrible, or it would be if he worked eight instead of five hours a day: and if he had the proofs of a book to correct in the evenings and tarred roads and a Brough for his spare afternoons. But there are none of these things. There is only one road and no motor bike. He has not been outside camp bounds. Imagine an airman six months at Cranwell without going out. Karachi Depot could not rival Cranwell in some respects. The great point of B Flight was that they worked together and slept together and could live together if they wanted. It made everybody keen to play up to the others.

Robert Graves had been commissioned to write Lawrence's biography. Graves would do his best to play the game. If he came to Cranwell Pugh should be nice to him. He was to be trusted. Pugh should give Lawrence's regards to the flight, or what was left of it. Was Cranwell still decent? No trumpeters, guards, roll calls, general nonsense? Had the band stopped playing the Lincolnshire poacher? Did the hot water still work? Lawrence particularly wanted to know if it was decently warm at reveille. Dusty would know. Lawrence used to bribe the stoker to do their fire first in the morning. Lawrence had heard that Nigger was the complete clerk. Did he carry an indelible behind one ear and a pen behind the other? He should be warned that Lawrence was keeping his hand in by doing as much logging of repairs and overhauls every week as Nigger did in six months.

July 1927

[Robert Graves replied to Charlotte Shaw's letter of 27 July pointing out that he had to complete his biography of Lawrence quickly. If she waited six weeks for instructions from Lawrence, her help would be too late.]

August 1927

[Karachi]

Charlotte Shaw

3.VIII.27

It was drizzling and Lawrence shivered with cold, the thermometer at 79 degrees. A wireless message had come to say that Carr had crashed (with no hurt to himself) in Austria. On the aerodrome in Karachi the six flares put out for Carr were burning magnificently. He would like to cry. A relay doleful letter. He wrote a less whimpering one last night to Ayot. They will probably reach her by different posts: but unless Graves slowed up, or they put Lawrence on guard again, in the nearest future, he will not keep on double-banking his efforts. The ouput looked so thin, sorted into two envelopes.

[In May, Flight Lieutenant C.R. Carr had failed in an attempt to fly from Cranwell to Karachi, achieving the longest non-stop flight on record before coming down in the Persian Gulf. This was a further attempt.]

Charlotte Shaw

Karachi

12.VIII.27

Lawrence was tired and wanted to turn into a lizard and find himself a long, cool, dark, twisty hole under one of the cactus clumps, and sleep there until the world was empty of his kind.

He had been working overtime at Graves' biography of him, which made Lawrence sorry to have been the innocent cause of it. Graves had done the latter half well, but inevitably used a lot of *Seven Pillars*, which was hard on Lawrence, because he had sacrificed a certain amount to keep it out of circulation. It felt like it was being dragged out of him line by line. He asked Graves, whenever it got bad, to go easy on the private stuff; but the book had been written in a great hurry, so it was done before he could answer Graves's questions. If he had been in England and could have seen Graves to talk to, he would have understood Lawrence's feelings and acted accordingly; but letters were helpless things.

The best thing in R.G.'s book was a dozen pages of child like notes on Lawrence's life at Cranwell written by a Sergeant (the last in command of B Flight) in sergeant language: but so simply, kindly and delightfully. It was ridiculously too favourable but his diaphragm was warmed by it.

[These were the notes by Sergeant Pugh included by Graves in *Lawrence and the Arabs*. These notes were annotated by Lawrence in *T.E. Lawrence to his Biographers*.]

Charlotte Shaw

[Karachi]

18.VIII.27

The Graves biography could help Lawrence underline some of the errors by Lowell Thomas and unsay some of the things which the Press had said. But the biography had been written against time and was already finished and partly in print. Reading it was a misery for him. Every page by RG had inaccuracies which Lawrence corrected until he was sick. 80% of the book was what he called a bare parody or précis of Revolt: it was not quite right to make so free with another's work. Some of it reproduced the Seven Pillars. He had begged Graves to leave that alone as it was meant to be private while he lived. The only merry part was a final section of a few pages by a Sergeant at Cranwell who wrote, in perfect airman style, a scrappy picture of Lawrence in camp. He sounded a most real and easy to live with person; and it delighted him. In retrospect he could see how much there was to say on the other side.

September 1927

Edward Garnett

[Karachi]

22.IX.27

'So your copy of my Uxbridge notes make such a slow progress. I am trying not to rewrite: but I have to rearrange extensively, and to cut out repetitions and expand the sentences which are in esoteric shorthand...I think the job may be worth its trouble. It seems to me to convey some of the reality of the Depot at Uxbridge. I called it to you an uncomfortable book once. It is. There is no trace of me in it, hardly a ghostly outline of the principal figure. It deals entirely in terms of 'us': and if one of us is mentioned by name, and gives a phrase or an act of his own, it is only to serve as mouthpiece of us. The unit in the notes is the squad. So it is a libel on the happiness of an airman's life e.g. at Cranwell.'

October 1927

Charlotte Shaw

[Karachi]

27.X.27

Years ago he promised Edward Garnett his notes on Uxbridge – the history of the 3 months' breaking-in to the RAF. Garnett had reminded him of this promise and so he had been making the notes legible for his eyes. They were only notes but the final impression was so drab that he felt he dare not send them without a few pages about the real RAF – the Cranwell season – which after Uxbridge was like the sun breaking through. He had a few pages of Cranwell notes but had also sent some to Charlotte when he first arrived there, dealing with colour hoisting parade, a guard, and Wing Commander Jago's sermon about Queen Alexandra. Could she have these copied and sent to him? There were only a few hundred words in all. He didn't send Charlotte anything after he settled down, but she asked him, at first, to tell her what the new life was. If he tacked these on after the Uxbridge notes E.G. would see that they were not the RAF but just Uxbridge, which was horrible.

December 1927

Charlotte Shaw

15.12.27

His letters to Charlotte were unworthy. Writing did not come to him by easy course of nature. If he thought for weeks he could store up a small heap of ideas. If he put them down one by one, after a while he had a rough meditation about what had been interesting to him. This he would write out twice or three times to get it into order and a logical sequence. That was the sort of letter she should get from him but he couldn't do it.

'Queen Alexandra' came to hand securely. That gave him (with the notes he already had and what Charlotte sent him) nearly all that he wrote at Cranwell about the camp. He would copy them, as 'solitary disjected chunks of words', into the back of Garnett's notebook. They would correct the drabness of the Uxbridge tale: for Cranwell was a warm and happy place, but not in temperature!

He asked Charlotte not to be hard on Graves' book. If Graves borrowed much of the *Seven Pillars* he did so with Lawrence's approval. Other parts he had toned down, such as the ride to Abdulla, with all the self revelation dissolved out of them. Graves had been trusted to do all this on his own and he deserved credit.

Charlotte Shaw

27.12.27

The three days at Christmas had been miserable for his eyesight. All the fellows he normally liked and enjoyed being with had been making fools of themselves. In England the Tank Corps had been like this, and almost worst one Christmas. At Cranwell there was nothing horrible. Last year he had been on the troopship and there were not so many drunks. But Drigh Road had been a degraded place that weekend.

He read Vansittart's Singing Caravan. His original copy had notes of some paragraphs of the *Seven Pillars* scribbled on its back flyleaves. They were put there as he flew between Paris and Crete in a Squadron of Handley Pages.

[An inscription in the front of Lawrence's original copy of *The Singing Caravan* reads: 'Carried with me on Handley-Pages from Paris to Egypt in 1919. Between Paris and Marseilles the chapter II of my *Seven Pillars of Wisdom* was written on a back cover of this book, now torn out. Its rhythm was derived from the beat of the Rolls Royce Eagle VIII engines of our machine. Other notes from the *Seven Pillars* are on the back flyleaf of this copy. Cranwell, 1926. TES.'

Dick Knowles

[Karachi]

30/12/27

Dear Dick,

As a rule I work at this machine for an hour a day, and as I get more intelligible on it I am beginning to write letters to the people to whom I am most in arrears. It is not a very good payment of dues, for either I am careful at framing my sentences - in which case spelling and sense go west: or I am spelling carefully, in which case the sentences mean little or nothing: or the meaning is excellent, but unintelligible below the errors in syntax and spelling. I leave it to you to divide this letter into these three categories. You have no idea how hard it is to do four things at once. Later, when I can hammer blindfold like a clerk (Group IV), my stuff will be itself again.

Life here remains as it was when I wrote to you the first and last times from here. A good place in which to mark time, for the food is good, and there is no attempt to control our deportment in camp, and the work is light (too light, I'm afraid... the excessive leisure takes much filling) and not uninteresting, for the officers are all full out for work; and I have found a sheltered occupation, which delivers me from working parade, first thing in the morning, and from most of the ceremonials. This is an extraordinary place for Ceremonies. An average of one posh visitor a month seems to come here, or to Karachi, and no performance is complete without the presence of the R.A.F. And India is a country of rifles, so that a parade is a military occasion. At all times of the year hundreds of us are being rafted down to the town in Leyland floats, to line streets or honour a cenotaph, or fire a feu-de-joie. From all these diversions of temper my little job as Key-orderly preserves me. In return I get up at reveille (easy...) and unlock the shops by 7 o'clock; and lock them up again in the dinner time, when work nominally ceases for the day. But often there is an afternoon shift, and for them again I open doors; and the rest of the time I have the keys in my control, and can use the shop and office as a playground. It was a comfort at Christmas time, when the camp turned very wet. Normally it is as dry as any camp I have met; but the mess, when it did break out, finally, was correspondingly worse... I think it was worse than Bovington in 1923, which has hitherto been my high-level of beastliness. No, upon reflection, it was not so bad as that.

Christmas day itself I spent in the guardroom, doing another man's turn. He thought I was doing him a kindness, he being a buffalo, an animal which likes dampness; I thought he was doing me a kindness; so the exchange was mutually satisfactory. The guard were all T.T., at least on duty, and no person came near us to bother us. So I think I scored. Guards are a beastly ordeal, for me. I get in a shaking funk before the mounting, and find it difficult to give the right salutes with a pop-gun at short notice, without muddling myself up. Sheer wind, of course, for actually I know the movements well. But something always comes to flurry me, when it is a performance with witnesses.

You were no doubt at Clouds Hill. I wish I could have been, for the day, though I make no doubt that the tenant (if any) has cleaned it up muchly. But all that has happened since I left England makes me pat myself on the back of myself, for my wisdom in running away. Cranwell would have stood, grumblingly, one book about me; when Graves added himself to the *Revolt*, they would have spat on me. When Lowell Thomas added himself to Graves, they would have spewed on me. It was hard luck, having the two of them at once; though in the end it will be best, probably. At least, nobody can do another, and the soul of the great British public will be turned with rage at its surfeit of my rareness and virtuosity, and will refuse for years to hear me quoted or mentioned. The BIGGER THE BOOM? THE BIGGER THE SLUMP... so that is comfortable. I hope you will take the crest of the market for the disposal of your *Seven Pillars*. If you ask me when the crest is or was, then I cannot tell you. Posh got £400 for his proofs... but they were a unique set. I have been a golden gander to lots of people; and if that spare copy of *The S.P.* at Oxford is not claimed by I come back, then it is going to give me a new bike in 1930, and maintenance money for it for two years. I hope the Matchless is going as it should; it sounded right. Just well run in, and nippy in type. When you are my age you will be sighing for heavier things, which are less acrobatic to ride, and suggest ease to their decaying owners. The point of glory in a Brough was that lazy touring speed, maintained, you felt, without effort on the engine's part, for all day.

I wonder where you go, about Winchester. One of my pet places used to be at Ringwood - or rather near it. The forest is fine about Picket Post; though perhaps this is hardly the time of year. We forget the seasons here, where the climate is always as near fine as can be, and the temperature pretty constant through the year, dropping ten degrees a night in summer, from 90° to 80°, and in winter sometimes falling as low as 60° at midnight. Also this place has no direct sun; the nearness of the sea gives us so much mist and there are such continual dust-storms in the Gulf, that the light comes to us always filtered, indirectly. I go about perversely wishing for a really hot day, one which would show the grumbling crowd how fortunate is the climate they have fallen into.

There used to be a little tea-cottage, the last house on the right as you reached the bridge out of Ringwood, on the Wimborne road. It was well run by an amusing woman - a type of 'new poor'. Do not forget, either, the dairy in Wimborne itself, which supplies the best Devonshire cream, under the pretence (and price) of Dorsetshire. I expect you find Salisbury too particularly military for your tastes to go wandering there. The best of Salisbury is the green grass round the cathedral, and some of the houses in the Close. Though there are good houses, old timber halls, in the town. I like Salisbury. Also I read in the papers that they are at last trying to do something to clean up the skirts of poor desecrated Stonehenge. It has become only its shadow, since the war, what with aerodromes and cottages and fences. Once it stood all by itself on its grey hill, as you came from Amesbury, and was magnificent.

There, I must stop talking. I often think of you, and always as a rather shapeless Sidcotted bundle, peering over the rim, or through the floor of a Virgin in mid air. Probably false: but my imagination makes those big machines wander out into the sky, once a month or so, for a day and a night, over England and Scotland, just droning away for hour after hour aimlessly among the clouds, burning so much petrol and oil, and coming home again for breakfast, and then bed, and afterwards more weeks to clean up for another try. Flying is probably by now only a boredom to you. It is more than a year since I got into the air on any pretext, and I look back upon it as one of the few 'different' things. If I had never flown (like most of the fellows here) I don't think I would dare go into the streets in blue uniform.

You wrote something about first going up. It stressed the lack of sensation, I expect. I felt that: but each flight since has felt stranger. The utter separation of the self from familiar things... but of course in your case your cockpit is only part of your job. I should not like to take my stool and table and ink-pot with me into space.

Yours

T.E.S.

Our library has started subscribing for *J O'Ls*... a result of my lending about those copies you sent me. Good effort.

January 1928

His Mother

[Karachi]

4.i.28

That is much better: when we do not write so rapidly, our letters have time to reach their destinations and answer their questions: so that we do not need to repeat everything many times. It is not as though I had much to say. Life with me is much the same, from week to week, or from year to year: in camp at Farnborough, or at Bovington, or at Cranwell, or at Drigh Road. One room is like another, in barracks, and one airman is like another airman. We do not have changes or adventures. We stay still, and are physically taken care of, like stock cattle.

I am glad you thought to leave England for a little. They say, in the papers, that it has been cold there, and wintry. It feels improbable, out here, where the climate is hardly varied from January to January, where it is never hot, and very seldom cold. Karachi seems to have struck the mean of the world's climates, and to exist in a perpetual temperateness of heat and sunshine. Yet it is a dreary place, because the weather is too same to have a character. Too long a succession Of perfect weeks brings monotony.

Italy, you have chosen: and Rome, of all places in Italy. Now I could have understood some little village in the hills. Did you ever read D. H. Lawrence's marvellous novel *The Lost Girl*... with its pictures of country life, very high up, in Italy? One of the most beautiful of modern stories, told by a master of English prose. You can get a 3/6 edition of it, published by Martin Secker. In such a house as that you might be quiet.

Yes, that sending of the parcel was a pity. I have been much troubled by parcels: the great warm heart of the British and American public seems to yearn over people who write, and they send me incongruous things: so I have my private way of getting the things I ask for: and the Post Office (which in India means the Customs) have my instructions not to notify to me the other things. I do not know what happens to them: perhaps they are sent back as not delivered (but the Stores will have their rules against that, for it would involve them in expense), perhaps they are sold out here to pay Customs charges. Also registered letters are not delivered to me. I found that they were only afflictions. My post is unmanageably great. I have had to make a rule not to spend more than 3/- a week in stamps and stationery, to answer the letters I get: and that means very many letters go without their replies. I cannot answer more than one in three of what I receive, and even what I do write is too much. It taxes my spare time valuelessly: for my opinions and ideas are not useful to anyone else, and it is no pleasure to me to put them on paper. Some day I dream of putting round a little printed card to everyone... 'Many thanks for your letter, which I should have endeavoured to answer, only that I have determined lately to write no more letters that are not of a strictly business character.' It would be a saving of time and tissue... but I am afraid of causing more talk.

N.

February 1928

David Garnett

[Karachi]

16.2.28

Garnett was over imagining the importance of Lawrence's Uxbridge notes. They were written as the basis of a projected book in 1922. The book would never come off because he liked the RAF too much to put a true account of it to a public which would not understand. He only suggested that Garnett should read the RAF notes to cure him of a lingering suspicion that Lawrence could write.

March 1928

David Garnett

[Drigh Road, Karachi]

15.3.28

I have today posted (as yesterday I finished) the RAF notes.... I never want to write a thing again. The notes eventually worked out at 70,000 words: the Uxbridge part was 50,000: and I added 20,000 on Cranwell, (built up out of contemporary letters and scraps of writing which I'd hoarded against such a need) to redress the uniform darkness of the Depot picture. Cranwell was a happy place. Will you let me hear of their safe arrival in your hand?..This afternoon I am going out into the desert with some paraffin and the original draft, to make sure that no variant survives...So before you get it your copy will be unique...I want it offered to Cape, for publication, in extensor, without one word excised or moderated... and I want him to refuse it, so as to free me from the clause in his contract of the *Revolt in the Desert*, tying me to offer him another book. I hate being bound by even an imaginary obligation.

[Lawrence burned the original notes and the rough pencil draft of *The Mint* at Karachi, so that only Charlotte Shaw's corrected typescript and Garnett's fair copy survived. He had, however, already sent Garnett a single sheet of the original notes in their pasted up form. Lawrence had also sent a page of the rough pencil draft to Charlotte Shaw, which she preserved with his letters. Lawrence told Garnett on 22 March 1928 that Charlotte Shaw had seen a draft of *The Mint*].

Hugh Trenchard

[RAF Drigh Road, Karachi]

17.3.28

Lawrence had posted his RAF notes to Garnett. In Karachi he worked on his original notes for months until they were 'all out straightly' in a little note book of 176 words (70,000 words) called *The Mint*, because they were all being stamped after Trenchard's image and superscription. It was a worm's eye view of the RAF – a scrappy, uncomfortable thing.

Charlotte Shaw

[Karachi]

20.3.28

Lawrence discussed the Uxbridge notes. (Lawrence had sent a rough copy of *The Mint* to Mrs Shaw some weeks earlier). Parts of the notes had shocked him, as much as the original experiences they tried to mirror. The second part was worse than the first and only the third part, Cranwell, was sunny. The RAF was now his very own service and he learned to fit in and gave up his rights to personality.

[As early as March 1928 in a letter to Sergeant Pugh Lawrence mentioned the possibility of a film about his life 'in which they propose to put a travesty of my regrettable self', but nothing came of this.]

April 1928

Sergeant Pugh

[Karachi]

13.4.28

He seemed to have answered Pugh's query re Miss Brown of Purley who wanted a photo of Lawrence. Let her cut one out of the *Daily Mail*. These flappers! A publisher wrote and asked if he had any little poems that Lawrence would let him publish ('a hen might as well lay cabbages as me write poetry') because if so he would send Lawrence the latest Brough Superiors for the years 1928-29-30-31-32. Lawrence told him that he had no poems and Karachi had no roads.

May 1928

A.W. Lawrence

[Karachi]

2.5.28

Lawrence told his brother about the RAF notes which he sent to David Garnett. The copyright was Lawrence's for life and would pass to his heirs for 40 years after his death. These notes (*The Mint*) would not be published during his lifetime. And he hoped that his brother would not (without the permission of the Chief of Staff of the RAF) publish them before 1950. They were very obscene.

June 1928

[His second posting was to Miranshah in Waziristan near the Afghan border to which he transferred in June 1928. Without the prospect of seeing his peers, letters offered the only method of contact. He received so many letters that he could answer only a small proportion of them, but he also wrote some very lengthy replies to his favourite correspondents including Charlotte Shaw and Sergeant Pugh. This is the period of some of his most frank and revealing letters and his decision to change his name by deed poll to T.E. Shaw.]

Sergeant A. Pugh

RAF Detachment Miranshah

9/6/28

Lawrence described how this was more like 'B' Flight but their number was 'A'. He had a change of Commanding Officer every few weeks. This was part profit and part loss. At Cranwell it would have been a dead loss. At Karachi it would have been a gain. Miranshah was very quiet and remote, which he liked, but he lacked music and books. If Mrs Shaw and the others sent him as many books as they used to send to Cranwell the local library could not hold them all. Miranshah was 300 feet up and cool with the temperature not over 100 at midsummer. But in winter it could be as cold as Cranwell.

David Garnett

Miranshah Fort, Waziristan

14.6.28

The Mint? Why I wrote it back in 1922. It feels incredibly far off...I should have written *an agony* after the Title: only for the third part, which is not unhappy. Actually the RAF is excellent living:- sometimes. Here, for example, and at Cranwell. I look back on Cranwell's eighteen months as the happiest I've ever spent....

Old Lincoln (the Steep Street is, or was, Ermine Street) delighted me. The cathedral, as you saw, I did not like. Yet perhaps its only because it succeeds too well. I do not think it disappoints as much as it chills. We come to it expecting to be chered: and it tells us that we are no good at all. (Reigius excepted: the Norman arches and the font, and the organ tones are lovely.

August 1928

E.M. Forster

Miranshah

6.8.28

Dear E.M.F.

Your wonderful letter about *The Mint* has given me about eight readings of unalloyed pleasure, so far. It is a gift that, of mine, of being able to read so loosely that I can go on reading a thing for time after time, and enjoy it always. Now I am going to read it again, time 9.

150

No, it is properer to write and thank you for it. It is just like the letter of one writer to another. Marvellous, that you and I should be on such apparent terms. I looked up to you for years as a distant but impeccable star. Now you are no further from me than the thickness of this sheet of notepaper, and my reluctance to cover it with black marks... and not impeccable, since I have found your critical judgement partial to my imperfections. However perhaps I am your blind spot.

Do not swoon with the eccentricity of this typing. I am doing it in the dark, and there is not a bell to ring at the end of lines. I only turn over when it stops on the far side. And I cannot feel with my finger-tips exactly where I am striking the keys.

The (Hitherto) youngest Garnett wrote me a most queer letter (it was a quite absurdly laudatory letter, too: only so queer. More like a woman than a man) about *The Mint* (forgive my egoism in talking about it all the time. To write an unpublished book is to hear nothing, except from you and the Garnetts and the Shaws, what sort of book it is... and one does wonder, you know). He said it was a study in pain, and that it had hurt him; I did not think it very horrible anywhere. Now there were things I did write about the Tank Corps which were horrible... but *The Mint* is not abysmally cruel or crude. Surely not. You get on the side I'd like to stand, when you deduce from it that cruelty is not universal, nor basic in humankind. I am sure it is not.

You put the first and second parts before the third, as writing. I am interested by that word. Every night in Uxbridge I used to sit in bed, with my knees drawn up under the blankets, and write on a pad the things of the day. I tried to put it all down, thinking that memory and time would sort them out, and enable me to select significant from insignificant. Time passed, five years and more (long enough, surely for memory to settle down?) and at Karachi I took up the notes to make a book of them... and instead of selecting, I fitted into the book, somewhere and somehow, every single sentence I had written at Uxbridge.

Now tell me. Did my mind select at the time... or is there no truth that art is selection... or does my book lack selection. Is the whole affair there, and the trees cluttered up by redundant twigs and blossoms?

I wrote it so tightly, because our clothes are so tight, and our lives so tight in the service. There is no freedom of conduct at all. Wasn't I right? G.B.S. calls it too dry, I believe. I put in little sentences of landscape (the Park, the Grass, the Moon) to relieve the shadow of servitude, sometimes. For service fellows there are no men on earth, except other service fellows... but we do see trees and star-light and animals, sometimes. I wanted to bring out the apartness of us.

You wanted me to put down the way I left the R.A.F., and something about the Tanks. Only I still feel miserable at the time I missed because I was thrown out that first time. I had meant to go to a Squadron, and write the real Air Force, and make it a book - a BOOK, I mean. It is the biggest subject I have ever seen, and I thought I could get it, as I felt is so keenly. But they broke all that in me, and I have been damaged ever since. I could never again recover the rhythm that I had learned at Uxbridge, resisting Stiffy... and so it would not be true to reality if I tried to vamp up some yarn of it all now. The notes go to the last day of Uxbridge, and there stop abruptly.

The Cranwell part is, of course, not a part, but scraps. I had no notes for it... any more than I am ever likely to have notes of any more of my R.A.F. life. I'm it, now, and the note season is over. The Cadet college part was vamped up, really, as you say, to take off the bitterness, if bitterness it is, of the Depot pages. The Air Force is not a man-crushing humiliating slavery, all its days. There is sun and decent treatment, and a very real measure of happiness, to those who do not look forward or back. I wanted to say this, not as propaganda, out of fairness, the phrase which pricked up your literary ears, but out of truthfulness. I set out to give a picture of the R.A.F., and my picture might be impressive and clever if I showed only the shadow of it... but I was not making a work of art, but a portrait. If it does surprisingly happen to be literature (I do not believe you there: you are partially kind) that will be because of its sincerity, and the Cadet college parts are as sincere as the rest, and an integral part of the R.A.F.

Of course I know and deplore the scrappiness of the last chapters: that is the draw-back of memory, of a memory which knew it was queerly happy then, but shrank from digging too deep into the happiness, for fear of puncturing it. Our contentments are so brittle, in the ranks. If I had thought too hard about Cranwell, perhaps I'd have found misery there too. Yet I assure you that it seems all sunny, in the back view.

Of Cadet College I had notes. Out of letters on Queen Alexandra's Funeral (Garnett praises that. Shaw says its the meanness of a guttersnipe laughing at old age. I was so sorry and sad at the poor old queen), for the hours on guard, for the parade in the early morning. The Dance, the Hangar, Work and the rest were written at Karachi. They are reproductions of scenes which I saw, or things which I felt and did... but two years old, all of them. In other words, they are technically on a par with the manner of *The Seven Pillars*; whereas the Notes were photographs, taken day by day, and reproduced complete, though not at all unchanged. There was not a line of the Uxbridge notes left out; but also not a line unchanged.

The only photographic chapter of *The Seven Pillars* was the account of the tribal feasts, in Wadi Sirhan, when we stuffed meat and rice till we were sick. For that I had photographic notes, which only required rearranging. I wrote *The Mint* at the rate of about four chapters a week, copying each chapter four or five times, to get it into final shape. Had I gone on copying, I should only have been restoring already crossed our variants. My mind seems to congest, after reworking the stuff several times.

To insist that they are notes is not side-tracking. The Depot section was meant to be quite a short introduction to the longer section dealing with the R.A.F. in being, in flying work. Events killed the longer book: so you have the introduction, set out at greater length.

'You hadn't, that is to say, communicated your happiness to me' - nor convinced my rational side of it. The happiness is real: but sensory, only, I think.

'*The Mint* is not so great a work as *The Seven Pillars*':- but possibly better, as Garnett thinks. It is so tiny a theme and work; perhaps I have a cherry-stone talent. *The Seven Pillars* is a sort of introspection epic, you know: and it would have taken a big writer to bring it off.

'There seems no reason why you shouldn't write all sorts of books'. Why, I feel as dry as a squeezed orange. I do not think it is at all likely that I will ever be moved to write anything again. *The Mint* dates from 1922, when I hadn't looked back in cold blood at *The Seven*

Pillars, and seen how they fell short of my fancied achievement. Too ambitious, the little soul was: and so he's come a fearful cropper.

There are now women free in Waziristan to explore: so that point does not yet arise. 1930 before I come home. 1935 (if I am lucky) before I get thrown out of the R.A.F... and then I have a promise of a job, as night-watchman in a City Bank. So life is all mapped out safely, for long enough ahead.

It is good to feel a little safe. Often I get sorry over all the chances of money I have thrown away. One does need money, to the bread and butter point, to keep one's behaviour decent.

The Mint mustn't be published till after 1950... when it will be so stale that nobody will much want to publish it. The new point of view, to which you (surprisingly... for I did not know there was one) allude, will be old, by then.

More and more thanks. You have given me vast and unalloyed pleasure.

T.E.S.

October 1928

<u>Corporal Trevarthan</u>

[This letter was donated to Cranwell College Library by Corporal Trevarthan's daughter, Mrs K. Pearce, on 29 October 2001].

Miranshah

16.X.28

Dear Corporal

We are all happy here. It is a good detachment. The cooking is [?] night off. He has two of everything and would go three, if the flesh wasn't so weak.

Also he and Corporal Stone have had three days each in dock with fever. I ran stores: the stores also ran, as Corporal Leitch says.

No rifle parades: we do not march to work. We breakfast and then trickle down. Mr Smethan is a treat. He has asked Wing to wash out guards: Wing replied that the Wing Commander was away.

So it not true that very shortly a lorry comes up from you to us? I'm still worrying about my hot bath. The weather here is getting chilly. What is needed is a drum. Have you any, not on charge? At Depot I had a 15 gallon Dope drum: that was very good: but it's the sort of thing only found at Depots. A petrol drum (4 gallon) would do: or two four-gallon oil cans, which I could have stuck together by the coppersmith for whom I rely on. Sergeant Major Bushen. I am sure he will want a coppersmith for that [?]

May I remind you also of my overalls? They could come up by lorry, too, I expect.

[?] sends his live. Corporal Stone is in Bannu, to check a broken case of photographic goods.

Au revoir

TES

5 Sqdn were much in credit on last month's messing. So we forgot about your C.R.A.s ? Tick?

[The news of a revolution in Afghanistan combined with the fact that he was based only ten miles from the Afghan border led to sensational stories in the British press claiming that he was actively involved. The Air Ministry acceded to the request of the Government of India that he should be removed from the sub-continent as soon as possible. Trenchard was prepared to offer him a posting in Aden or Samililand but Lawrence opted to come home.

When Lawrence returned to England in 1929 he was posted to RAF Cattewater (Plymouth) where he became close friends with the Commanding Officer Sydney Smith and his wife Clare. Lawrence was one of the RAF support team involved in the races for the Schneider Cup and he helped to design fast modern air-sea rescue boats. This took him to Southampton, Cowes in the Isle of Wight, Felixstowe and Bridlington. Apart from his time at Carchemish and to a lesser extent at Cranwell these were, on the whole, his happiest years. He was also happy in extending the circle of his friends including Lady Astor, Henry Williamson and Frederic Manning].

November 1928

Charlotte Shaw

[27 November 1928]

Two years after he left Cranwell he referred to his 15 months there as one of the two golden periods of his life (the other was Carchemish).

February 1929

Ernest Thurtle

14 Barton Street, Westminster

9/2/29

Lawrence was told very distinctly that his visit to the House of Commons to meet Thurtle (Labour MP for Shoreditch) was not approved. Lawrence had been delighted, by lending Thurtle his two books, to give himself away completely. Lawrence asked Thurtle to be uncommonly discreet over *The Mint*, the RAF book.

March 1929

F.L. Lucas

RAF Cattewater Plymouth

26.3.29

Lawrence was interested that Lucas felt the RAF (*The Mint*) was less 'big' than the Arab Revolt (*Seven Pillars*). Of course it was not. Damascus and Cranwell were different, but if Cranwell felt less then that was because it had been less well conceived and written down.

Others besides Lucas had been troubled by the gap between the Uxbridge Depot and Cranwell Cadet College. He was very unhappy at Farnborough and decided not to put it on record. From the Tanks he returned for three days to Uxbridge and went thence to Cranwell which gave him the chance to carry the story straight through. He could have expanded the 'explanation' (in *The Mint*) into greater length and detailed the Farnborough and Tank Corps digressions. He had some raw notes but they were pretty grim reading.

He was glad that Lucas felt the difference between Cadet College & Depot. EM Forster had said that Cadet College didn't come through as a happy place. Lawrence had re-read the manuscript and was inclined to disagree with him. It seemed to contain better 'bits' than the first two parts. No doubt they were too 'bitty': a whole Cadet College would be longer than Depot. He was always apart and intact but to see another airman in the street was like one ship sighting another at sea.

February 1930

Frederic Manning

[William Rothenstein, *T.E. Lawrence by His Friends*: 'Then there was Frederic Manning. Lawrence, who seemed to have read everything, knew Manning's *Scenes and Portraits* almost by heart. Like Max Beerbohm, he thought this book contained the strongest and subtlest prose of recent times. I have already described elsewhere how the two met (*Men and Memories*, Vol.II); how Lawrence, eager to interest Manning, started to talk again and again of his Arabian days, and was interrupted each time by Manning, equally anxious to talk of himself. This was the only occasion on which I knew Lawrence ready to spread his peacock tail; but he was not given the chance.'

Lawrence wrote to Rothenstein: 'Wasn't it delightful to find Manning coming out so suddenly as a real flesh and blood figure. Beautiful as are *Scenes and Epicures*' – he means *Scenes and Portraits* – 'ever so much more worthwhile is *Her Privates We*.']

[In October 1915, Manning enlisted in the 7th Battalion of the King's Shropshire Light Infantry. Ten years after the Great War, Manning wrote his classic account of ordinary infantrymen serving on the Western Front. It first appeared anonymously as *The Middle Parts of Fortune: Somme and Ancre.* In January 1930 an expurgated version in one volume appeared under the title *Her Privates We* by Private 19022. Lawrence wrote to David Garnett:

'*Her Privates We* knocked me all of a heap with delight. It's the true and honourable thing, so far as the "other ranks" are concerned. I never thought to see it. That's what my little *Mint* should have been and wasn't'.

Manning wrote to Lawrence from Edenham, Bourne, in Lincolnshire on 7 March 1922. This is possibly the earliest correspondence between them. The friendship was not to be renewed until the 1930s. Manning retired to comparative seclusion at Bourne, the place which gives its name to the hero of *Her Privates We.* Following its publication, Lawrence made contact with Manning after an eight year interval.]

[25 February 1930]

The airmen are reading the *Privates* avidly...Everyone to whom I write is loudly delighted with the *Privates*...Of course I'm ridiculously partial to it, for since 1922 my home has been in the "ranks" and Bourne says and thinks lots of the things I wanted to have said.

March 1930

Frederic Manning

[21 March 1930]

I have read it [*Her Privates We*] once more since last time, and everybody in the hut seems to have read it. You see, I live cheek by cheek with the privates. They are very honest and cleanly people, I fancy. If I can get my copy of it back, I'll try to persuade you to look at some notes I made in 1922 upon life in the RAF as a recruit. I wasn't cheerful like Bourne but had a rotten time, and so my story is dismal: only I think it is true as far as it goes.

May 1930

Frederic Manning

[15 May 1930]

After the Arab business I rather foreswore saddles. The RAF is a socket in which I fit safely; after many tribulations, as you will discover if P.D[avies] lets you read my *Mint* which describes how the Air Force rounds off its pegs to fit into their holes.

[Manning made his eagerness to read the typescript of *The Mint* known to Lawrence].

June 1930

Frederic Manning

[24 June 1930]

The Mint shall be sent to you, when it is presentably printed by P.D's care: for that I need to make £100...and the summer is too rare to waste at a table.

August 1930

<u>Frederic Manning</u>

[It was Lawrence's intention to arrange a very limited printing of *The Mint* and he received an estimate from Peter Davies of £120 for 12 copies]

[7 August 1930]

I have had a disappointment over those RAF notes of mine...suddenly I realised how scrappy and arty and incompetent they are. They are not worth printing: which is fortunate for I am no nearer the £120 that the printing of twelve copies was to cost.

[Manning replied to Lawrence on 13 August 1930: 'I should be enormously interested to see *Mint* in type-script, however greatly I may deplore the decision not to print...On the other hand, I do not see why you should spend £120 to print 12 copies for a gift to your friends: it is quite enough for you to give them the book.'

When Manning reissued *Scenes and Portraits* in a second edition, a further essay entitled 'Apologia Dei' was included, dedicated to T.E. Shaw.

Manning wrote to Lawrence again on 29 October 1930: 'The child I am fathering on you ['Apologia Dei'] has gone to the printer...You have broken faith with me about *Mint*, or so I think; but perhaps you were only waiting until I had disentangled myself from the divine mysteries of creation. Well, God bless you in all your ways *Mint or no Mint*. As I put the last words to the 'Apologia Dei' yesterday they fired a royal salute in the Park. Wasn't it nice of them?']

June 1931

<u>Charlotte Shaw</u>

26/VI/31

Lawrence commented on the request by the Cadet College at Cranwell for a lecture from George Bernard Shaw. Reputations had changed. Lawrence imagined GBS before a Service audience twenty years ago and laughed.

January 1932

<u>Frederic Manning</u>

[Manning's correspondence with Lawrence was punctuated by his disability and deteriorating state of health and he spent considerable periods of time convalescing abroad].

[2 January 1932]

Time has made you very nomadic. Do you go back to The Bull, at Bourne?...It seems queer, to imagine you in that spot, which used to be just a slowing down on my trips from Cranwell to London. One used to close throttle outside Bourne, for the turn in its wide road.

[At the time of his death, Lawrence's Clouds Hill library contained all the published works by Frederic Manning including his Life of *Sir William White, Pioneer of Naval Architecture* inscribed 'To T.E. Shaw from Frederic Manning, 20.11.32.]

June 1933

George Brough

East Cowes, 13.6.33

I read the article in the *Motor Cycle* and was disappointed. That is no way to taste the merits of a B.S. By the way, did you ever see the note of a ride to Lincoln from Cranwell that I gave to the RAF College magazine a year or two ago? It was more my notion of what Broughing should be. Captain de la Bere, the Editor, would probably show you the article, if you asked him nicely. I did not keep a copy...Ten years ago (nearly) I wrote a set of articles on the joys of riding – but the *Motor Cycle* would not have them. This is the survivor.'

November 1933

K.W. Marshall

[17 November 1933]

[The November 1933 issue of the *British Legion Journal* contained an article called 'Service Life', which Lawrence was alleged to have contributed. In reality, the text had been taken from three of the Cranwell chapters in *The Mint*. These had been sent in to the journal by someone who had been allowed to read the typescript without Lawrence's knowledge. The RAF authorities were very angry, and feared that some of the less acceptable Uxbridge chapters might also find their way into print. Lawrence wrote:]

I've got into awful trouble: with the Air Ministry, for publishing opinions about service matters without permission – with Lord Trenchard, for publishing part of *The Mint* against my most solemn promise to keep it private till 1950 at least – Jonathan Cape, for piece meal disclosure of matter upon which they hold an option. In fact my name is mud, everywhere, and I may be civvy next week because of it...They all want me to let the police follow it up – and that would mean courts and reports.

[Eventually, the matter was smoothed over without any further action, and the *British Legion Journal* published an apology in a later issue.]

Rupert De La Bere

[Professor at Royal Air Force Cadets College, Cranwell]

13 Birmingham Street, Southampton

26.xi.33

Dear Prof., Yours is the unkindest cut of all! What has happened is briefly this:-

Twelve years ago I wrote some notes on the RAF Depot...and in 1925 I added a word on Cranwell and sent it to Trenchard. A 'book' of 80,000 words, only notes: no continuity or development. To Trenchard I faithfully promised that it should not be published.

Various people have read it (Sir John Salmond holds it now): one chapter was sent by me to your *Journal* – an innocuous chapter.

[This refers to chapter 16 of *The Mint* titled 'The Road'. Renamed 'Ramping', Lawrence sent this chapter to Rupert de la Bere on 8 October 1930, for publication in the *Journal of the Royal Air Force College* over the initials 'J.C.' It was published in the Spring 1931 issue of the *Journal*].

An Irishman is lent the script by a friend of his to whom a friend of mine had without telling me lent it...sub-loan upon sub-loan. "Hot stuff" says the Irishman and copies...how much of it? God knows...but the *Legion Journal* is then sent a précis of the last three chapters by him, and comes out with a mash of it as an article by me.

Thunder from the Commissioner of Police [Trenchard]: from the Air Ministry...my head astonished but unbowed. The *Legion Journal* apologises next month. The Irishman has left his rooms – no address – and is laughing, probably. I am the poorer by three chapters, a visit to London, seven stamps (no, eight now) and three telegrams.

So the *RAF College Journal* will *not* reprint it. In its mangled form it does not appeal to its author! Conceit, that is. Probably it is better in petto.

Has Dunn told you he has found a publisher? Good for him. Garnett called the stuff pretty good. I saw D. in his Squadron at Lympne: very amusing. He was like a slightly irascible bantam-cock in a large harem of hens – who looked up or down to him with vast fluttering respect. From the officers I gathered that he keeps *them* in order, too. Only the adjutant escapes criticism, so long as he gives D. Dual and plenty of it! Yours

TES

Philip Sassoon, Evan Charteris and I spent a giddy afternoon in the cellars of the Tate Gallery, choosing pictures for Cranwell. Chambers of horrors, littered with *worse* pictures than those on show! We got to twenty (it must be a large college) and then felt faint. I hope you don't get them all. We nearly sent you one of myself in blue uniform, looking very bad tempered. You could have labelled it 'Cadet College 1925-1926'!

May 1934

George Brough

Southampton, 3.5.34

'I was in Wolverhampton for a while, looking at some engines of Henry Meadows – and at Lincoln before that. So I took the chance of passing near Nottingham to look in (during a beastly wet day, of course) and see the new marvel being born. It looks most promising – and most expensive. I shall be broke but happy. Please take your time over it. The old hack has done only 20,000 miles, and is running splendidly.'

[The 'old hack' was George VII which TEL had ridden since March 1932. This was to be Lawrence's final Brough motorcycle on which he died in May 1935.]

July 1934

Frederic Manning

[Manning spent a considerable time in Australia, eventually leaving for England on 11 April 1934].

[25 July 1934]

I shall come to Bourne for soon I am to collect a new motor bike from Nottingham which is next door to Bourne. It was to have been tomorrow, but is now postponed, for a fortnight or more. That gives you nice time and go and come: for it is almost sure to be a month. Your return to England makes it feel, somehow, better furnished!

October 1934

Florence Hardy

[Written on the back of a letter from R. De la Bere, Professor of English at Cranwell, as the best way of getting a boy into the College. Lawrence had evidently written to him to get this information for Mrs Hardy.]

13 Birmingham Street, Southampton

19.X.34

Dear Mrs Hardy

De la Bere is 'Professor of English' at Cranwell, the RAF Cadet College. I wrote to him weeks ago about your nephew, the 'Master Hardy' of this reply, and am sorry to be so slow in getting the result. I am away almost constantly, now, and find it more and more difficult to deal with necessary letters.

I think it is a good letter, with information in it for the Dorchester schoolmaster and yourself. De la Bere will continue it, if more is needed.

Yours sincerely

T.E. Shaw

November 1934

Frederic Manning

[In November 1934, Lawrence was posted to the Marine Craft Detachment at Bridlington, East Yorkshire. He wrote to Manning, almost certainly the last letter his friend was to receive from him].

Ozone Hotel, Bridlington

16.XI.34

Alas you see, it never came off. My visits to Cranwell and Nottingham were postponed and then came a sudden transfer to this unfashionable winter resort.

[Manning's last letter to Lawrence is dated 21 December 1934 and carried the usual season's greetings. When Manning returned to Bourne after a visit to London he fell seriously ill with influenza and was admitted to the Butterfield Hospital in Bourne. He recovered, but had not long been back at 'Gleneden', his home in Bourne, when he caught pneumonia. His doctor sent him for treatment in London where he died on 22 February 1935.

Lawrence had been due to retire from the RAF on 25 February, but had actually left five days earlier because he had not used up his full leave entitlement. He had left Bridlington by bicycle, travelling slowly southward in the direction of Dorset and Clouds Hill. He meant to call on friends on his way, and his first stop was at the RAF Staff College at Cranwell. Here was a particular friend, Rupert de la Bere, the Professor of English and History whom Lawrence had helped to edit the Staff College Journal. After this, Lawrence had gone to Cambridge, to visit his brother at the University].

February 1935

Peter Davies

[28 February 1935]

On Tuesday I took my discharge from the RAF and started southward by road, meaning to call at Bourne and see Manning: but today I turned eastward instead, hearing that he was dead.

[William Rothenstein, *T.E. Lawrence by His Friends*: 'It was over Manning's death I last heard from Lawrence. When Manning died in early 1935, there was no obituary notice in *The Times*. I drew the Editor's attention to this neglect and telephoned a short notice to the office, at the same time telegraphing to Lawrence, urging him to follow up the lines which were printed. Not only did I receive no answer, but Lady Manning complained of Lawrence's silence. I again wrote, addressing my letter to Mrs. Hardy's care, and this time heard from Lawrence in terms which were strangely foreboding.']

May 1935

William Rothenstein

Clouds Hill, Moreton, Dorset

5.V.35

Dear W.R.,

Manning died as I was on my way to Bourne, to visit him. I turned off and rode down here. Your two letters came. Between them I had to go to London and I called at Airlie Gardens: vainly, as usual. I suppose you are still chained to your College. Now Mrs. Hardy has sent me your last note. I am sorry to appear so remiss; but my discharge from the R.A.F. (which had to come) has rather done me in, so that I no longer have the mind or wish to do anything at all. I just sit here in this cottage and wonder about nothing in general. Comfort is a very poor state after busyness.

As for Manning, I cannot say how sad the news made me. He was a lovely person, and it is hateful to see him go out, unfinished. But gone he very definitely is. It makes one feel as though nothing can matter very much.

If I come to London again soon I shall ring your bell once more. Patience will tell, in the end. Only I do not expect to come up yet awhile.

Yours ever

T.E. Shaw

[He had written previously to Rothenstein in a similar spirit. 'It is a sorrowful thing when a Hogarth, Hardy or G.B.S. dies; but it satisfies another facet of my mind. It's all over and they are out of it without failure; we are safe with them. Men run about always on the edge of the precipice and when they are safely dead we breathe again; if we have cared for them.'

A fortnight after getting the letter about Manning, Lawrence himself lay dead at a military hospital in Dorset.']

Postscript

As well as Lawrence's letters and *The Mint*, we also have other contemporary accounts by Leslie Webb, Rupert de la Bere, and Sergeant Pugh who all served with Lawrence at Cranwell.

There are also the letters from Lawrence to his biographers, Robert Graves and Liddell Hart, which reference *The Mint* and the Cranwell years.

In addition, a number of articles have been written about Lawrence's time at RAF Cranwell, including: Peter Gray, *Lawrence of Arabia's Lincolnshire Posting* (1996); Leonard Rivett, *Lawrence of Arabia - Ross and Shaw in the Royal Air Force* (1996); and Allan Warburton, *A Legend in Hiding* (1996).

Sergeant Pugh: *Lawrence and the Arabs* (1927)

The account of Sergeant Pugh's time with Lawrence at Cranwell was recorded by Robert Graves in *Lawrence and the Arabs* (1927).

Lawrence was asked by Graves to comment on this biography, including the section by Sergeant Pugh, and these comments were included in *T.E. Lawrence to his Biographer Robert Graves*, published in 1938.

Robert Graves, *Lawrence and the Arabs*: 'Sergeant Pugh, of his Flight at Cranwell, in Lincolnshire has written me a letter about Shaw in the RAF, which I print as it stands.'

The amendments by Lawrence to Graves are given in square brackets for deletions and *italics* for additions.

Arrival at Cranwell

As far as my mind takes me back, it was in the first week of September 1925 that he came to the camp, and although many had heard of his 'carrying-on', few had seen him. He was met with all kinds of looks (suspicious): was he finding out who's who and what's what of the RAF? Is that why he was discharged previously? (amazement): we had heard he was a man with a terrible scowl of harshness, etc., etc. (wrath): he is some ex-service guy pulling our legs; and yet! You know his carriage, slight, mild, unassuming, why did he set the camp alive in excitement just to see him?

First Fatigue (I was taking names)

Perhaps a dozen men were to have a 'go' at cleaning the camp fire buckets. Taking names (you know why) he happened to be the first on the roll and, asked his name, promptly sprang to attention, giving his particulars. The second and third names were taken before the S.M. snapped at those two for not doing likewise and commented on the fact that S. had shown them his military training, by saying 'take an example of Shaw, you are letting yourselves down' and possibly stronger words were used. (His start at one told.) Having occasion to call

163

and view the work in progress (and between you and me to get a good 'close up' of this man nobody could weigh up), there he was with bath brick, polishing and rubbing as though his life depended on the result (eagerness personified) and laughing his heart out in some crude joke of his work mate; an aircraftman of, to say the best, poor intellect who stood by while our friend grinned and worked.

Credit from the Tank Corps

It soon flashed through the camp that he was in credit to the tune of £50 from the Tank Corps and at 'stand easy' when ordering tea and cakes from the canteen, he asked for about four or five extra teas and wads (cakes). Asking a few of the (secretly scrutinising) airmen to 'muck in,' at least three 'lots' were left in sheer wonder and almost embarrassment; smiles and expressions, 'Deep B.' Etc., being used.

Church

Our camp church he liked – that was all. Always a true soldier preparing for and marching to same, when his turn for it came along. But it was a d-d shame that men of the calibre he went with, should be compelled to listen to the 'something rot' that they were attending; for Sermons were not Shaw's strong point. Generosity itself for a just cause. Apparent stupidity (which was amusing to all who 'eyed him') for any cause concerning his presence in the above mentioned place of worship. Politics clashed with divinity – Shaw's view.

S. joins up in RAF Second Time

An amusing item was told of his second admission to the RAF. All recruits must pass an educational test before admission. S. had to do a paper of a visit to some place or other and accomplished this with such speed, tact and general show of a born author, that the Officer i/C. asked him why he came to join up and yet could turn out his 'stuff' with so much apparent ease. His reply was 'Chiefly a mental rest,' which took the wind completely out of the officer's sails, and yet the mask of mildness on his face floated him clear of trouble.

[Lawrence, *T.E. Lawrence to his Biographer*: 'This rejoining yarn really was rather funny. I went up to West Grayton, in RTC uniform, to transfer. For educational test they gave me an essay (on my favourite game or some such rot). I wrote the necessary few perfunctory sentences, just to show that I was able to read and write. The examining officer read it, looked at my name, looked puzzled, called me out: said "Have you been in the RAF before?" "Yes Sir." "Some years back?" "Yes Sir." "Under another name?" "Yes Sir" "Did you then write an entrance essay on your native place?" I gave up, completely floored. The fellow had remembered it all those years, without any knowledge that I had any particular history behind me. It's the greatest literary compliment I've ever been paid.']

A lot of heart to heart talk took place about various authors to whom he might apply for a job. Finally he was shown a list of RAF trades and I swear he would tackle the lot in turn and decided to be a full blown Air Craft Hand, which means he does all kinds of fatigues and is treated as though he were a mere nothing in uniform.

'B' Flight, Cranwell

Being posted to 'B' Flight and the way he behaved during his stay was worth a guinea a box. Every conceivable kind of job was put before S. as the office 'boy' of our flight. (I could give you a real good list of his duties which he was to do.) He had every job well mastered in a week and 'taped' for any clerk who might follow. Our Flight Lieutenant took to S. and at once realised the asset he must mean to the flight. What 'got him' was that S. had more power for getting things than he had himself. (I'm speaking dead honestly now.) He did not on any occasion ever let anyone think that what was given at all was given through thoughts of what he might do or say. His sheer force of personality got him, as you may say, undreamed of odds and ends necessary for us in our work, which seemed unattainable to any Sergeant to say the most, and never an aircraft hand. To know him was to be drawn by his magnetic personality and the heavens fell through, that alone is what made the airmen scratch their heads and THINK.

A Gramophone was bought

There is a good story on its own. A beautiful machine with Records. At first we held aloof wondering what class of music appealed to S. – Mozart, Beethoven, Tannhauser? (excuse my ignorance of the classical variety). It left us guessing, but we soon woke up to the fact that he pulled our legs by ordering some of the most awful sounding records possible to get, yet his face was a blank. Should we laugh? Moan? Or what? That broke all the ice barrier of wondering which had built up between the airmen.

He Starts

No clock was ever made to beat S. for awaking when he wanted, be it any hour. How was it done? Sailors they say do manage it, but at regular intervals. With S. any time was his time. But always before reveille. Baths are his god. He bribed the 'civvie' stoker to attend to the fires for his bathing 'Saloon' before the others; and to see him enjoy a real Turkish variety, gradually cooling to D. Cold, was to know when a man is happy. Duty compelled me to have a week of his routine before 6 am. So this is authentic. Bath is S.s' second name.

To show there is no ill feeling he starts one of the most appalling records on the market and to hear the various good humoured grumblings of the flight will send S. in fits of laughter. 'Onward Christian Soldiers' was his weak or strong point. National Anthem he reserved for medical inspection in the huts on Mondays. Rude but true. A rather sleepy (at the night time) sailor, whom S. loved to tease was presented by him, S., to a most glorious hand knitted pair of pink woollen bed socks. He had them specially made in our Town.

Broughs

S. had a Brough-Superior 1926 model. You might call that machine his house. To see him ride was enough. To see that baby on a machine like that at speed made the population gasp. Brough junior says that he is the opposite number to his 'bus' – 'Two Superiors.' An insight concerning both is the following:

[The following account differs materially from the original manuscript printed by Garnett in *The Letters of T.E. Lawrence*, p. 495]

Out riding one summer evening, he came across a smash up between a car (driven by an oldish man) and a pedestrian. When the unconscious pedestrian had been [safely disposed of] *stowed in the back of the car for carriage to hospital*. S. was asked to swing the car for the old boy. Nervousness and excitement caused [him] *the driver* to leave the ignition fully advanced and on S. swinging the starting handle flew back and broke S.'s right arm. Without so much as a sign to show what had taken place S. asked if he would mind retarding the offending lever, and swung the car with his left hand. After the car was at a safe distance, S. got *an AA Scout* [a man] to 'kick over' his Brough, and with his right arm dangling and changing gear with his foot S. got his bus home and parked without a word to a soul of the pain he was suffering. Through some unknown reason the MO was away [for over an hour] *and it was next morning* before his arm could be 'done'. That is a man – S., I mean.

[Lawrence, *T.E. Lawrence to his Biographer*: 'It was not set till next morning as a matter of fact].

 S. had intended doing a 'pull off' from an aeroplane with me and descending by parachute. Unfortunately his arm spoiled it for the pair of us. (Personally, I was relying on his personality to get permission for the 'drop'), so you see how everyone 'fell' for him through his ways. Have served a little while in the RAF but never before have I seen a man refuse to go to Hospital with a broken arm. Yet S. did and 'got away with it'. Having after 10 days got into the style of writing with his left hand, the good work went on. His skill and supervision in his position astounded one and all. He will want to cancel this but let me tell you as his friend that his broken arm was the 33rd broken bone he had at various times, including 11 ribs.

[Lawrence, *T.E. Lawrence to his Biographer*: '? I've lost count, myself'.]

The last sentence must be known whether he approves or not. In his book *Seven Pillars of Wisdom* he mentions a fact about his capture by a Turkish officer and his treatment under his captor's hands. A bayonet has been forced after two attempts between his ribs – those scars are on his body still and are very noticeable at once when he is stripped.

'Office Boy'

As previously stated S. carried out every duty, job or any mortal thing that came his way with amazing speed and accuracy that often we wondered at his reserve power which pointed him out as differently as though he was miles above our standard at anything we tackled. His letters were the joke of the flight, because at every post something or other turned up. Am convinced that had he been given more spare time, the load of letters would not have been littered all over the trays, tables and pigeon holes – in fact they were everywhere. Mind you his kit was kit, but correspondence he could not keep in check. To see him sign a cheque on his book account (*Seven Pillars*) for a large amount, with his left hand after his accident, made me wonder what proof the bank held of the genuineness of the signature. They used to get through without a line or word of doubt.

Fires

S.'s job during cold weather would be to light the fires in the offices. Coal was usually difficult to obtain, but nothing would prevent the fires from being lighted. One day he pulled down a dead tree actually in the Air Officer Commanding's private plantation, walking past flights and offices till he reached the 'B' Flight, perspiring like a bull and all smiles. Anyone would think he walked about invisible. He invented a 'Shaw mixture' of old oil from aero engines, sawdust and coal dust and mixed it like mortar. So with his trees and mixture fires were kept roaring all day long.

Nights Out

Asked his idea of a good night out, he told me that to take a man *pillion* on his Brough to a decent town [and give him] *for* a good feed and general good time was OK to a limit. That limit was that his companion on those rides must *preferably* be [a man who had a criminal tendency] *mildly a ruffian*, for preference, and his pleasure was derived in studying the man's peculiarities unseen to the man himself.

[Lawrence, *T.E. Lawrence to his Biographer*: 'I prefer my modification. The other phrase means too much.]

'There are too many honest men in this world and a few more rogues would make the world a very interesting place.' Never sly, he would weigh up a cute scoundrel and gently smile at the result of his observation.

[Lawrence, *T.E. Lawrence to his Biographer*: 'Please modify this paragraph yet further, in which he describes my taking out for a trip, to Nottingham or somewhere, a fellow from the camp: on condition that he was more or less of a ruffian. I took out most of B Flight, one time and another: and they were all of them very decent fellows. Sergt. Pugh's note refers to a Corpl. in the Pay Section, whom I took out twice or thrice, as a reward for his looking after my credits, and backing them for me. Admitted he was a vulgar fellow: but I am interested in all sorts, and experienced enough to chance my arm against such. Don't let B Flight think I thought them rough or ruffianly. I liked them and admired them.]

[Graves, *Lawrence and the Arabs*: 'Shaw told me himself that he took out nearly all B Flight at one time or another: all very decent fellows, he said, whom he admired very much. Sergeant Pugh has made a joke read too seriously, I think.']

Promotion

At the beginning of each quarter a return is to be submitted stating the particulars of men recommended for promotion. Talking it over with the Flight Commander, he asked for S. to see if he had any views on the matter. S. emphatically refused to hear of any advance, a thing which made the Flight Commandant nearly curl up, laughing.

Night Riding

It sometimes took place that S. felt like a blind into the night, summer or winter, and would cover as many miles as safety permitted, arriving in camp dog tired and dirty yet cheery and stroll to the canteen for a couple of packets of 'Smith's Crisps' - chipped potatoes. That would invariably mean his supper. Yet he would be loaded up with food things for his room-mates. Fruit he loved, and would go a long way for a good apple. Other fruits he liked, but the best was the apple.

Offer of Air Officer Commanding

The Air Commodore at Cranwell offered S. his house for the purpose of spending Christmas, but no! He was an Aircraft hand and as I've said before he kept his place as such, never allowing anything to break him from his position in the RAF.

It seemed his sole purpose was to be an airman of the lowest grade and rank and to be left alone with his Brough at B Flight, Cranwell. He was hero worshipped by all the flight for his never failing cheery disposition, ability to get all he could for their benefit, never complaining, and his generosity to all concerned till at times it appeared that he was doing too much for everyone and all were out to do the best for him. Quarrels ceased and the flight had to pull together for the sheer joy of remaining in his company and being with him for his companionship, help, habits, fun and teaching one and all to play straight. He fathered us and left us a sorrowful crowd awaiting letters or his return.

Flying and Scrubbing

When opportunity permitted he made a point of flying with all the officers in the flight so that each knew him well and in my opinion were proud of the fact, the way they used to smile when he climbed in with them. Flying is a very old hobby of his but although he has crashed 7 times, still goe4s on. He even used to leave the office at times, shove overalls on, and away out into the hangar, scrubbing and washing machines down although there was never any need to do so. Just to feel that he could do any job that came along. The number of times he has corrected mistakes and styles of mine are innumerable but I'm afraid I've slipped back during his absence. His languages got us beat, although he would not shoot out anything out of lace unless asked, in that respect.

Scrounging

The hut table could be improved upon, so forthwith S. and a party went away with it to exchange it for a lovely one in the mess deck. He made his only mistake by taking one that was marked by birds, and was 'rumbled', but as usual got away with it. The Quartermaster was a good sort. S. said so.

S. has been known to lift all manner of articles for our use, sometimes going so far as to speak to the victim and walk away with anything he fancied would be of use to us. Never for himself.

Coal

A good incident took place when the strike was on; all coal issues were stopped and B Flight had *only* a lot of coal dust and slack.

S.'s sheer cheek got to work, and calmly filling a huge bucket with dist he inquired the name of a Big officer who had stopped the issue. Walking point blank to his office, he *found that the officer had not stopped his own coal ration, so he* exchanged his load for some wonderful pieces of coal as big as himself. No one had found out who changed the dust yet. His comments were a broad grin and silence.

Civil Police

[Graves, *T.E. Lawrence to his Biographer*: 'Sergeant Pugh had given me the following note about Lawrence at Cranwell:]

He was [stopped by a 'copper' on point duty for furious driving] *held up on three separate occasions by the same 'copper' on point duty in a traffic muddle* in Town (Sleaford) and reported the matter to the Superintendent.

[Lawrence, *T.E. Lawrence to his Biographer*: 'For "Stopped for furious driving in the town (Sleaford)" – this has never happened to me. Read: "held up on three several occasions by the same constable on point duty in a traffic muddle:"]

He pointed out that police were the servants of the public, paid by the public, and he did not think that the 'copper' on point duty knew his job, that he was decidedly inefficient and a 'Swede' (Airman's term for villager). The Super. and S. had a grand argument, but S.'s eloquence floored the Super. And left him wondering what the RAF had enlisted. *That 'copper' is now permanently excused traffic control.*

[Lawrence, *T.E. Lawrence to his Biographer*: 'Add: "This constable is now permanently excused traffic control". But the point of this story will be lost on most of your readers: they do not know what cavalier treatment fellows in uniform receive, usually, at the hands of jacks in office. The Cranwell people were astounded that I was not arrested for making a protest at the inefficiency of a police constable. Government is the enemy of the poor.]

[Graves, *Lawrence and the Arabs*: 'The point of this story may be lost on most of my readers who are unaware of the cavalier treatment that men in uniform usually get at the hands of jacks-in-office. The Cranwell fellows were astonished that Shaw was not arrested for making a protest against the inefficiency of a police constable'.]

Air Display

He took all the flight and wives to Hendon by charabanc although I personally know that his ambition was to charter an Imperial Airways machine and 'do' it by air, but he was let down for a 'Kite' at the last minute.

Both going and coming he did not sit down for more than an hour, continually watching traffic and direction, and never turned a hair when the remainder slept or curled up, tired.

Jobs

On the summer holidays coming round he told us he had got the offer of a job as a Steward aboard a liner going to USA, but finally turned it down owing to work on his book. (Wish this had come off.)

A Visit

[He visited the Union Jack Club once just to try it.]

[Lawrence, *T.E. Lawrence to his Biographer*: 'As a matter of fact in London I usually stopped there.]

He used to Brough down to 'Smoke' (London) most Saturdays to look after his book being printed, sleeping at the Union Jack Club. One night it was full, but they shoved him in somewhere. He came back and gave us his views. He said what with sleeping in a dormitory with a drunken sailor one side and a 'blind' marine on the other there was nothing to do but swear.

[Graves, *Lawrence and the Arabs*: 'Here ends Sergeant Pugh's account'].

[Graves, *T.E. Lawrence to his Biographer*: 'The following additional notes were given me by Sergeant Pugh, but I did not use them in my book. They may be of interest here':]

Tate Art Gallery

On one occasion of leave he happened to walk into the above and stood by his portrait hanging in there. At the same time it was crowded with people, some admiring and some doing the other, which our man stood, looked, listened, smiled broadly and walked away. Such, as he said, is fame. On some later occasion he was invited to a private show of Art and his bust by Kennington stood on view. Admiral Beatty stood by and turning to Shaw said, 'What a horrible looking fellow'. Later he was introduced to Beatty! with curtains for the latter.

Tax Collectors

S. had not been here long before he had a letter from an Income Tax collector asking for the sum of £10 to be forwarded. S. thought for a few seconds, then he went to the Pay Office to have an allotment made out to the collector for the sum of 6d per week to be drawn at the post office and so pay off his amusing debt.

[Graves, *T.E. Lawrence to his Biographer*: 'Undated, and enclosed in the packet returning me my last batch of typescript:]

I thought Segt. Pugh's stuff great fun. I have changed a thing or two in it, for correctness sake, or to hide a name...

[Lawrence to Graves, *T.E. Lawrence to his Biographer* 1 October 1927:]

I got your letter with the prints of me on my 'bike', last Saturday. They shall be returned to Sergt. Pugh...

[Lawrence to Graves, *T.E. Lawrence to his Biographer* 7 December 1927]

Sergt. Pugh carries off great honour for his pages. I hope they will not get him a court-martial. I don't suppose anything will come to me of it...

Ruper de la Bere: 'Aircraftman T.E. Shaw in Lincolnshire' (1935)

Captain Rupert de la Bere was Professor of English at the Royal Air Force College, Cranwell, from 1921 to 1938. De la Bere did not contribute to *T.E. Lawrence by his Friends*, but an article he published in the Autumn 1935 issue of the *Journal of the Royal Air Force College* , 'Aircraftman T.E. Shaw, A Last Conversation', provides more information about this little known friendship. A version of this article, 'Aircraftman T.E. Shaw in Lincolnshire (A Last Conversation)' also appeared in *The Lincolnshire Magazine*, Vol. 2, No.7, Sept. – Oct. 1935:

'I had known Colonel Lawrence on and off for fifteen years. He was at Cranwell some years ago as an aircrafthand and he paid me a long visit at the College only a few weeks before his death. We all knew who he was when he served at Cranwell (as far as I recollect from 1922-26), and most of us respected his incognito.

We knew that he did not wish to mix with officers, because he wanted to avoid what was still in the front of their thoughts, and to forget certain beastly experiences recorded in his great book. He was happier in the light hearted conversation of young airmen, who had not known the dangers and discomfort of war. We bade him "good morning" when we passed him, but we never discussed anything that might bring back to him those memories. We used sometimes to speak to him at length, but it would be on service topics; we always treated him as if he were a conventional airman.

He once took, of his own free will, a most interesting part in a course I was giving to Officers at Cranwell, on Imperial Geography, and gave a discourse on the Middle East which will never be forgotten by those who heard it.

Once or twice I when wanted his advice on a point of scholarship, I used to write him a note. He would send me an elegant reply and when he was writing *The Seven Pillars of Wisdom* he sent me the printer's proof, in which I drew his attention to one or two small errors. I reproduce a copy of a letter [see below] in his fine writing in jet black ink, in which he allowed me to reproduce an extract, and in which he made some typical comments on the Desert Campaign.

I remember that the proof had been roughly bound by Lawrence himself, and on the outside he had written, mischievously, a title – *The Complete Aircrafthand*. This book he afterwards presented to the College Library. We bound it more suitably and, though anyone can read it, and many officers and cadets have availed themselves of the opportunity, we have insured it for £250, and keep it under lock and key. It is valuable, being unique owing to its amount of autograph. The text of the book is remarkable, incisive, clear, unsentimental. It is an amplified form of *The Revolt in the Desert*.

It was written by Lawrence in a room at Leadenham. It is written in the manner of Doughty, Burton and Philby, with that mastery of English which the desert seems to induce.

At Cranwell, Lawrence served in B Flight, and was of great assistance to Flight Lieutenant Green, his Flight Commander. He was, indeed, the complete Aircrafthand. His kit was always scrupulously clean, brightly polished and neatly turned out. In the Flight Office he was responsible for the tidiness of the room and the lighting of the fires. He kept the log books with meticulous care, to the joy of the Flight Officers, and he never shirked a fatigue. He was always scrupulously correct in his demeanour. I have seen him cheerfully sweeping out the Officers' Mess after dance. I have also seen him, during the interval in the morning, carrying about six cups of tea at once to his fellow airmen, a bit of conjuring done without that strain on the face habitual to conjurers and ventriloquists.

Indeed, the things I remember about him best were his conspicuous health and good cheer, which were an answer to those who rebuked his lowly status. I used to see him swinging along the station roads with a young orderly, the picture of happiness, both men at ease, talking hard. It was amusing to think that an Aircrafthand and a Fellow of All Souls could have so much in common. But Lawrence had something in common with everyone, and he entered the ranks just as in medieval times, many learned and successful men entered a monastery or an Order like the Templars.

He rode a speedy motorcycle and went at a dangerous rate. He was fond of the Lincolnshire roads. His motorcycle, an annual loan from the manufacturers, was a Brough Superior. On this bike he nearly killed himself while he was here, but was not at all perturbed. Indeed he made a remark to his rescuer which showed what little store he set by his life. Another day, in cranking a car, he broke his wrist, but without a word of complaint to the owner of the car, he went off to our Hospital and was treated by Wing Commander Huntley. As soon as Huntley had gone, Lawrence walked out of the hospital, much to the alarm and despondency of the staff. The reason he gave was that he could not stand the constriction of the ward; he suffered from claustrophobia, and wanted to return at once into the open air or bigger rooms.

After Lawrence left Cranwell, I did not see him for some years, although we exchanged quite a number of letters, all of which I have kept and treasure, except those which I have reluctantly given to my friends. For these letters have that air about them which has preserved letters in the past. Most letters go to the waste paper basket after a week or two but others are self-preserved for us. Lawrence's are beautifully written in jet black ink, and are delicately phrased, and there is always something rare in their message, and in the words which convey it.

Some years ago, I was having tea in my quarters at Cranwell, with a party of cadets, when to our pleasure and surprise Lawrence came in. He just said "You know who I am." He had come up from Bristol non-stop on his motor bike. I hurriedly ordered from the Mess, which he could not enter, food, and indeed, gave him a very good tea, as he was famished and very thirsty. He became most cheerful and talked to us at length and with much range and precision, about his ideals in classic art. He must have been with us about an hour and a half. I remember we talked after the figure of Queen Nefertiti in the Berlin Museum. Later I asked him what he thought of Epstein's work at St. James's station. He replied that although these sculptures were ugly out of their context, they were appropriate in a cubist building.

During the next years that followed when Lawrence had left Lincolnshire, I continued to correspond regularly with him in connection with the *College Journal* for which he wrote anonymously, more than one article. One of the last articles he sent me after I had written for it, was from a remarkable translation of the Odyssey. I wrote to him at once urging him to begin the translation of the Iliad; partly because he was the man for such work and could have produced something worthy, and partly because it would have paid him. I thought he might need the money. This rendering of the Odyssey was in a volume de luxe. I could not afford the book myself, but by the generosity of the author and the printers, I was given the loan of it for a fortnight, and was able to show it to many officers and cadets, who took the pleasure in the elegance of this text and the beauty of the type. The book was afterwards on view in the British Museum, as a specimen of British bookmaking at its best.

Lawrence told me, when he was in Lincolnshire a few months ago, that he spent a whole day over ten lines of translation and wrote two copies of them before he made the final fair copy. Similarly he said of the Arabs, that the secret of handling them was an unremitting study of them. This attitude to scholarship makes *The Seven Pillars of Wisdom* on of the greatest books in the world.

The last time I saw Lawrence was last March [1935], a few weeks before his death. My room was full of people, and as I walked towards the door talking to one of them I saw Lawrence standing humbly outside.

He was untidily dressed in ancient flannels and a coat and muffler, which had seen very much better days. I know that at least one of my visitors wondered, as he passed by, who was this slipshod apparition. Although I had not seen Lawrence for some time, and he had aged and lost much of his youth, I recognised him at once and had pleasure in showing him round the College and of talking to him on all sorts of topics, for about an hour and a half.

I offered to lend him my car to show him round the station, but he would not accept. I took him first to see the pictures on the walls of the College, in the choice of which he had played a big part [see letter from Lawrence to de la Bere dated 26 November 1933]. We talked together of Tuke, whom we had both known at one time. Tuke is the painter of the sailing ship scene in the first of the Cadets' ante-rooms. Tuke had used Lawrence as a model in his youth; and I had watched him at his easel.

After going through the ante-rooms, we went to the Cadets' Quarters and spoke to "Colonel" Young, who, of course, recognised his visitor, and two other College servants whose names I have forgotten.

Then I took him to the Main Lecture Hall, and the Library, where I introduced him to Captain C.W. Pollock and Mr L.E. Fisk. While he was in the Library I showed him our copy of The Seven Pillars of Wisdom. He studied this book carefully and explained to us the significance of some of the illustrations. He was a modernist in art.

I asked him why he did not re-engage in the Royal Air Force. He told me that if he signed on for another 12 years, he would be to elderly for the ranks. He added with a smile, that he had already reached the giddy height of Aircraftman Class I. He said that the idea of a man of 60 being in the ranks was preposterous. I suggested that he should apply for promotion, and take the necessary examinations. He said that the educational difficulties were too great.

This was a typical remark made mischievously by a man who was an international scholar in Arabic and Archaeology, a good linguist in several languages and a Fellow of All Souls. I suppose a Fellowship of All Souls is the highest academic honour in the world.

I do not know how the train of conversation started, but presently we asked him what he was going to do to balance his budget in the future, and he told us he had 25/- a week to live on and he thought that enough for any man. I remarked that he would never be able to maintain his motor bike on it. He replied that he was giving up this bike, and he showed me his push bike on which he had already come a great distance and on which he was proceeding to Cambridge. I felt sorry to see him so worn, and I thought, tired.

He told me that if ever he went short of money he could always translate books from German and French, and I urged him once again to translate the Iliad, and not keep his talents laid up in a napkin. We discussed at length my excavation of a Roman Villa at Haceby. We talked at length, too, about what he was going to do when he left the Service. He told me that he was very tired and getting old. In fact, he was 47 years of age, but there was no doubt that he was looking more tired and bleached than when I saw him last.

I asked him if he would attend our College Literary Society one evening, and I think he would have come but he said: "For the moment I am 'Other Ranks' and I do not feel happy in the company of officers." But I gathered he would come one evening as he was always interested in the College.

[*Journal of the Royal Air Force College*, Autumn 1935: 'In March this year the late A.C.1 T.E. Shaw visited the College. He had left the Service after 12 years in the Royal Air Force, and was meditating a tranquil and philosophic life somewhere on Egdon Heath in the Hardy Country. He spent an hour and a half going over the College, in which he had always taken an active though quiet interest.']

So we have lost one of the great figures of the century – a man whose death was signalised by eulogies from the Sovereign downwards. For after his death, the King, who is more conversant with facts and men than most, sent this message to Lawrence's brother:-

"The King has heard with sincere regret of the death of your brother, and deeply sympathises with you and your family in this sad loss. Your brother's name will live in history and the

King gratefully recognises his distinguished services to his country and feels that it is tragic that the end should have come in this manner to a life still so full of promise."

Mr Churchill wrote of him: "I fear, whatever our needs, we shall not see his like again."

Lawrence had the qualities of great personal bravery, initiative and learning, whether he was designing a strategy, leading a charge, or digging an ancient site. He spoke with a modulated voice and with a twinkle always in his eyes. What he said, like what he wrote, had a natural finesse, and impressed itself on the memory.

There was no mystery at all about him. If he was a mystic he was a practical mystic. A romance about him was conjured up for young men and maidens by a cheap American journalist. He was one of the great men who could mix freely in all classes of society, but he preferred the company of his intellectual inferiors. He wanted rest and oblivion after all the troubles, mental and physical, which he had endured in Transjordan and Arabia.

Some years ago, I had gone up with some Cadets from our Literary Society to see Marlowe's *Dr Faustus* at Oxford, and on the following Sunday I was at a loose end. As chance would have it, I turned my steps to All Soul's College, and when I got into Porters' Lodge, one of the batmen – or scouts as they call them at Oxford – asked me if I should like him to show me around.

I accepted the offer and found out by accident a few minutes later that he had been Lawrence's scout. After showing me round this beautiful College, which is remarkable for having no undergraduates, he showed me several relics of Lawrence, including a dagger of solid yellow gold, which he had given to the College, together with other mementos.

He also showed me the original of Augustus John's drawing in the frontis-piece of *The Revolt in the Desert*, and told me that an American tourist had offered him £25 for it. I advised him not to sacrifice it. But what interested me most was a letter written by Lawrence which I was allowed to read.

In it he described how he had received that day several decorations from His Majesty, and, after walking across the Tower Bridge, had dropped them one by one into the Thames, beyond the reach of the drag-net.

Everybody knows how, as a white Arab, he had hoped to build up an Arabian Empire or a succession of Arabian states, from Mecca to Cilicia; from the Red Sea to the Shatt-el-Arab; and from the coast of Palestine to Persia. He had made a number of promises to the Arabs, and had been unable to fulfil them. He had been repulsed by the policies of Sykes and Picot, and the sentiment of Balfour and Rothschild. He felt, therefore, that he had let down the Arabs. Whether he had exaggerated the ambitions of the Arabs by his promises does not matter: nor whether he had alienated the goodwill of the French who, he told me, refused him a passport.

While I have been in Lincolnshire, I have heard so many foolish criticisms of him, that I have been dismayed by the critics' lack of imagination. Many people contended that he should not be in the service, because he would not wear any ribbons. They were obsessed with paragraph this and sub-paragraph that, forgetting that it was a distinction to have such a man in the service in any capacity, particularly, perhaps, as an Aircrafthand. Besides, no one who knew Lawrence would think or say that, judged by the most utilitarian standards, he was unworthy of his pay, rank and place in the service.

To critics of a higher category, particularly to historians who have the privilege of being wise after the event, it may be said that Lawrence backed the wrong horse; that he should have conciliated the support of Ibn Saud, not of the frail Sharifian family; that he should not have alienated the French, nor made such exaggerated promises to the Arabs. It may be that the Arab campaign was only a minor campaign. But their contentions, whether correct or not, miss the true significance of this man. A man may be great in failure.

In conclusion, if any mystery has been conjured up about Lawrence, the mystery has been useful in this materialistic age, which requires a little mystery and romance. But those who knew Lawrence best, know that there was no mystery about him; that he was just a charming man, and a great intellectual to whom nothing was difficult. He continually surprised one by some new achievement, by an unexpected aspect, by some remarkable phrase or sentiment. Everyone liked him and respected him. It may be that he courted publicity by his studied obscurity. But if he did, he despised himself for it; and none of us is infallible. Besides, all must be forgiven to a man who has made history. He performed exploits unsurpassed in guerrilla warfare, when he harassed and paralysed, with 3000 Arabs, more than 12 times their number of Turks. He evolved a new theory of war; he substituted for concentration, dispersion. He practiced a kind of bloodless strategy by which he paralysed his opponent by an intangible ubiquity. All will pardon this man if he was occasionally impish, exasperating and baffling, and if sometimes he cultivated an aura of mystery.

When I last saw him he was just going off on his push bike from Cranwell to Cambridge. I offered again to drive him round the camp but he seemed reluctant. I offered to get him some food from the Fancy Goods Store, but he was not interested in food.

He had a long conversation with me on the steps of the College. I remember the last words which I said to him were urging him not to waste his life as a modern Diogenes, but to get down again to a worthy and useful work. But he just laughed in that serene and boyish way of his and pedalled off.'

[There is a framed copy of the letter from Lawrence to de la Bere in the library of the RAF Cadet College, Cranwell, with the following caption: 'This is a letter written by Colonel T.E. Lawrence to the editor of the *Royal Air Force College Journal* granting him permission to reproduce a chapter of *The Seven Pillars of Wisdom* and answering one or two questions which the editor had raised about the Desert Campaign'].

"Thank you very much. I hope you will cut out 'Prince of Mecca', for that is an American invention and impossible in fact. 'Emir Mekky' = Prince of Mecca and denotes actual temporal overlordship. It could not be an honorific – and King Hussein was never in the mood to honour me. We did not get on together.

Alas I was not among the first to enter Damascus; indeed my position there was very equivocal. I found an empty will amongst our leaders, when they got there – and knowing there were things urgently required I compelled them to do as I wanted. That was all.

Otherwise there is nothing which is not a fair expression of opinion. Of course I do not share your view of the literary merit of the book. It seems too literary for a memoir, and too truthful for literature. However that doesn't much matter.

The AOC asked me for a copy for the C.C. library, and this I've sent him. So you will be able to look at it, when you wish.

The facts about publication are that this full text will not be published in my lifetime: but about 150 copies are going to friends of mine, without reservations: so knowledge of it will soon get about. They will be distributed in the end of November. An abridgement is to be published by Cape in March 1927 and the serial publication of 40,000 words of this abridgement can be begun by the *Daily Telegraph* after Dec. 15 next. So your long quotation shouldn't appear before the D.T. has had its whack. After that do anything you please. Other people will be doing the same.

TES"

[This letter was written in the summer of 1926 after Lawrence had donated a copy of the *Seven Pillars* to 'Biffy' Borton who deposited it in the College Library, where it remains to this day. Rupert de la Bere wrote a review of *The Seven Pillars of Wisdom* which was published in the *RAF Cadet College Magazine* in Spring 1927:]

'A Great Book: *The Seven Pillars of Wisdom*, by Col. T.E. Lawrence (now serving in the Royal Air Force under a thin incognito)...This, of course, is the account given by himself in a book – now in private circulation – which, both for dramatic interest and literary beauty, will take its place with Doughty's *Arabia Derserta* among the masterpieces. In 652 pages, Col. T.E. Lawrence...modestly relates his share in doing what no other man...could have done...in firing the tribal Arab with a sense of nationality and in welding a race naturally so divided, for a hundred different reasons of clan, religion and region, into a unanimous pan-Arabian force...

No book could give a warmer or a fuller impression of Arab life. Here, I think, it best to quote five pages from Chapter XLVII, describing a function in which a few of us have participated once. 'Feasting' (an extract from *The Seven Pillars of Wisdom*)..

But now the fingers that gripped the rifle have taken up the pen and brush; and the result is an artistic unity which, for its literary and historical merits, will take high place among the masterpieces of our tongue.'

Lord Halifax: 'Lawrence of Arabia' (1936)

[*Journal of the Royal Air Force College*, Autumn 1936]

(Being an address delivered by Lord Halifax in St Paul's Cathedral at the unveiling of a Memorial to Colonel T.E. Lawrence on 29 January 1936)

'Thus he came to join the humblest ranks of the Royal Air Force, the youngest of the Services. The future lay with youth, and here for Lawrence was the very embodiment of youth, with all its life before it....These years from 1922 to 1934 among the unnamed rank and file were perhaps the happiest of his life.'

Robert Graves: *T.E. Lawrence to His Biographer* (1938)

[Graves, *T.E. Lawrence to his Biographer*: 'Lawrence now sent me the manuscript of his book, *The Mint*, a contemporary account of his recruit's training in the RAF at Uxbridge in 1922. I had not known of its existence. He asked me for my opinion. In the main I liked it very much, better than *Seven Pillars*, because it had obviously been written straight off, not brooded over. (There was one particularly good chapter about Queen Alexandra's funeral-parade)...I said that I hoped he would not tease at *The Mint* as he had done at *Seven Pillars*: there was no mystery about good writing, given something to say – all there was to be done really was to write with ink on paper....I offered to get *The Mint* privately printed, at my expense, in ten copies not for sale...He replied:]

Miranshah

6.XI.28

This is two excellent letters you have given me about *The Mint*. The poor little thing interests me: because it's my only effort at really writing something about nothing. *Seven Pillars* was a historical necessity: I don't call it an option: but *The Mint* was a pure wantonness. I went to Uxbridge with the deliberate intention of writing something about service life: and I put down these notes evening after evening in the hut, with the blankets up to my chin, writing on the support of my drawn-up knees. They are the perfect exemplar of journalism, in its antique sense: and it interests me very much to find that you and Garnett and Forster (three very different people) all see something in them...

About printing *The Mint*, as you suggested:- thanks very much, but no. 'They' would hear of it, and say I'd written another book: and *The Mint* is 1922, and not a book. It's better left as a manuscript diary. Diaries exist in thousands, and are thought no harm of...

[Graves, *T.E. Lawrence to his Biographer*: 'I left England in October 1929 and except for a brief visit in September 1930, when he and I met for the last time, did not return there until forced to leave Spain by the civil war...

Nearly all of Lawrence's letters to me of 1931 and 1932 have since gone astray. Towards the end of 1932 he was sent some critical work that L.R., myself and some others were engaged in...His reaction as of low brows to high brows surprised me...I wrote to tell him that I felt that he was not playing the game, in assuming that plain-man tone with such forced ingenuousness: during all my years of association with him he had behaved as my intellectual equal. The change was sudden; and unfair, because sudden. Had all the past interest in my work been just another kind of game? He replied:]

Plymouth

24.1.33

Come off it, R.G.! Your letter forgets my present [state]. It is so long since we met that you are excused knowing that I'm now a fitter, very keen and tolerably skilled on engines, but in no way abstract. I live all of every day with real people, and concern myself only in the concrete. The ancient self-seeking and self-devouring TEL of Oxford (and TES of the *Seven Pillars* and *Mint*) is dead. Not regretted either. My last ten years have been the best of my life. I think I shall look back on my 35-45 period as golden...

[Graves, *T.E. Lawrence to his Biographer*: 'A publisher wrote to me, as Lawrence's biographer, asking whether there was any chance of publishing The Mint, and whether I would approach Lawrence about it...I forwarded the letter to Lawrence, who replied:]

Clouds Hill
Moreton
Dorset

30.VII.33

That enquiry about the Mint amused me. I am still RAF, so no question of printing it can arise. Nor will it arise when I leave...for I have vested the copyright in the Chief of Air Staff for the time being. Also I have lost the typescript! Or rather, it was in the hands of Sir Geoffrey Salmond, the late CAS, when he suddenly died: and nobody knows where he put it...

[Graves, *T.E. Lawrence to his Biographer*: 'He had all the marks of the Irishman: the rhetoric of freedom, the rhetoric of chastity, the rhetoric of honour, the power to excite sudden deep affections, loyalty to the long-buried past, high aims qualified by too mocking a sense of humour, serenity clouded by petulance and broken by occasional black despairs, playboy charm and theatricality, imagination that over runs itself and tires, extreme generosity, serpent cunning, lion courage, diabolic intuition, and the curse of self doubt which becomes enmity to self and sometimes renouncement of all that is most loved and esteemed.'

Liddell Hart: *T.E. Lawrence to His Biographer* (1938)

[Liddell Hart asked Lawrence to comment on the draft of his book which was eventually entitled *T.E. Lawrence: in Arabia and After* and published in 1934. These comments were recorded in *T.E. Lawrence to his Biographer Liddell Hart* which was published in 1938.]

[Talks with T.E. Shaw during week end of 12 May 1929:]

Brough, motor manufacturer, whom he has helped in design, gives him each new model (part-worn) whenever one comes out. Has done 94 mph on road on present one. Averaged 54 mph Durham-Cranwell – highest average, but usually reckons on 40 mph average. Slows to 35-40 at crossroads and careful in traffic and corners. Love of speed...

[Talk with T.E. Shaw, Inverness Court W2, 25 October 1929:]

He has only had 2 skids in last 5 years. Once at Cranwell, bringing back sausages for supper and struck ice patch at 45 mph in dark – he went to one grass border and eventually found bike on other. Second time going up Highgate Hill (just before going to India), skidded on tramlines and sheered all side off the bike...

[Talks with T.E. Lawrence 27 May 1933:]

The Mint, an account of life in the RAF, written in 1922, 1923 and 1925. First and main part about life at Uxbridge Depot, showing moral effect of Bonham-Carter. Later chapters about Cranwell to show happier contrast – if artistically spoils.

[Letter from Lawrence] Bridlington, Monday, 14.VIII.33

Transferred from RTC to RAF for remainder of engagement: was sent to Uxbridge for one day to drawn airman's kit: then posted to Cranwell. My term of service was 7 active & 5 reserve, from March 1923. While in India, I extended, to serve my 5 reserve years in active.

Aircraft-hand (general purpose unskilled man) in B. Flight, of the Cadet College. Each flight had half a dozen training machines for the cadets to learn flying: and three or four instructors, and a dozen or fifteen airmen (one third fitters, one third riggers, one third aircraft-hands) to look after the machines. We did anything there was to do.

Was posted overseas to India direct from Cranwell. Sailed in Dec. 1926 and upon arrival at Karachi was sent to RAF Depot at Drigh Road there.

[Hart: 'On August 20 he came to spend the day with us at Farnham, and here went through the last chapter, "Fulfilment", and the Epilogue of *T.E. Lawrence: in Arabia and After*.]

Re *The Mint*, 'a book which TE considers his *finest piece of work*...' TE underlined the words here italicised and substituted *'best writing'*.

[Talk with T.E., Bush Hotel, Farnham, 20 August 1933]

Motorcyle: Christened one of the first 'Boanerges', because so thunderous. Now calls them George's. Present one is George VII. Next year's model expected to do 150 mph. Wonders whether Brough will trust him with it. Enjoys motoring so much that would not charge Air

Ministry with the 1d. a mile strictly due to him for journeys on duty. Used to do about 400-600 miles a week when at Cranwell. If missed a week, his delight was immense on getting in the saddle again.

The Mint: Now in Sir J. Salmond's possession.

[Extracts from revised draft of *T.E. Lawrence: in Arabia and After*]

Chapter XXII ('Fulfilment'). On his hard experiences at the Uxbridge Depot of the RAF: 'But it was at least the means of inspiring a book which TE considers his best writing, superior both in a literary and a philosophical sense to the *Seven Pillars of Wisdom*. He wrote the greater part while actually living the life he records, so that no lapse of time affects the photographic accuracy, but when he rejoined the Air Force in 1925 he added further chapters on his life at Cranwell which form a happy contrast to the portrayal of Uxbridge. Artistically, TE considers that the addition tends to spoil the effect, but it is characteristic of his fairness that he should have made it. Whether the book will ever be published, only the future can tell. One difficulty, apart from TE's indifference, is that it "out-joyces" James Joyce in the fidelity of its record of barrack-room conversations.'

TE crossed out this passage, and wrote in substitution: 'as he emphasised at the time in a diary which he maintained throughout the experience. These notes were added to later, at Cranwell where the atmosphere was happy; but they remained notes, without any attempt at formal composition. Incidentally in reproducing barrack-room conversation they out-joyce Joyce.

Mr. Jonathan Cape years later learnt of the existence of this manuscript diary (which TE prefers to the SP as writing), and suggested that it might fulfil a clause in his contract for *Revolt in the Desert*, giving the firm an option on the next book. The author agreed instantly and submitted the notes for approval, with a statement that his terms for them were a million pounds down in advance, and 75% royalty! Mr. Cape was not able to raise the million pounds before his option expired.'

[Letter from Lawrence] Southampton, March I, 1934

The book [*T.E. Lawrence: In Arabia and After*] came to me as an advance copy. Very Big and very solid, said I. Till now I have only run through the pictures and glanced at the maps, which seem to fill their purpose satisfactorily. I suppose reviews will begin to roll along next week. I shall be in Lincoln or Newcastle or Wolverhampton, out of sight and minding. For your sake I wish the book well (self-devoting of me!) but my judgement tells me that people will not want more yet about so hackneyed a subject. Now had you torn me to shreds in the Lytton-Strachey fashion: aha, that would have been a spectacle.

[Liddell Hart met Lawrence for the last time on 22 March 1935].

On Monday, May 13th, returning home about 7.30pm, I was told by my secretary that the Air Ministry, first, and Alan Dawnay, later, had telephoned to say that TE had met with an accident when riding back, on his motor cycle, to his cottage at Cloud's Hill from Bovington camp, and that he was lying gravely injured with a fractured skull in the Military Hospital there...TE had pitched on his head after a violent swerve in trying to avoid a butcher's boy who was cycling along the road in company with another boy...

Days of anxiety followed...All the time he lay unconscious, and it was clear that his head injuries were very severe. There seemed a glimmer of hope, as his vitality was astounding, but on the Saturday congestion of the lungs developed, and at about a quarter past eight on Sunday morning, the 19th, death came. A post-mortem examination showed that the brain was badly lacerated; even if he had survived he would have lost speech and memory, and been paralysed.

The funeral was arranged for Tuesday, May 21st. Most of those who went came direct to Moreton Church, but a few gathered beforehand at the cottage. On the way there from London one drove along the Salisbury-Blandford road, TE's favourite speed stretch, where the switchback contour peculiarly gives the sensation which is described as that of 'moulding the hills and dales'...

Shortly before 2pm a light motor hearse passed the cottage with TE's plain unmarked coffin. We set off in cars and then went ahead to the church at Moreton...Most of the friends went into the church, but I waited until the hearse arrived, and then followed it in with Jack Salmond and Scott-Paine. Augustus John trod on the heels of the bearers – Newcombe, Eric Kennington, Ronald Storrs, Pat Knowles, Aircratman Bradbury, and ex-private Russell of the Tank Corps. (They were chosen with the idea of representing six different phases of TE's career.) The service was simple and brief; the parson faltering as if overcome by the occasion or emotion.

At the end the coffin was carried out, down the steps and placed on a 'trolley' which the bearers pushed along, the rest of us following – out of the churchyard gates and along the wooded lane to the new cemetery. It had only a few graves. The coffin was lowered into the leaf-lined grave, the service continued, and then we took a last look at the small coffin before breaking away.

M.S.: 'T.E.L.' (1949)

[*Journal of the Royal Air Force College*, November 1949].

You, when the world was old, and tired, and wise,
And mirth forgotten, and adventure dead,
When even children walked with slow, staid tread,
And old men taught that war's proud songs were lies;
Scorning this travesty of life in death,

The stifling safety of a senile serf,
You, in the oldest corner of the earth
Sought youth, and smiled to taste its quickening breath.
And, warring in those vast and golden plains
Where time was born, or sifting wisdom's sands
With prince and prophet, held life in your hands,
And stormed the heavens with your psalm of praise
And when, the wheel spun, death stood at your side,
Laughed in the old God's face, and laughing, died.

M.H.G. Allison: 'Lincolnshire's link with the Lawrences' (1968)

[*Lincolnshire Life*, Vol. 8 (8), October 1968]

'Coming to Cranwell in August 1925, T.E. found it "a comfortable, peaceful, cleanly camp.' The countryside was "a queer change from the richness and beauty and colour of Dorset. Lincolnshire is like a picture of a dead earth in green and gray. You feel the curve of the great ball in the wideness of all the local views".

Old Lincoln delighted him – except for the minster. "The cathedral I did not like. Yet perhaps it's only because it succeeds too well. I do not think it disappoints as much as it chills. We come to it expecting to be cheered: and it tells us that we are no good at all."

In a letter to E.M. Forster, T.E. mentions "little Smith, the bearded bookseller of Lincoln." (Mr Smith kept the Cathedral Bookshop at the time). It so happened that T.E. and E.M. Forster together visited the bookshop. Subsequently Smith asked T.E. the name of his companion; on hearing who it was, the bookseller ordered a small consignment of Forster's books; he sold them quickly and ordered a larger consignment which also went well. A useful bit of business!

T.E. on occasions spent the night in a lodging house on Steep Hill, Lincoln. The house, No. 33, was kept by a Mrs Dugdale. She recalled that one night he arrived having motor cycled a long distance in the pouring rain. Mrs Dugdale had a meal ready and said to Lawrence, "Now just go to the sink and wash your hands and face before you sit down." "Good heavens, woman," said T.E., "God's been washing my face all the way here."

The Cranwell interlude in T.E. Lawrence's service life was a happy one...It was during this period that he wrote, "The weather barometer points to 'stormy'. My private indicator is set at 'calm'." William Dodds, for many years manager of the Regal Cinema, Lincoln...was stationed at Cranwell at the same period and retains the memory of T.E. as a quiet and pleant personality. Lawrence left Cranwell for India at the end of 1926.'

Winston Kime: 'David George Hogarth' (1980)

[*Lincolnshire Life*, Vol. 20 (9), December 1980]

'Lawrence of Arabia... was one of the almost legendary fighting men emerging from World War 1. After leaving the Army, his longing for anonymity led him to enlist as an aircraftsman in the RAF and, whilst serving at Cranwell, he spent a lot of time roaring about the Lincolnshire countryside on a high powered motorbike...Lawrence's exploits...have been recorded in numerous books and war histories...but considerably less has been written about a man born in Lincolnshire who was Lawrence's early mentor and who introduced him to the Middle east and guided his camel tracks across the sandy wastelands...Doctor David George Hogarth, archaeologist, traveller and scholar...'

Denis McDonnell: 'Lawrence Link is Remembered'(1994)

[*T.E. Notes*, February 1994]

'Tomorrow, the chairman of the city council's recreation, leisure and tourism committee, Councillor Trevor Rook, will unveil the...plaque on the wall of Brown's Pie Shop at 33 Steep Hill. This...commemorates the city's link with Lawrence of Arabia. It recalls:

"On this site in 1925 soldier and author T.E. Lawrence lodged while serving at R.A.F. Cranwell. Around this time he wrote his book, Seven Pillars of Wisdom, the legendary account of his leadership of Arab insurgence against the Turks in Syria during World War One."

The plaque – 16 inches in diameter – is in cast aluminium with gold lettering on a dark green background. In the October 1992 *T.E. Notes* issue there appeared an article entitled "T.E. Slept Here?" in which John Lord gave us a little history of the structure at 33 Steep Hill. Seems it was originally called the "Fox and Hounds" (but John wasn't sure) before his parents took it over in 1970 and made it into a toy and book shop. After that, it became what it is now, i.e. a restaurant by the name of Brown's Pie Shop. According to John Lord: "T.E. apparently occupied the front upstairs room with a bay window (and simply carved wood chimney piece)".

Denis McDonnell: 'T.E. and the Royal Air Force College at Cranwell' (1994)

[*T.E. Notes*, February 1994]

'The Royal Air Force College at Cranwell is a famous landmark in RAF history. Its origins lie with the Royal Naval Air Service who in 1916 formed a flying training station there to train officers and cadets to fly aeroplanes, kite balloons and airships. On 1 April 1918 the Royal Flying Corps and the Royal Naval Air Service were amalgamated to form the Royal Air Force. At the end of the First World War, Major General Sir Hugh Trenchard, Chief of Air Staff, was determined to reinforce the RAF as a single independent force and proposed a cadet college at Cranwell which he favoured due to its remote location and the flatness of its airfields. His wishes prevailed and on 5 February 1920, the Royal Air Force College, Cranwell was opened...

The new extension to the College Hall Library, opened in 1965, is known as the Lawrence Room. In it have been collected all items of College property associated with T.E. Lawrence, including books, pictures, and a manuscript letter written by him to the editor of the College Journal.'

[The portrait of TEL in the Lawrence Room is a copy of an original by Augustus John and it was presented to the College by Rupert de la Bere who was Professor Of English and History at Cranwell from 1921 to 1938].

Leslie Robert Webb: 'Lawrence of Arabia' (1995)

[The following account was written for Mrs Khinlyn Fern in September 1995].

'My introduction to Lawrence of Arabia was at the end of August 1925. At that time I was a leading Aircraftsman in the Quarter Master Stores at Cranwell. It was routine for new arrivals to report to the Quarter Master stores for issue of bedding and allocation of hut sleeping quarters. Accordingly a new arrival presented himself on this particular day, I having served his requirements, needed to record his particulars in the Store Register.

My first question was, what's your name? Shaw was the reply. Your number? (Service number), 352 and then a pause of at least 6 seconds duration before he added the last 3 figures (085) of his service number. I gave him a mild rebuke, and told him also, that it was the first thing taught me when joining the RAF, and to do himself a favour and practice it. He just gave me one of those looks and replied apologetically "I do find it difficult to remember it at times", at this time I did not have a clue as to who he was; just another "irk" recruit from the Depot I thought.

Returning to the next stores hut, my colleagues were in conversation with a group of "customers" that had gathered during my short absence. Among the gathering was a couple of "old sweats" who were expounding their knowledge as to the identity of the new arrival. That was the first time I had heard of Lawrence of Arabia. To me this new recruit at Cranwell sounded something out of the ordinary to the normal recruit from the Depot. Throughout the next 18 months that I served with Shaw at Cranwell, I found him to be very likeable and friendly chap with a great sense of humour.

He was a frequent visitor to the QM stores which consisted of a pair of sleeping Quarter Huts converted for storage purposes. The Hut Numbers were 128 and 131 and numbered in multiples of 3. To me Shaw was just another one of the happy gang in West Camp Cranwell. What I have to say about him are facts, and not what I have heard from someone else or read in a book. I was 20 years of age in 1925 and my classification was LAC bobbing on promotion to Corporal. The officially recognised Quarter Master was a Sergeant Billie Williams, a great character. I had two airmen to assist me and as the Air Force used to put it, that constituted the establishment for the QM stores.

Whenever Shaw was on the scrounge he would ask the QM Sergeant first of all in order to avoid getting me into any trouble as a result of his activities. I was simply delegated to execute the deed. He had that something about him, that he always managed to get whatever he was after and it was always on behalf of his fellow tenants in Hut 105. "What's the chance of a bucket of coal, Les? The lads are very cold and no fire", or "We have run out of cleaning materials in the Hut, or a couple of electric bulbs have been broken."

I will always remember the exchange of tables as described by Sgt Pugh, the swap was organised by Shaw assisted by a couple of the characters in Hut 105. Whatever Shaw got up to, it was always on behalf of someone else. I can only recall Shaw wanting something for himself, and this was for a part worn Great Coat (overcoat). It was to be a couple of sizes larger than normal to hold his spare frame because he intended to have it fleece lined. The requirement was duly completed and he rewarded me with a ten shilling note of appreciation. Shaw always biked in uniform and in the winter months such protection must have been very welcome.

More than often Shaw made for the long straight Leadenham Road when leaving the camp. It was one such occasion that "Smudge Smith" a diminutive cockney character in B Flight was invited by Shaw to jump on the pillion. Off went the pair of them tearing down the road at speeds of 80-90 mph. Shaw was so pleased with the performance of the Brough with a passenger aboard that he carried onto Nottingham, where he pulled into a posh hotel. Smudge recounted the story to me the next morning: "We walked into the restaurant and seated ourselves at one of the tables, a geezer turns up who Shaw said was the head waiter; a meal was ordered by Shaw for both of us. Before the head waiter signalled someone to serve us he wanted the money first. Blimey, I've never seen so many knives and forks around the plates, I didn't know where to start".

One of the huts was converted for garaging our bikes and many hours were spent tinkering and tuning our machines mainly Douglas AJS-Francis Barnet types. Shaw was a regular at the garage. We all envied his Brough but none denied the man who rode it. Shaw was a popular chap and liked by us all.

Reading *The Mint* for the umpteenth time I re-lived the harsh treatment he received on entry to the RAF. Bear in mind it was only a matter of four months that I followed Shaw after his posting from Uxbridge to Farnborough. I too went through a repeat of the treatment experienced by Shaw. I too hated the RAF because I felt I had been conned by those faceless people who publicised what a wonderful life it is in the Royal Air Force. Join the RAF see the world and fly was the theme.

The drill instructors were a mixture of NCO's whom we termed "yard dogs". They were transfers from the Guards Regiments for the purpose of putting some discipline into this new "Air Force lot". The Depot Commandant was a Group Captain Bonham-carter a badly wounded and one legged character from World War 1. He was a much hated and feared man. Chief trainer of the guard dogs was a Flight Lt Wombwell an ex ranker. During my last week or so at Uxbridge, I was now skilled in the art of square bashing, this resulted in me being selected for the formation squad to take part in the wedding procession of Elizabeth Bowes Lyon and the Duke of York. It was only a matter of a few days later that my posting came through for Cranwell.

I relived the journey from Uxbridge to Cranwell so aptly described by Shaw in The Mint. My experience at Uxbridge reminded me of the expression many of my fellow sufferers made practically every day: "Dear Mum, Sell the pig and buy me out". Mum replied "Pigs dead soldier on". I woke early the morning following my arrival at Cranwell and the only sound was the strong wind whistling through the eaves and doors of the Hut. No bugle calls, no duty NCO's rushing around banging on doors and tables yelling "wakey wakey rise and shine".

I had the whole of the reception Hut to myself. After leisurely washing and shaving myself I took a peek out side for a sniff of the Cranwell air. This surely was paradise itself. A fellow Aircraftsman was passing who I immediately recognised. It was "Tich" Skelton, son of a near neighbour in my civvy street days who had joined the RAF a couple of years earlier. "Tich" was a cook and butcher which is a trade in the RAF and for which a rate of 3/6 per day is paid, and your classification is that of an aircraftsman 2nd class (AC2). This same rate of pay is applied to all tradesmen such as Clerks, Storekeepers, Drivers, Fitters etc.

Shaw entered as an Aircraft hand which means a trade less occupation for which 3/- per day was paid. "Tich" was on his way to the cookhouse (early shift) to prepare breakfast and invited me to accompany him. He beckoned me to a corner of the Kitchen where another couple of cooks were preparing food. "Tich" placed a large plate in my hands containing two fried eggs and several rations of bacon whispering "get that down you before the first rush arrive".

The AOC (Air Officer Commanding) was Air Commodore "Biffy" Borton who I never saw all the time I was at Cranwell. I would imagine he must have been a very kindly man because this station was so typical of the life I thought it was going to be when I joined.

At about 9 am I reported to the Station SM at the Orderly Room. This was followed by a brief interview with the Adjutant who welcomed me to Cranwell and my duties at the QM stores. I would estimate the total strength of the NCO's and other ranks in West camp was 150. This would be approximate strength of a squadron made up of 3 Flights A, B &C. Our job was to look after the Aircraft and the Officer Cadets who fly them.

East Camp was about half a mile down the Camp road and consisted of a "Sparks" School (wireless training), the Camp laundry, and several large stores, such as Clothing, Equipment, Fuels etc. It was also the terminus for a single line track of our train between East Camp and Sleaford (the local town) and named by East & West Camp personnel "The Flying Swede".

1926 has now drawn to an end and about this time we saw little or nothing of Shaw. I got my promotion and early in the new year I was posted to RAF Apprentices' School, Halton. The last I saw of Shaw was a photograph in the Daily Mirror or Sketch of him climbing a rope ladder to board a ship destined to sail for India. So it was goodbye to a very likeable man and a good friend.

Before closing down on this narrative I must tell you of one story that was told at Cranwell and it is the only one I would be ready to believe about Shaw. King George V was holding an investiture at the Palace to which Shaw was invited. The King was about to invest Shaw with some high honours when Shaw interjected and told HM what to do with them, politely of course. Shaw was so incensed with the British and French governments who had "ratted" on the promises that Shaw had made to the Arabs on their behalf.'

Allan Warburton: 'A Legend in Hiding' (1996)

[*Lincolnshire Life*, April 1996]

'Lawrence of Arabia...described the two years he spent at Cranwell as amongst the happiest of his life...Although everyone on the station knew the real identity of their famous recruit they respected his need for some sort of personal privacy and, indeed, helped to shield him from inquisitive reporters...Lawrence often rode to Hertfordshire to visit the Shaws, but on one occasion a trip landed him in trouble; he returned late to Cranwell and was put in the guardhouse by the guard commander who didn't believe that Lawrence had been "taking tea with George Bernard Shaw"!..The two happy years that Lawrence of Arabia spent at Cranwell helped to restore him to some form of sanity: maybe the clean Lincolnshire air and the clear skies had something to do with it.'

Leonard Rivett: *Lawrence of Arabia - Ross and Shaw in the Royal Air Force* (1996)

[12 June 1996]

'Lawrence left Uxbridge...He was amazed and impressed by the change when he arrived at Cranwell...Sixteen slept in a small hut, the beds down each wall, with a table and two forms and a square stove in the middle...The hangar was a girder sheathed in iron with a concrete floor without one pillar or obstruction and at night looked like a palace...The airmen worked eight hours a day in the workshop; before and after that they did their own cleaning, bed making, hut tidying; another hour and a half...But Lawrence loved it. Everywhere he found a relationship and had no loneliness any more...He had found contentment and happiness.'

Peter Gray: 'Lawrence of Arabia's Lincolnshire Posting' (1996)

[*Lincolnshire Past & Present*, No. 25, Autumn 1996]

'On 24 August 1925 a lone airman, weighed down with bayonet, full kit and equipment, trudged up to the gates of RAF Cranwell after a long, hot journey from London. He presented his papers to the sergeant; these identified him as Aircraftman 2nd Class T.E. Shaw...He became part of B Flight which consisted of 14 aircraftmen, a corporal and a sergeant, all based in the primitive facilities of Hut 105. Lawrence received no special privileges and his daily routine was that of any normal recruit: hut chores, parades, guard duties, lectures, aircraft maintenance...The former Commandant at Cranwell records: "He was extremely tactful and never did anything to call attention to himself. I think he disliked publicity and shunned it, but while he was with the air force and I knew him, he did nothing to court it."

Likewise his flight sergeant was to say: "It seemed his sole purpose was to be an airman of the lowest grade and rank and to be left alone with his Brough at B Flight, Cranwell. He was hero-worshipped by all the flight for his never failing cheerful disposition, ability to get all he could for their benefit, never complaining, and his generosity to all concerned..."

While at Cranwell Lawrence...was also preparing *The Seven Pillars of Wisdom* for the printer. This first limited edition was to be published privately by subscription...Besides the subscription copies (128 copies at 30gns each) Lawrence gave away a further 62 to friends and relatives. Sir Hugh Trenchard received one of these gift copies inscribed thus: "Sir Hugh Trenchard from a contented, admiring and, wherever possible, obedient servant, T.E.S. 5.XII.26".

During his Lincolnshire posting he was an especial favourite of the station's telegraph boy; each telegram delivered to A/c Shaw – and there were many – earned the lad a tip of a shilling, which considerably boosted his half crown a week pay.

Cranwell's rural situation not far from the Great North Road permitted Lawrence plenty of opportunity to ride his motorcycle...George Brough had even designed and built several Brough Superiors for him...they allowed Lawrence the freedom of travel – sometimes at speeds approaching 100 mph – down to London and back in one day, or to speed along the country roads of Lincolnshire, untroubled by heavy traffic...

Lawrence...sailed to India on 7 December 1926, leaving behind fond memories of his Lincolnshire posting...he wrote in a letter to a friend: "The RAF is still my spiritual home, and I'm awfully sorry to leave Cranwell where I've had the best year I ever remember to have had..."

Edwin Rose: 'Lawrence of Arabia – a different viewpoint' (1997)

[*Lincolnshire Past & Present*, No. 27, Spring 1997]

Lawrence had originally enlisted in the RAF in 1922 as John Hume Ross. The Recruiting Interviewing Officer, Capt. W.E. John's (author of the *Biggles* books), told his side of the story in *Popular Flying* (July 1935) and *Flying* (20 August 1938).

'Johns found that the personal details given by Ross were false and so refused to enlist him, not knowing his true identity and suspecting he was an escaped criminal. Within an hour "Ross" returned with an order from the Air Ministry that he must be accepted into the RAF; but then the doctors refused to pass him as fit. A special doctor was duly sent from the Air Ministry to do so. When Johns complained to his commanding officer, he was told, "Watch your step. This man is Lawrence of Arabia. Get him in or you'll get your bowler hat." Johns wrote "Lawrence went on and wherever he went, word of who he was preceded him." Eventually it was revealed that it was Air Vice Marshal Sir Oliver Swann who had prepared Lawrence's false papers and even suggested the name Ross.'

Adam Newell: 'Lawrence of the RAF' (2006)

[*RAF Magazine*, September 2006]

'Still using the pseudonym of Shaw, he was posted to the cadet College at Cranwell in August 1925, where he became an aircrafthand in B Flight. His duties included pushing the aircraft (Avro 504Ks, Bristol Fighters, DH9As and Sopwith Camels) in and out of the hangars, recording flying times in the cadets' logbooks, and hand swinging the propellers of the training craft. Since the end of the war, Lawrence had been writing (and rewriting) *The Seven Pillars of Wisdom*. Publication was set for 1927 and to avoid the inevitable publicity he requested an overseas posting'.

Mrs E. Hoggett: Horse Drawn Tea Waggon at RAF Cranwell

[Undated letter to RAF College Cranwell Library]

My maternal grandparents were married at the register office St George's Square in London on 13 April 1895. My grandfather William Hoggett was a private in the Coldstream Guards whose address was given as Wellington Barracks. My grandmother Lizzie Seth was in service in James Street, Buckingham gate. My grandparents were amongst the first people to cross Tower Bridge on the day that it officially opened. After military service my grandfather became a prison officer at Wakefield, Yorkshire where my mother was born. He later moved to Preston in Lancashire where my aunt and three brothers were born. When my grandfather died in 1922, Nan (my grandmother), two daughters and the youngest son came to live in Lincolnshire at Rauceby Bottoms near Sleaford to be near her sister who lived there with her family.

With the bit of money that was inherited from my grandfather, Nan invested in a horse drawn tea wagon which was sited at RAF Cranwell. Nan was a lovely happy soul, full of fun with a big heart. Unfortunately she was too generous with the credit that she allowed her customers, many of whom, when they were eventually posted, omitted to settle their debts, so eventually the enterprise failed.

As children Nan frequently regaled us with tales of these times and she was very proud of the fact that Lawrence of Arabia was one of her regular customers. There are some photographs showing Nan and my aunt in the van, with servicemen posing in the front. One of the airmen eventually married my aunt but, most interestingly is that the hatless airman in the centre of one of the photos is none other than A/C Shaw, aka Lawrence of Arabia.

Chronology

Based on chronological table in *T.E. Lawrence by His Friends*, edited by A.W. Lawrence, 1937.

Event	Date
Born Tremadoc, North Wales	**16 August 1888**
Oxford City High School	**September 1896 – July 1907**
In northern France studying castles	Summers 1906 & 1907
Jesus College, Oxford (1st Class Honours in Modern History)	**October 1907 – June 1910**
In France studying castles	Summer 1908
In Syria studying castles	Summer 1909
Wrote his thesis *Crusader Castles*	Winter 1909 - 1910
At Jebail in Syria studying Arabic	**Winter 1910 - 1911**
Excavating at Carchemish (Jerablus) under D.G. Hogarth and R. Campbell Thompson	**April – July 1911**
Walk through northern Mesopotamia	Summer 1911
Excavating in Egypt under Flinders Petrie	**Beginning of 1912**
Excavating at Carchemish under C.L Woolley	**Spring 1912 – Spring 1914**
At home in Oxford	Summer 1913
Survey of Sinai	January – February 1914
At Oxford and London completing *The Wilderness of Zin* (archaeological report on Sinai co-written with Woolley)	**Summer 1914**
At War Office, commissioned	October 1914
In Egypt as Intelligence Officer	**December 1914 – October 1916**
On special duty in Mesopotamia	March – May 1916
Journey to Jidda with Ronald Storrs	October 1916

First meeting with Feisal	October 1916
Joined Arab Bureau	November 1916
Attached to Arab forces	**December 1916 – October 1918**
Akaba expedition	May – July 1917
Akaba falls, first meeting with General Allenby	July 1917
Promoted to Major	Summer 1917
Deraa episode	November 1917
Present at official entry into Jerusalem	December 1917
Battle of Tafileh	January 1918
Promoted toLieutenant-Colonel	March 1918
Enters and leaves Damascus	1 – 4 October 1918
Present at meetings of Eastern Committee of War Cabinet	**October – November 1918**
With Feisal in France and Britain	November – December 1918
In Paris for Peace Conference	**January – October 1919**
Journey by air to Egypt	May – June 1919
At All Souls College, Oxford (as Fellow) and in London	1919 - 1921
Adviser to Winston Churchill, Colonial Office	**1921 - 1922**
On missions to Aden, Jidda and Transjordan	August – December 1921
Resigns from Colonial Office	July 1922
Joins Royal Air Force as John Hume Ross	**August 1922**
Discharged following press disclosure of his identity	January 1923
Private T.E. Shaw, Royal Tank Corps	**March 1923 – August 1925**
Acquires cottage at Clouds Hill, near Bovington Camp, Dorset	
Aircraftman Shaw, Royal Air Force	**August 1925 – March 1935**

Sent to RAF West Drayton to be processed as a recruit, then a brief spell in Uxbridge, 18 August 1925.	August 1925
Posted to the Cadet College at Cranwell, Lincolnshire on 24 August 1925	**August 1925**
To E. Palmer 25 August 1925 To Florence Hardy 26 August 1925 To John Buchan 27 August 1925 To A.P. Wavell 29 August 1925 To Robert Graves 29 August 1925 To S.C. Cockerell 29 August 1925	August 1925
To E. Palmer 7 September 1925 To E. Candler 22 September 1925 To Charlotte Shaw 28 September 1925	September 1925
To Charlotte Shaw 17 October 1925 To Robert Graves 21 October 1925	October 1925
To Francis Rodd 3 November 1925 To Edward Garnett 3 November 1925 To Charlotte Shaw 5 November 1925 To Francis Rodd 6 November 1925 To Florence Hardy 9 November 1925 To Charlotte Shaw 17 November 1925 To Francis Rodd 21 November 1925 To Edward Marsh 21 November 1925 To Lionel Curtis 24 November 1925 **Burial of Queen Alexandra 27 November 1925** To E.M. Forster 29 November 1925	November 1925

To Charlotte Shaw 9 December 1925	December 1925
To E. Palmer 10 December 1925	
To William Roberts 10 December 1925	
To Lionel Curtis 14 December 1925	
To Charlotte Shaw 26 December 1925	
To his Mother 28 December 1925	
To Sydney Cockerell 29 December 1925	
To Alec Dixon 29 December 1925	
To Raymond Savage 30 December 1925	
To Charlotte Shaw 4 January 1926	January 1926
To R.V. Buxton 4 January 1926	
To D. G. Hogarth 14 January 1926	
To J. B. Acres 15 January 1926	
To Charlotte Shaw 15 January 1926	
To Charlotte Shaw 19 January 1926	
Florence Hardy 20 January 1926	
Met the Shaws at Ayot St Lawrence 23-25 January	
To Francis Rodd 28 January 1926	
To H.J. Cape 28 January 1926	
To Charlotte Shaw 8 February 1926	February 1926
To Florence Hardy 13 February 1926	
To C.E. Wilson 19 February 1926	
To Charlotte Shaw 22 February 1926	
To H.J. Cape 22 February 1926	

To Lionel Curtis 8 March 1926	March 1926
To S. L. Newcombe 10 March 1926	
To F.L. Lucas 14 March 1926	
To Charlotte Shaw 15 March 1926	
To Whittingham & Griggs 15 March 1926	
To Charlotte Shaw 18 March 1926	
Revolt in the Desert (popular abridgement of Seven Pillars of Wisdom) was made by Lawrence in seven hours at Cranwell on March 26 and March 27 1926, with the assistance of two airman friends, A/A Knowles and A/c Miller. **The text they produced was submitted to Cape on 30 March 1926.**	
To Edward Garnett 6 April 1926	April 1926
To Charlotte Shaw 6 April 1926	
To his Mother 20 April 1926	
To Charlotte Shaw 20 April 1926	
To E. M. Forster 26 April 1926	
To Charlotte Shaw 26 April 1926	
To Charlotte Shaw 29 April 1926	
To Charlotte Shaw 10 May 1926	May 1926
To Charlotte Shaw 20 May 1926	
To Florence Hardy 20 May 1926	
To J. G. Wilson 25 May 1926	
To H.H. Banbury 25 May 1926	
To Charlotte Shaw 26 May 1926	
To Francis Yeats Brown 26 May 1926	

To Charlotte Shaw 3 June 1926	June 1926
Met the Shaws at Ayot St Lawrence 5-6 June 1926	
To Charlotte Shaw 8 June 1926	
To Charlotte Shaw 11 June 1926	
Met the Shaws at Ayot St Lawrence 13 June 1926	
To Charlotte Shaw 17 June 1926	
To Florence Hardy 21 June 1926	
To Charlotte Shaw 24 June 1926	
To Charlotte Shaw 1 July 1926	July 1926
Lawrence took B Flight and their wives to Hendon by charabanc to see the annual air display 3 July 1926	
To his Mother 6 July 1926	
Met the Shaws at Ayot St Lawrence 11 July 1926	
To Charlotte Shaw 20 July 1926	
Met the Shaws at Ayot St Lawrence 25 July 1926	
Lawrence gave a copy of *Seven Pillars* to 'Biffy' Borton at RAF Cranwell 15 August 1926	August 1926
To Rupert de la Bere (undated)	
To Charlotte Shaw 22 August 1926	
To Charlotte Shaw 24 August 1926	
Lawrence drew up his last Will & Testament 28 August 1926	
Lawrence thought that copies of *Seven Pillars* would be ready for dispatch to the binders 15 September 1926.	September 1926
To Robert Graves 16 September 1926	
To Charlotte Shaw 24 September 1926	

Seven Pillars was still not ready when Lawrence learned that he had inadvertently libelled Ronald Storrs. The offending passage had to be rewritten, and then, since the type had been distributed, four pages had to be reset, proofed and reprinted 25 September 1926. To George Brough 27 September 1926	
To Charlotte Shaw 2 October 1926 To Charlotte Shaw 5 October 1926 To Charlotte Shaw 14 October 1926 To Mrs Friedlow 14 October 1926 To D. Knowles 18 October 1926 To M. Pike 18 October 1926 **Met the Shaws at London 20 October 1926** To Charlotte Shaw 26 October 1926 To T.B. Marson 26 October 1926	October 1926
To Charlotte Shaw 1 November 1926 **Lawrence began the month's leave to which he was entitled before going to India 4 November 1926** **Met the Shaws at London 4 November 1926** **Met the Shaws at Ayot St Lawrence 7 November 1926** **Met the Shaws at London 11 November 1926** **Met the Shaws at Ayot St Lawrence 13-14 November 1926** **Met the Shaws at London 19 November 1926** To Lord Trenchard 20 November 1926 **Lawrence sent a copy of *Seven Pillars* to Lord Trenchard 22 November 1926** To Lord Trenchard 29 November 1926	November 1926

Met the Shaws at London 24 November 1926 To Charlotte Shaw 30 November 1926	
To his Mother 1 December 1926 **Met the Shaws at London 1 December 1926** To Charlotte Shaw 2 December 1926 To Robert Graves (undated) To Dick Knowles 3 December 1926 To Francis Rodd 3 December 1926 **Lawrence sailed for India from Southampton in the troopship _Derbyshire_ on 7 December 1926** **Stanley Baldwin's incomplete copy of the _Seven Pillars_ was sent through John Buchan on 14 December 1926.** To Charlotte Shaw 16 December 1926 To Sergeant Pugh 16 December 1926	December 1926
Subscribers' edition of _Seven Pillars of Wisdom_ completed and distributed	**December 1926**
In India. _Revolt in the Desert_ published and later withdrawn; _The Mint_ completed; brought back to England following press stories claiming he was involved in a rebellion in Afghanistan	**January 1927 – January 1929**
To J.S. Hollings 11 January 1927	January 1927
To Charlotte Shaw 23 March 1927	March 1927
To Charlotte Shaw 7 April 1927 To Sergeant Pugh 27 April 1927	April 1927
To Jonathan Cape 25 May 1927	May 1927
To John Buchan 20 June 1927	June 1927

To Robert Graves 28 June 1927 To Sergeant Pugh 30 June 1927	
To Charlotte Shaw 3 August 1927 To Charlotte Shaw 12 August 1927 To Charlotte Shaw 18 August 1927	August 1927
To Edward Garnett 22 September 1927	September 1927
To Charlotte Shaw 27 October 1927	October 1927
To Charlotte Shaw 15 December 1927 To Charlotte Shaw 27 December 1927 To Dick Knowles 30 December 1927	December 1927
To his Mother 4 January 1928	January 1928
To David Garnett 16 February 1928	February 1928
To David Garnett 15 March 1928 To Hugh Trenchard 17 March 1928 To Charlotte Shaw 20 March 1928	March 1928
To Sergeant Pugh 13 April 1928	April 1928
To A.W. Lawrence 2 May 1928	May 1928
To Sergeant Pugh 9 June 1928 To David Garnett 14 June 1928	June 1928
To E.M. Forster 6 August 1928	August 1928
To Corporal Trevarthan 16 October 1928	October 1928
To Charlotte Shaw 27 November 1928	November 1928
To Ernest Thurtle 9 February 1929	February 1929
At various air stations in England working mainly on high speed marine craft	**March 1929 – March 1935**
To F.L. Lucas 26 March 1929	March 1929

To Frederic Manning 25 February 1930	February 1930
To Frederic Manning 21 March 1930	March 1930
To Frederic Manning 15 May 1930	May 1930
To Frederic Manning 24 June 1930	June 1930
To Frederic Manning 7 August 1930	August 1930
To Charlotte Shaw 26 June 1931	June 1931
To Frederic Manning 2 January 1932	January 1932
To George Brough 13 June 1933	June 1933
To K.W. Marshall 17 November 1933 To Rupert de la Bere 26 November 1933	November 1933
To George Brough 3 May 1934	May 1934
To Frederic Manning 25 July 1934	July 1934
To Florence Hardy 19 October 1934	October 1934
To Frederic Manning 16 November 1934	November 1934
To Peter Davies 28 February 1935	February 1935
Retires to Clouds Hill	**Spring 1935**
To William Rothenstein 5 May 1935	**May 1935**
Has accident on motor cycle near Clouds Hill	**13 May 1935**
Dies in Bovington Military Hospital	**19 May 1935**
Funeral at Moreton, Dorest	**21 May 1935**

Sources

T.E. Lawrence

T. E. Lawrence (1926) *Seven Pillars of Wisdom*

352087 A/c Ross (1955) *The Mint*

J.C. [It was signed pseudonymously with the initials J.C. It may be a coincidence that these were the initials of his parents' family names, Junner (or Jenner) and Chapman], 'Ramping', *Journal of the Royal Air Force College, Cranwell,* Vol. XI, No.1, Spring 1931

T.E. Shaw [T.E. Lawrence], 'Ramping', *Journal of the Royal Air Force College*, Autumn 1935 [reprint of Spring 1931 article with proper recognition of author]

'S' [T.E. Lawrence], 'Putting the Weight in Ancient Days', *Journal of the Royal Air Force College*, Spring 1933 [excerpt from *The Odyssey*]

[T.E. Lawrence] 'Ramping' T.E. Lawrence, *The T.E. Lawrence Society Journal*, 2:1

[T.E. Shaw] 'Brough versus Biplane: a chapter from the Lawrence of Arabia story', *Motor Cycling*, 21 May 1959

Articles

M.H.G. Allison, 'Lincolnshire's link with the Lawrences', *Lincolnshire Life*, Vol. 8 (8), October 1968 [D.H. Lawrence and T.E. Lawrence in Lincolnshire]

R. De la Bere, 'A Great Book', *RAF Cadet College Magazine*, Spring 1927 [Review of *Seven Pillars of Wisdom*]

Professor R.D.L.B (De La Bere), 'Aircraftman T.E. Shaw ', *RAF College Magazine*, Autumn 1935

Nicholas Birnie, 'T.E. Lawrence and Frederic Manning', *The Journal of the T.E. Lawrence Society*, Vol. 1, No. 2, Winter 1991-2

Professor R. De La Bere, Aircraftman T.E. Shaw in Lincolnshire (A Last Conversation), *The Lincolnshire Magazine*, Vol. 2, No.7, Sept. – Oct. 1935

Charles Findley, 'The Amazing AC2', *Royal Air Force Flying Review*, January 1958

Peter Gray, 'Lawrence of Arabia's Lincolnshire Posting', *Lincolnshire Past & Present*, No. 25, Autumn 1996

Lord Halifax, 'Lawrence of Arabia', *Journal of the Royal Air Force College*, Autumn 1936 [text of speech at St Pauls]

Mrs E. Hoggett, Rauceby, *Horse Drawn Tea Waggon at RAF Cranwell*, [Undated letter to RAF College Cranwell library]

A.F. Johnson, 'Aircraftsman Shaw', *Royal Air Force Review*, 1948

Winston Kime, 'David George Hogarth', *Lincolnshire Life*, Vol. 20 (9), December 1980 [Hogarth, archaeologist, traveller and scholar, was Lawrence's mentor and friend].

Lord Kinross (JPD Balfour), 'Aircraftsman Shaw', *Royal Air Force College Journal*, March 1944

'T.E. Lawrence and Rupert de la Bere', *The Journal of the T.E. Lawrence Society*, Vol. II, No. 1, Summer 1992.

Mike Leatherdale, 'Lawrence and his Brough Superiors', *The Journal of the T.E. Lawrence Society*, Vol. 1, No. 2, Winter 1991-2

A.W.H.M., 'Aircraftsman Shaw – A Memory', *Journal of the Royal Air Force College*, November 1949

M.S. 'T.E.L.' [a poem] *Journal of the Royal Air Force College*, November 1949

Denis McDonnell, 'Lawrence Link is Remembered', *T.E. Notes*, February 1994

Denis McDonnell, 'T.E. and the Royal Air Force College at Cranwell', *T.E. Notes*, February 1994

Adam Newell, 'Lawrence of the RAF', *RAF Magazine*, September 2006

Leonard Rivett, *Lawrence of Arabia: Ross and Shaw in the Royal Air Force*, 12 June 1996

Edwin Rose, 'Lawrence of Arabia – a different viewpoint', *Lincolnshire Past & Present*, No. 27, Spring 1997

Allan Warburton, 'A Legend in Hiding', *Lincolnshire Life*, April 1996

Leslie Robert Webb, *Lawrence of Arabia* [a memoir of T.E. Lawrence written for Mrs Khinlyn Fern in September 1995].

Flight-Cadet A. Will 'Revolt in the Desert', *RAF Cadet College Magazine*, Autumn 1927 [review of *Revolt in the Desert*]

Books

Michael Asher (1998) *Lawrence: the uncrowned King of Arabia*

Bodleian Library (1988) *T.E. Lawrence: the legend and the man* [Exhibition Catalogue]

C. Boon (1997) *'Monday is Market Day'...Memories of Sleaford*

Malcolm Brown (2005) *Lawrence of Arabia: the life, the legend*

Winston Churchill (1937) *Great Contemporaries*

Richard Graves (1976) *Lawrence of Arabia and his world*

Robert Graves (1937) *Lawrence and the Arabs*

E.B. Haslam (1982) *The History of Royal Air Force Cranwell*

H. Montgomery Hyde (1977) *Solitary In the Ranks: Lawrence of Arabia as airman and private soldier*

J.R. Ketteringham (2002) 'Thomas Edward Lawrence', *Lincolnshire Natives and Others*

Ronald Knight (1985) *Colonel T.E. Lawrence visits Mr & Mrs Hardy*

Ronald Knight (1988) *T.E. Lawrence and the Max Gate Circle*

Philip Knightley & Colin Simpson (1969) *The Secret Lives of Lawrence of Arabia*

Michael Korda (2011) *Hero: the life and legend of Lawrence of Arabia*

A.W. Lawrence (1937) *T.E. Lawrence By His Friends*

Rodney Legg (1988) *Lawrence of Arabia in Dorset*

John Mack (1976) *A Prince of our Disorder: the life of T.E. Lawrence*

P.J. Marriott & Y. Argent (1996) *Last days of T.E. Lawrence*

Philip O'Brien (1988) *T.E. Lawrence: a bibliography*

Clare Sydney Smith (1940) *The Golden Reign: the story of my friendship with Lawrence of Arabia*

Terence Rattigan (1960) *Ross*

John Rennison (2003) *The Digby Diary*

Andrew Simpson (2008) *Another Life: Lawrence after Arabia*

Desmond Stewart (1977) *T.E. Lawrence*

Lowell Thomas (1924) *With Lawrence in Arabia*

P. Tunbridge (2000) *With Lawrence in the Royal Air Force*

S. Weintraub (1963) *Private Shaw and Public Shaw*

Michael Yardley (1986) *T.E. Lawrence: a biography*

Letters

Malcolm Brown (1988 & 2005) *The Letters of T.E. Lawrence*

David Garnett (1938) *The Letters of T.E. Lawrence*

Robert Graves & Liddell Hart (1938) *T. E. Lawrence to his Biographers*

M.R. Lawrence (1954) *The Home Letters of T.E. Lawrence and his brothers*

Jeremy & Nicole Wilson (2000) *T.E. Lawrence Letters Volume One: Correspondence with Bernard and Charlotte Shaw, 1922-26*

Jeremy & Nicole Wilson (2003) *T.E. Lawrence Letters Volume Two: Correspondence with Bernard and Charlotte Shaw, 1927*

Newspaper Cuttings

'Lincoln links with Lawrence of Arabia', *Sleaford Standard*, 22 December 1972

Michael Dawney, 'Hero's halcyon days at Cranwell', *Sleaford Standard*, 18 August 1988

'Well, now we know', *Lincolnshire Echo*, 11 May 1992

'Plaque marks historic spot', *Lincolnshire Echo*, 19 July 1993

Shelagh McIntyre, 'Week in Ancaster', *Sleaford Standard*, 3 June 1994

Pat Nurse, 'Lawrence of Cranwell', *Lincolnshire Echo*, 9 November 1996

'Back on map as plaque restores Lawrence link', *Lincolnshire Echo*, 27 October 1998

'Former postman mourned', *Lincolnshire Echo*, 17 February 1999

'Mystery woman in life of Lawrence of Arabia', *Lincolnshire Echo*, 29 May 2002

Emma Pearson, 'How Lincolnshire legend still inspires film makers', *Lincolnshire Echo*, 23 May 2006

Lisa Porter, 'Lawrence's lost letter for sale', *Sleaford Target*, 26 May 2010

Gavin Cordon, 'Payments to a mystery Miss Bryan confuse the legend of Lawrence', *Independent*, 29 May 2002

Chris Hastings and Charlotte Edwards, 'TE Lawrence's 'mistress' was an orphan', *The Sunday Telegraph*, 9 June 2002

Neil Tweedie, 'Mystery of woman paid wages by Lawrence of Arabia', *The Daily Telegraph*, 29 May 2002

Martin Bright, 'Who was the secret 'wife' of T.E. Lawrence?' *The Observer*, 26 May 2002

Maurice Chittenden and Gareth Walsh, 'Secret Lawrence "wife" was just a taxing affair', *The Sunday Times*, 2 June 2002

John Crosland and Michael Horsnell, 'Did Lawrence of Arabia secretly wed this woman?', *The Times*, 29 May 2002

James Bone and Michael Horsnell, 'Landlord link to home of mystery lover', *The Times*, 29 May 2002

'Lawrence Sale', *Lincolnshire Echo*, 12 April 2008

The Pateran Press – Other Books by John Pateman

Bren Gunner on Manoeuvres: Arthur Pateman Goes To War: The story of Arthur Pateman and his time in the Royal West Kent Regiment in Palestine, Malta, Samos, Leros and a POW camp. £12.50

Canadian Corner: The story of the Canadian Corps in the Great War and the Commonwealth War Graves Commission cemetery at All Saints churchyard, Orpington, Kent. £7.50

Charles Dickens and Travellers: Extracts from the works of Charles Dickens concerning Gypsies and Travellers. £7.50

Dippers Slip: the life and times of Noah Pateman: The story of Noah Pateman and his family and their life in Orpington and the Crays. £12.50

Fordcroft: The story of a small working class community in St Mary Cray, their lives and living conditions. £7.50

Hoo, Hops and Hods: the life and times of Robert Pateman: The story of Robert Pateman and his family and their life on the Hoo Peninsula. £12.50

Lincolnshire Asylums: The story of The Lawn (1820), St John's (1852), Rauceby (1902) and Harmston Hall (1930). £7.50

The Ontario Military Hospital: The story of how the Great War hospital was built in Orpington in 1916 by the Government of Ontario. £7.50

Orpington at War: The story of the men who died in the Great War and between the Wars who are remembered on War Shrines, War Memorials and War Graves. £7.50

Orpington Man: the life and times of John Pateman, Volume One 1956-74: The story of John Pateman and his family and their life at Oakdene Road and the Ramsden Estate. £7.50

Orpington War Memorial: The story of the men who died in the Second World War and in later conflicts who are remembered on Orpington War Memorial. £10.00

Patemans By Census: The story of the Pateman family as recorded in the national census between 1841 – 1911. £12.50

Patemans By County: The story of the Pateman family as recorded in the births, marriages and deaths registers for England from 1837. £15.00

Patemans in Kent: The story of the Pateman family in Kent as recorded in the births, marriages and deaths registers for England from 1837 and the national census 1841-1911. £7.50

Petten Grove: The story of a street on the Ramsden Estate in south London and the people who lived in it from 1956 – 2003. £7.50

The Ramsden Estate: The story of how the Ramsden area of Orpington was developed from open farmland into a large post-war council housing estate. £12.50

The Royal West Kents in Orpington: This is the story of the men and women of Orpington who fought and died in The Royal West Kent Regiment in both World Wars. £7.50

St Mary Cray Cemetery: The story of a Victorian cemetery in Star Lane and the fallen from RAF from Biggin Hill who were buried there in World War Two. £7.50

Seven Steps to Glory: Private Pateman Goes to War: The story of Walter Pateman, a Kent Gypsy who fought and died in the Great War. £7.50

Strewing the Pateran: the Gypsies of Thorney Hill: The story of the Pateman family of Gypsies who lived in the New Forest. £7.50

Ten Pound Pom: Victor Poxon Goes To War: The story of Victor Poxon and his life in the Royal Navy and Australia. £7.50

Three Years on the Western Front: Gunner Rodbourne Goes to War: The story of Albert Rodbourne, one of the first men in St Mary Cray to volunteer to fight in the Great War. £12.50

Tugmutton Common: the life and times of William Pateman: The story of William Pateman and his family and their life at Locksbottom, Farnborough. £10.00

What Dark History is This? William Pateman and the Gordon Riots: The story of William Pateman, a ringleader in the Gordon riots which rocked Georgian London. £7.50

Copies of these titles can be purchased online from Lulu.com or by post from 11 Windsor Close, Sleaford, Lincolnshire, NG34 7NL. Please make cheques payable to John Pateman and add £2.99 for postage & packing.